The Medication Question

A Norton Professional Book

The Medication Question

Weighing Your Mental Health Treatment Options

For Patients and Their Families

Ronald J. Diamond, MD

W. W. Norton & Company
New York • London

For information about permission to reproduce
selections from this book, write to
Permissions, W. W. Norton & Company, Inc.,
500 Fifth Avenue, New York, NY 10110

For information about special discounts for bulk
purchases, please contact W. W. Norton Special Sales
at specialsales@wwnorton.com or 800-233-4830

Manufacturing by RR Donnelley, Bloomsburg
Book design by Joe Lops
Production manager: Leeann Graham

Library of Congress Cataloging-in-Publication Data

Diamond, Ronald J., 1946–
 The medication question : weighing your mental
health treatment options / Ronald J. Diamond. — 1st ed.
     p. cm.
 Includes bibliographical references and index.
 ISBN 978-0-393-70630-7 (pbk.)
 1. Psychopharmacology. 2. Psychotropic drugs.
 3. Mental illness—Treatment. I. Title.
 RM315.D488 2011
 615'.78—dc23

                              2011015983

ISBN: 978-0-393-70630-7 (pbk.)

W. W. Norton & Company, Inc., 500 Fifth Avenue, New York, N.Y. 10110
              www.wwnorton.com
W. W. Norton & Company Ltd., Castle House, 75/76 Wells Street, London W1T
3QT

1 2 3 4 5 6 7 8 9 0

This book is dedicated to my wife, the love of my life,
the reader of my manuscripts, and, even more important,
the reader of my soul.

A good wife, who can find?
Her worth is far above rubies.
The heart of her husband trusts in her.
And nothing shall he lack.
—Proverbs 31

Contents

Acknowledgments

The most enjoyable part of writing a book is writing the acknowledgments. It feels good to be able to thank those people who helped in my thinking and writing. It is also nice for those people who have seen various ideas and drafts to finally see the published result. Inevitably, not everyone can be listed, and many people whose ideas are part of these pages are not able to be included. I apologize ahead of time for any lapses of memory that may have omitted some names.

The Mental Health Center of Dane County has been my professional and intellectual home for more than 30 years. It is a special place that tries very hard to live by the values of respect, recovery, and cultural competence. The staff and consumers at the MHCDC have been my teachers. There are too many to name all of them individually, but I want to especially mention my personal support group, including Bill Greer, Tim Otis, Gerry Brew, Gail Marker, Brad Schlough, Sue Moran, Kristen Esbensen, Andrea Jacobsen, Bob Factor, and Pam Smith. They and my other colleagues over the past 30 years have all given me part of what I have poured into this book. I especially want to thank Linda Keys and Lynn Brady for their excellent strength-based case management of me. They help me to stay organized, support my strengths, and are gentle in their admonishment of my failings.

This book started as an idea from Deborah Malmud, my editor at W. W. Norton. She went over the outline, came up with the title, and very gently pushed me along. It would not have happened without her. In this, as in my other writing, my thinking has been strongly influenced by Pat Deegan and the other people who developed the ideas of psychiatric rehabilitation, William Miller and his colleagues who developed motivational interviewing and Marsha Linehan and the group who worked with her to develop Dialectical Behavioral Therapy. My thinking about recovery began with Paul Carling and the Center for Community Change, the think tank that he developed and that operated for a period of time in the 1980s. This was the forum that first introduced me to the concepts of recovery and shared decision making. I also trace much of my professional thinking to my friend and mentor, Len Stein, my father, who taught me to think about common problems in uncommon ways, and my mother, who tried to teach me how to listen. Finally, I want to thank the people who read and commented on various versions of this book, including Linda Keys, Gail Handley, Pam Valenta, Aaron Mandel, Pilar Gomez, Ken Herrman and Cherie Diamond.

Preface

How do we decide on the role of psychiatric medication in our healing? When should psychiatric medication be considered, and when should it not be an option? Many of us will need to grapple with the decision of whether to take a psychiatric medication. If we are not faced with this decision ourselves, our family members or friends may ask our advice. There are a number of books that give information about psychiatric medications, including my own book *Instant Psychopharmacology* (now in its third edition). These books make information about medications accessible to people who are not physicians.

This book has a different focus. This book is not about the psychiatric medications themselves; rather, it is a book that goes through the thought process of how to decide whether or not to use a psychiatric medication. It is written for people who are thinking of using a medication, and it is for their families who may be involved in this decision. What can these medications do to help us, and what can they not do even if we want them to? When is it worth taking a psychiatric medication, and when is it not? This is a book that can help you be more involved in decisions that directly affect you. Until recently the decision of whether or not you should take a medication was your doctor's decision. He or she would make a diagnosis and come up with a solution. This was never a very good approach to medical decision making, and it is now even less acceptable. More information is available about medication, both in books and on the Internet. There is also more concern about risks and side effects. Potential users of these medications, or "patients," want to be part of the decision about whether or not a medication makes sense for them. It is my strong belief that a person who is actively involved in his or her own treatment is more likely to have a better outcome than a person who is the passive recipient of treatment. It is no longer acceptable to "medicate" a person; rather, the job of physicians is to provide enough information and consultation so that someone can make an informed and active decision about his or her own treatment.

The words used to describe this approach are "shared decision making" and "collaborative treatment." A Google search will bring up websites and books and other resources that describe and promote these ideas. This book is very much part of this rapidly evolving set of ideas that assumes that patients will want a much more active role in their own treatment and that treatment is much more likely to achieve better results if the patient is an informed and active part of the decision process. The decision about whether or not to use psychiatric medication may be influenced by your doctor, or therapist, or spouse or friend. In the end, this should largely be the decision of the person who would be taking the medication. For some illnesses, medication is more clearly an important part of effective treatment. In some cases, the decision to use a medication may not just be that of the patient, but it may be influenced or even determined by family or the courts. Even in those situations where the decision about the use of medication is not entirely under the control of the patient, being informed and involved can still help lead to a better and more effective decision. The goal of this book is to help you make a more informed and thoughtful decision about whether you may want to use a psychiatric medication as a solution for your specific problem.

Medications are tools that can help to solve a problem. Medications by themselves are not "good" or "bad"; they are only useful or not useful. My advice is that you should not start by thinking about a medication; instead, start by thinking about the problem. What is the problem that you would like help with, and is medication a good tool to help with this problem? Are there other tools, in place of medication or in addition to medication, that may also help? What are the reasons to avoid or at least think carefully about using medication as part of the solution to this particular problem?

The Medication Question

Introduction

WHY TAKE A PSYCHIATRIC MEDICATION?

Why take any medication? What do you want a medication to do? At first this seems like a pretty simple question. You take a medication to cure an illness. If you have pneumonia, you take penicillin because you want it to cure the pneumonia. On reflection, though, it is not clear why most of us take medications. Most medications are taken for chronic conditions: conditions without an obvious cure. We take medications for high blood pressure, high cholesterol, diabetes, arthritis, and many other medical diseases without much hope that the medications will lead to a cure. We take medications for chronic diseases for many different reasons: because we hope that it will help us to live longer, avoid disability, have less pain, keep the underlying illness from getting worse, prevent a stroke or heart attack, or allow us to keep working.

Even for the same illness, different people will have different reasons to take medications. One person is more concerned about not dying from a stroke, while another is more worried about becoming disabled. One person is more concerned about going blind from untreated diabetes, while another person is more concerned about dying from a heart attack connected to the diabetes. One person is very concerned about being in pain, while another is more focused on not being able to work because of pain. Our reasons for wanting to take medications are not the same; they are related to who we are and what we think is most important in our lives. The reasons why we do or do not take a medication are closely connected to our personal values.

All of us have a wide variety of diseases that would perhaps respond to medication, but we often decide that the disease is not that serious and that medication is not necessary. How do I decide whether to take a medication for my constipation, or stuffy nose, or minor headache? We may have a disease that would seemingly respond to a medication but decide that taking a medication is not "worth it." This may be because we believe the risks or side effects of the medication outweigh the help it may provide. We may decide to avoid medication because we believe the problem will go away by itself and we would prefer to use a "natural response" rather than taking something "artificial." It may be that even if a medication would help a bit, we do not believe that it would help enough to make a real difference.

People differ greatly in their willingness to take medication. Taking penicillin for pneumonia is an easy decision for most of us, but it is less clear whether everyone would be willing to take a medication to lower blood pressure when the blood pressure is not that high and it is not currently causing any problems. High blood pressure increases a person's risk of having a stroke, but for one person, the risk of stroke seems a long way off and taking a medication does not seem very important, especially if there are side effects. For another person with the same high blood pressure, the chance to decrease her risk of stroke by taking a medication and tolerating a few minor side effects seems very well worth it. When the problem is something as subjective as pain, the question becomes even more confusing. One person is willing and even desirous of taking medication to decrease even minor pain, while another would prefer to tolerate very significant amounts of pain before resorting to a medication. Some people will take a pain-relieving medication as soon as they begin to hurt. Others will resist using a medication until the pain is so severe that they cannot go to work or otherwise function. Some people like the idea of a medication as being a solution to their pain, while others would strongly prefer a non-medication medicated solution.

Some people want the fastest, easiest treatment possible, and if this means taking a medication, then so be it. Other people are willing to use a solution that may take longer but is likely to last longer. Still other people may feel strongly that they want a "natural solution" to the problem, although the definition of "natural" is often unclear. For one person, vitamins are natural; for another, herbs are okay; and for another, anything that is from an ayurvedic healer is acceptable. The same person who wants to avoid medication because it is "unnatural" may or may not be abusing alcohol, marijuana, or other drugs. We have very strong feelings about these issues, and none of us are completely consistent in our beliefs. Some people have great trust in physicians and traditional medical care, while others are suspicious of anything that is connected to the mainstream healthcare industry.

Beliefs about the nature of the problem also matter. If I believe that I am depressed because I have just lost my job, I may not see that medication is going to help very much. If I believe that my lack of sleep is causing my depression to get worse, I may be willing to take a sleeping pill, even if I think that my depression is related to my loss of work. On the other hand, if I believe that losing my job has changed my brain chemistry so that it has now become harder to look for a new job, I may want to try a medication even if there is agreement that the loss of the job started the problem. I may believe that I hear voices because I have a mental illness or because I am spiritually connected to ancestors who talk to me. I may believe that my child is having trouble at school because the school is not well designed to meet his needs. Alternatively, I may feel that his problem in school is caused by a genetic, biological abnormality that is evident not just in school but in all areas of his life. Many important problems may have multiple causes. For example, I may believe that my child's behavioral problem is caused in part by the school and in part caused by his biological difficulty sustaining concentration. If so, I may decide that a medication is useful even as I work to improve the school's response to children who have less ability to maintain concentration. The issue is whether a medication is likely to help, not whether it is the only solution.

A belief about cause does not necessarily suggest a particular treatment. I may be very anxious because I am worried about my job; I may take a Valium-type medication because I know that it will help decrease my anxiety. I do not believe that I have a "Valium deficiency problem" or even an illness, but I may believe that a medication is both appropriate for my problem and likely to be helpful. A stimulant is likely to help my child concentrate better at school, whether or not I believe the problem is with him or with the school. The fact that a medication may help does not necessarily mean that we would all choose to use it. Many of the people who argue against the widespread use of stimulants in children agree that they can work, but even if they work they have enough potential risk that we may want to find an alternative solution.

SPECIAL COMPLEXITIES WITH PSYCHIATRIC MEDICATION

The discussion outlined above becomes even more complicated when we think about psychiatric medication. Psychiatric problems tend to be more poorly defined than medical problems. It is sometimes more difficult to be clear about what "getting better" or "getting worse" means or about how much these changes are impacted by medication. There is often confusion and even disagreement about the nature of the problem and whether it is the kind of problem that is likely to respond to a medication. At times, a physician feels that medication is an obvious solution, but at other times it is the patient who is very focused on medication. Often there is disagreement about how much risk or what side effects the person taking the medication should be expected to tolerate. More often with psychiatric medication, there is pressure from family or friends or the psychiatrist to use medication even if the consumer is reluctant.

BE CLEAR ABOUT THE PROBLEM

Before thinking about which medication to use or even whether to use a medication, think about the problem that you may want the medication to help solve.

- **How big is the problem?** How much does it interfere with your life or other things that you want to do? For example, anxiety can be a minor annoyance or it can significantly interfere with your life. It can be limited to causing some minor distress, or it can interfere with your ability to function at work or even keep your job. In extreme cases, feeling anxious can keep you from leaving your home.
- **What do you know about the problem?** What does it keep you from doing? When is it present, and when is it not present?
- **Have you had something like this in the past?** If so, what happened? Did it get better on its own, or did you learn to live with it? Did you take medication in the past, or did life circumstances change to help make it better without medication?
- **What have you already tried to make this problem better?** People rarely think about medication as the first solution to a problem. You may have tried to calm yourself down, talk to friends, listen to music, meditate, or tried a wide variety of other potential solutions. Which helped a bit, and which not at all?
- **What else could you try that you have not already tried?** Is this because these other solutions require too

much work, or is it because you do not believe they will
help or they have not helped in the past?

- **What else could be making the problem worse?** Could
  there be an undiagnosed medical illness or some major
  life stress causing the problem? Is alcohol or drug use
  causing the problem or making it worse?
- **What happens if this problem does not get better?**
  How much will it interfere with your life if things do not
  improve? What are you willing to put up with in terms
  of risks and side effects to try and make the problem better? What are you willing to change in your life to make
  the problem better?

Once you are clear about the problem, it is easier to think
about what "getting better" means.

What does "getting better" mean to you?

As discussed at the beginning of this introduction, "getting better" means very different things to different people. So what
does "getting better" mean to you, in relation to your particular
problem? Does it mean feeling better or having a better subjective sense of well-being or less subjective sense of distress?
Does it mean being able to enjoy things more, to have more
energy, or to concentrate better?

What would you be able to do if you were feeling better?
Would you be able to stay out of the hospital, read a book, or
go back to work? Does it mean being able to function better at
work or at home? Does it mean being able to do things you cannot now do or that you can do only with difficulty? The more
you are clear about what "getting better" means, the more likely
you will be able to find a path that will get you closer to your
goal.

Create your own list of "target symptoms"

It is important to identify "target symptoms" that are as specific as possible. The idea of "target symptoms" will be discussed in more detail in Chapter 8; they are an important part of determining whether a medication is really helping. "Improvement" does not mean the complete elimination of symptoms. How would you know if you were "getting better," and how would you know if you were "getting worse"? For a person who is chronically and persistently suicidal, "better" may mean going an entire day without suicidal thoughts, and "getting much better" might mean going an entire week without suicidal thoughts. If a person is hearing voices that are intrusive and bothersome, "getting better" may mean the voices recede enough to allow the person to be less distracted when having a conversation or reading a book.

Develop a very specific list of behaviors that would let you and people around you know if the medication is working. Sometimes these targets are things you want to be able to do, and sometimes they are a decrease in a symptom that is causing distress. For example, if the medication were working, I would be able to do one or more of the following:

- Enjoy reading a book;
- Be less distracted by the voices in my head, even if they are still there;
- Go a day at a time without feeling suicidal;
- Have fewer panic attacks; or
- Be able to concentrate enough to function better at work.

It is useful to be very concrete about these target symptoms. It is also helpful to be realistic. If a person has been persistently suicidal for a long time, it would be hoped that with treatment the person would no longer feel suicidal, but an initial "target" might be to go a day or perhaps a week without feeling suicidal. Accomplishing a target does not mean that the problem is fixed or gone; it only means that the problem is better in some measurable or observable way. The voices may still be present, but are they any less bothersome? I may still have some panic attacks, but are they less frequent or less severe? I may still be very concerned about people trying to poison me whenever I eat, but can I overcome this fear to eat anyway, even when other people are around?

It is important to come up with appropriate target symptoms. They must relate to changes that are important to you. It does little good to change something if it is an area that you do not care about. And it must be something that is a realistic target for medication. It is useful to work with a prescriber, people who know you, and your therapist to come up with these target symptoms. Some kinds of changes are easier than others. You may want a medication to change or improve things in areas where medication would be less likely to be effective. Thinking of and tracking target symptoms is a way of monitoring whether the medication is working. It is important to come up with target symptoms that will help you measure change if it does occur. For example, if your target was "getting a job," you may feel better, be able to concentrate better, and be less bothered by people putting ideas in your head, but you still may not have a job. Based on just looking at that one target, which is not quickly attainable, you may decide the medication is not working.

Learn about the medications that you are thinking about taking

What kind of medication might help the particular problems that you want help with? How well do these medications typically work, and how long do they typically take to work? What are the risks of these medications, and what are the potential side effects? Are there some side effects that seem particularly bad to you, and is there any way to choose a medication that might work while avoiding these specific side effects? Is there a range of many different medications, or is there one or two that seem most appropriate? What happens if you stop the medication, or if you drink alcohol while taking it? What other questions do you have about the medications that are being suggested? Where can you go to get your questions answered?

There are many different ways to get information about medication. Visiting your physician is a good way to start gathering information. Chapter 10 discusses how you can work more effectively with your physician. Pharmacists can also be useful. There are numerous books designed for people who are not doctors. *Instant Psychopharmacology* (3rd ed.) is a companion to this book and is designed to provide more information about individual medications. There are many websites as well: some have reliable information, and some provide information that is more polemical than scientific (see the Resource List for recommended sites).

Another source of information about medication is friends. Friends and family often have their own views about whether medication is "good" or "bad." Many people have their own medication horror stories or medication breakthroughs. People assume that their experiences will apply to you. Personal stories and experiences of friends will, of course, influence you. However, it is important to remember that our problems and our solutions and our experiences with medication may be very different from those of our friends.

Medications are typically labeled as antidepressants or antipsychotics or mood stabilizers. These common labels refer to the initial uses of that medication. In practice, medications may be used to treat a variety of disorders in addition to their initial use. For example, many of the antidepressants are very effective in treating anxiety disorders, even in people who are not depressed. Antipsychotic medications can be very effective mood stabilizers, even for people who have no psychotic symptoms. Some medications initially developed to control high blood pressure are now used in the treatment of posttraumatic stress disorder (PTSD). People often become upset when they are prescribed an antipsychotic that is labeled for use for schizophrenia, when that is not their problem or their diagnosis. Many medications have a range of problems that they can treat, and it is important to learn what a specific medication can do that would be useful for you.

ALL MEDICATIONS HAVE RISKS AND SIDE EFFECTS

All medications have side effects, and all medications have risks. Besides doing what we want them to do, medications do all kinds of other additional things throughout the body. Even aspirin and Tylenol have risks. The issue is whether the side effects or the risks are "worth it" to the person taking the medication. When does the potential help from the medication outweigh the potential risks and side effects?

For example, it may be worth taking a very dangerous medication with many side effects if that medication is likely to cure an otherwise fatal cancer. It may not be worth taking even a fairly safe medication if it is not likely to do much good or if the problem that one is taking it for is not that big. Even a relatively low-risk medication may not be worth taking in order to cure a mild headache that is likely to get better on its own. The issue is not whether a medication has risks or side effects: all medications do. The issue is whether the risk and potential side effect burden of this medication, at this time, is worth it to this person. How much help is this medication likely to provide, and how big is the problem that the medication may help solve?

Some side effects are rare but can be very serious. Others are more common. Just because a side effect is listed as a possibility does not mean that you will have it. Medication information handouts often give the percentage of people who experienced a side effect in research studies. Most people do not develop the side effects that are listed. On the other hand, if you do get a side effect, even if it is very rare, for you it is 100%. If a specific side effect is not listed, this does not mean that it is not possible. Some side effects are so rare that they may not be recognized as being connected to the medication. Some side effects only appear after a long period of time. If you are having a reaction that you think is connected to a specific medication, you could be right and it could be connected, even if it was not listed as a side effect. On the other hand, it may not be related to the medication even if you feel it is. It is important to talk with your physician about the problem and see if together you can figure out whether the problem is related to the medication.

MEDICATIONS ALONE ARE ALMOST NEVER ENOUGH

It is very unusual for any medication to solve a problem by itself. Usually, medication can help in some specific ways that need to be combined with other kinds of solutions. For example, a person who is depressed because he is out of work may have so little energy and motivation that it is almost impossible to keep looking for work; he may not be able to concentrate enough to look through want ads or fill out job applications. An antidepressant medication may help this person increase energy and motivation, and it could help to improve concentration, even though the person is still unemployed. If the person sits back and waits for the medication to work, he is likely to wait a very long time. But if he uses the boost in energy and motivation to force himself to start applying for jobs again, and if he forces himself to be more active and hopeful, then he reinforces the effect of the medication and is much more likely to get over the depression. Most of the time, when medications are helpful, they are most helpful when combined with other problem-solving strategies. The idea of combining medication with other problem-solving strategies is discussed throughout the book and is also the focus of Chapter 11.

Problems are often circular. A person drinks because he is depressed, but the alcohol greatly adds to his depression. A person is too anxious to leave her apartment, but the longer she stays in her apartment without going out, the more anxious she becomes when she tries to leave. At times, a medication may help a person to break out of these endless circles, but again the medication is never going to fix the problem without the person taking an active role in changing his or her behavior.

Plan a "Medication Trial"

Once you have decided on the size and nature of the problem you want help with, have thought through a number of different approaches, have figured out what part of the problem may actually respond to medication, and have figured out specific target symptoms, what do you do next?

It is important to plan a medication trial. Such a trial requires a number of decisions that will be discussed in more detail in Chapter 9. The outline of a trial should be considered as you go through the first part of this book.

1. An effective trial requires deciding how long it may take to see if the medication is going to work. It makes little sense to start taking a medication and then stop it after 3 days if it is going to take 3 weeks to see whether it is going to work. Part of planning a medication trial is being willing to stay on the medication long enough to see if it is going to do any good. Part of planning is to decide on a safe time to begin. When possible, do not start a new medication right before a big trip or some other important event. Think about starting a medication trial when other events are less likely to confuse the outcome of the medication trial.

2. Planning a medication trial requires discussing side effects with a prescriber. Decide as much as possible which side effects you would be willing to tolerate if they do occur and which ones would cause you to stop wanting to take the medication.

3. Planning a medication trial also means deciding on your commitment to the trial. Are you willing to take the medication every day for the period of the trial, or twice a day, or whatever is required?

4. Finally, part of a "medication trial" is making a commitment to do those other things, in addition to medication, that are likely to make an improvement possible. This may mean a commitment to push yourself to spend more

time with friends, to exercise, or to not use alcohol. This is not really just a medication trial; it is a trial to improve your problem and typically medication is just a piece of it. Decide as part of the trial what you are willing and able to do to increase the chance that the medication will work in ways that are important for you.

Medications do not work for every problem, and they do not work for every person. Even if a medication trial is well thought out and designed, in the end the medication may not do what was hoped. One of the most difficult parts of a medication trial is not continuing the medication or adding another medication but deciding that the medication is not working and should be stopped. This should ideally be a collaborative decision made among the person taking the medication, the prescriber, and other members of the person's support system and treatment team.

Decide if a trial of medication is "worth it"

The process of deciding whether to use a psychiatric medication does not start by thinking about medication. It starts with thinking about the problem you want solved: what kind of problem, how big is it, what else have you tried? It includes a careful consideration of what "getting better" means, and it means coming up with appropriate target symptoms to help monitor whether the medication is actually working. And it involves planning what a medication trial will look like: how long will it take to see if the medication is working and what else you need to do to increase the chance that the medication will help.

It is still important to consider whether a medication trial is "worth it." What are the likely benefits of the medication; how is the medication likely to help? What are the risks and possible side effects from the medication? On balance, is the potential help worth the risk and burden? If the problem you are trying to fix is big, and other solutions have not worked, then a medication trial may well be worth it.

It is hard for any of us to stay completely objective about the decision to use psychiatric medication. Our personal values about psychiatric medication are a strong influence. Balancing the risks and benefits is at the core of the decision of whether or not to use a psychiatric medication. The question is not "Does this medication have potential risks or side effects?" The answer to this question is always "yes"; all medications have at least some risk. There may also be a risk in not trying a medication if your problem is serious and medication could help you. The question to ask yourself is, "What risks are worth taking, for me, at this time, based on my particular weighing of all of the pros and cons?"

1

Anxiety

Anxiety and fear are normal feelings that warn us of danger and prepare us to be ready to react. Anxiety is a signal alerting us to danger that forces us to pay attention. It is difficult to ignore serious anxiety; it takes over our thinking. These feelings and reactions are part of our biology, and they allow us to survive.

Like most biological systems, anxiety has a wide range of intensity. One can experience mild anxiety or overwhelming anxiety. Anxiety can be focused on a specific problem, or it can become generalized and disconnected from any specific trigger. While anxiety can be useful and life-saving, those parts of the brain that process potential threats can also go awry and cause problems. The "anxiety system" can alert us to a threat, but the signal can become so intense that it interferes with our ability to concentrate and cope effectively with the threat. The anxiety system can be triggered inappropriately; wires can get crossed, and a person can experience intense, crippling anxiety even when there is no objective threat. While anxiety is a normal part of human biology, an *anxiety disorder* is an intense, persistent feeling of worry that causes significant distress and that interferes with functioning, and it occurs in the absence of an obvious or rational threat.

Anxiety disorders are a set of distinct syndromes, each with specific diagnostic criteria. They include panic disorders, phobias, obsessive-compulsive disorder, posttraumatic stress disorder, and generalized anxiety disorder. Research is providing us with a clearer understanding of the underlying brain changes connected to each of these anxiety disorders (Stein & Rauch, 2008).

Most people who complain of "anxiety" do not have one of these specific disorders. Rather, they have stress in their lives that is beyond what they can easily cope with, and as a result they may feel anxious. The distinction between anxiety caused by stress and anxiety caused by a biological disorder is not always clear. In extreme cases, it is usually obvious. A person who has no past history of serious anxiety and who has just been told he might have cancer is likely to be very anxious. This anxiety is related to a real threat. On the other hand, a person with severe obsessive-compulsive disorder (OCD), who feels compelled to repeat the same behavior over and over to avoid feeling overwhelming anxiety, has anxiety that is disconnected from any real threat. Differentiating between stress and an anxiety disorder is more difficult if a person is generally very anxious and is in a situation where this is a real threat, such as being told he may lose his job.

The interaction becomes more complicated when a person has an objective cause for anxiety as well as an underlying anxiety disorder; each can make the other worse. For example, a person who has severe and frequent panic attacks may also be at real risk of losing her job because of all the sick time she has taken. A person may be threatened with eviction because of the water damage he has done to the floors and walls of his apartment because of his incessant handwashing connected to his OCD. Real stress makes anxiety-related disorders worse; anxiety disorders can lead to real stress. In the waxing and waning of anxiety over time, it can be confusing to know which came first and how best to intervene.

DESCRIBE YOUR ANXIETY:
UNDERSTAND THE PROBLEM

It is difficult to come up with a good solution to a problem without first understanding the problem you are trying to solve. It is tempting to just pick a solution and go with it. As a clinical psychiatrist, I see many patients who essentially say, "I feel anxious; give me a medication that will make me to feel less anxious." Sometimes that may turn out to be a pretty good solution, but often it is not. Even if a person decides he or she wants to use a medication, it is difficult to know which one to use without understanding the nature of the anxiety. You are more likely to come up with better solutions to a problem if you can first accurately describe the problem. Whether you are going through this process by yourself, with a friend or spouse, or with a therapist, spending the time and energy thoroughly understanding the problem will be time and energy well spent. This does not mean taking a year to analyze everything possible, but it does mean looking at your anxiety and its relationship to your life in as focused and objective a way as possible.

What is the problem?

The first step to finding a solution is to understand the problem as clearly as possible. There are a number of questions that you can ask to help describe the nature of your anxiety. Some of the answers will be obvious. Some of the questions may require that you think about your anxiety in a new way.

- What is the nature of the anxiety?
- Does it fit into one of the defined anxiety disorders, or does it seem "atypical" and does not quite fit any one of them?
- Do you have more than one kind of anxiety, and does that confuse the picture?
- How does your anxiety feel? Can you describe it?
- When does it occur? Are you anxious all of the time, or does the anxiety occur just at work or at home? At what time of day? What are you doing when it occurs? Is there any pattern to it that you can describe?
- Is there an obvious (or perhaps less obvious) cause for

the problem with anxiety? Certainly, life stresses can cause anxiety. Is there a problem with other people in your life, or work, or money, or some other obvious major issue?

- What is your past history of anxiety? Have you been similarly anxious throughout life, or is this feeling new?
- What were the possible causes of other periods of anxiety, and how did the anxiety get better? Did it seem to get better on its own, or did it only get better after there was some life change, or after you took some action? What helped when you had anxiety in the past, whether it was this kind of very severe anxiety or even milder anxiety?
- What did you do to cope with anxiety in the past? Did you start exercising, or did you start a medication? Did you move to a new city or quit a stressful job? How well did these past solutions work?
- Have you had any major traumatic experiences? Some people experience life events that can be related to current anxiety, even years later. Severe stress and trauma can have long-lasting consequences. Some kinds of anxiety are specifically related to past traumas, while others seem less directly connected.

How big is the problem?

Are you coping reasonably well with the anxiety, or is it causing real distress or significantly getting in the way of how you want to live your life? Is this level of anxiety something that can be ignored, or is it something that you need to do something about? How much is it interfering with your life? What is it keeping you from doing?

If the level of anxiety is a minor annoyance, then you may still want to do something about it, but the amount of effort and risk you would be willing to tolerate might be relatively small. If the anxiety is causing a major problem in your life, then it may be worth spending more energy to try and change it, and it may be worth tolerating more side effects or risks so that you can get your life back.

What have you done to try and decrease your anxiety?

If the anxiety seems related to your job, have you thought about what you could do to decrease stress at work? This may mean changing jobs, changing something about the job, or working to change some part of your attitude about your job. Have you tried to talk with anyone else about the stress? What kind of problem solving or brainstorming have you tried? Often we feel stuck in a problem and it is hard to come up with solutions that may be more obvious to someone outside of our own situation. If you are obsessing about a particular set of thoughts, what have you done to try and distract yourself? If the problem is that you are having frequent panic attacks, what have you already done to try to decrease them?

Does your anxiety make sense to you?

What do you think may be causing the anxiety, or making it worse? Are there things going on in your life that make it clear why you are feeling so anxious? Does your anxiety seems disconnected from life events, or does the level of the anxiety seem out of proportion to the stress in your life? When does it occur: all of the time, just at work, or at random times no matter what you are doing?

Are you doing anything that may be making the anxiety worse?

Are you putting yourself into situations that increase your anxiety? Are you pushing yourself or doing things that may be making your anxiety worse? Are you using drugs or alcohol or other substances that may be increasing your anxiety? Caffeine is a common drug-related cause of anxiety (and sleep disruption), and amphetamines and cocaine can certainly cause anxiety. Drug and alcohol withdrawal can also cause symptoms of anxiety. For example, a heavy drinker who drinks every night but does not drink during the day when he is working will experience withdrawal every day, and this could easily be labeled as anxiety. Similarly, a heavy smoker can experience tobacco withdrawal when required to go a few hours without smoking.

Could a medical illness or a prescribed medication be causing the anxiety or making it worse?

Many medical problems can cause what appears to be an anxiety disorder. A thyroid that is too active can cause symptoms similar to generalized anxiety disorder, as can medication given to correct an underactive thyroid. Breathing problems can be experienced as anxiety. A rare tumor that secretes epinephrine can cause symptoms that look like a panic disorder. Similarly, many prescription medications can cause symptoms of anxiety, including medications taken for asthma or high blood pressure, as can some over-the-counter medications (such as decongestants) or combination medications (such as Excedrin). Is a medical assessment indicated? You are much more likely to get a better medical assessment if you can be as clear as possible about the exact nature of the problem. If you want to talk to your physician about possible causes of your anxiety, it is important to describe the symptoms of the anxiety as clearly as possible, how it started, when it comes and goes, its pattern of occurrence, and any other associated symptoms. The better your description is, the more likely that your physician will be able to do the appropriate examination for the specific concern.

What are you doing to take care of yourself?

What helps you to feel better? How do you take care of yourself, and are you actually doing those things? Exercise, meditation, and talking to friends can all help some people; sometimes they can help a lot. It is easy to get so focused on the anxiety that we forget to take care of ourselves.

What would "getting better" and "getting worse" mean to you, around this particular problem?

Would "getting better" mean subjectively feeling better, missing fewer days at work, functioning better at work, or being able to drive a car or go to the mall? As specifically as possible, think about what getting a bit better would look like and think about what getting a lot better would look like. Also, what would getting worse look like? It is useful to be as behaviorally specific as possible. Think about not only how you would feel, but also what behaviors a friend would see in you if your anxiety decreased or increased.

Stress-Related Anxiety

There can be a fine line between anxiety that is related to real life stress and anxiety that is related to an anxiety disorder. It is useful to think about stress before reading about each of the specific anxiety disorders. Standard psychiatric diagnostic criteria sometimes make it seem as though there is a clear distinction between anxiety from stress and an anxiety disorder. Real people are usually more complicated than this; in the real world, stress is often mixed with a disorder, and people often have elements of different disorders at the same time.

Stress-related anxiety is not a formal psychiatric diagnosis, but it is a common problem nonetheless. If you are very anxious about some work-related issue, it may make sense to start by talking to your supervisor, problem solving with a friend about various options, or thinking about what you could do to decrease the work-related stress. If you are feeling stuck, it may be worth talking to a therapist to brainstorm options, especially if you find yourself stuck in a behavioral pattern, like always taking on more and more responsibility or commonly feeling unfairly criticized by coworkers. Even if you are pretty clear that the problem is related to work and not you, it is worth trying to find new ways to cope and to adopt new behaviors that may elicit different responses from others. It may not require something as drastic as changing your job; it is surprising how small changes in attitude or in your own behavior can change the responses of others and help decrease your own anxiety.

Using medication for stress-related anxiety

Because stress-related anxiety is caused by a real-life situation, the appropriate goal for medication is to help you change
your life in ways that would generate less anxiety. If the anxiety is very intense and causes significant distress or problems
with functioning, and if there are other life-changing strategies
underway, then the short-term use of a medication may make
sense. If there is no other strategy underway to deal more effectively with the stress, then medication can easily become the
only treatment, and then it can end up making real change less
likely. The more there is a clear strategy and a clear time line
for how long you expect to need the medication and how you
would know if it is working, the more likely medication is to be
useful. If you are actively working on those issues causing your
anxiety, then short-term use of medication to help with sleep or
help with anxiety can be very useful. Chapter 9 goes into detail
about how to set up a medication trial to increase the likelihood
that medication will be useful.

Even if anxiety seems to be caused by some real life stresses,
such as financial, family, or work issues, medication can be useful if it helps you to cope with these life issues more effectively.
If you are not able to sleep, a few days of taking a sleeping pill
may be beneficial. If you are so anxious you cannot concentrate,
sometimes a few days of taking an antianxiety medication may
really help. If the basic problem is something going on in the
world or your reaction to something happening in the world
that you cannot control, medication only makes sense if it will
help you figure out how to cope with such stresses more effectively. If the medication is seen as the solution, it will almost
never work because the underlying issue will remain and eventually the medication will never be able to do enough to keep
the real issues from re-emerging.

While there are a number of different classes of medications
used to treat other kinds of anxiety, the benzodiazepines are the
primary medications used for stress-related anxiety by someone
who does not have a problem with alcohol or other substance

abuse. This class of medications includes diazepam (Valium), lorazepam (Ativan), alprazolam (Xanax), and others. While the current antianxiety medications do not have high abuse or addiction potential for most people, abuse and addiction is possible. Most people can use alcohol without it becoming a problem, but if someone becomes addicted to alcohol it can become a very bad problem. In the same way, most people can use a benzodiazepine for years without becoming addicted to it or without having to increase the dose. There are some people who become dependent on a benzodiazepine just as some people become dependent on alcohol. This is a particular risk for someone who already uses alcohol or other drugs to excess.

If alcohol or other drug use is part of the problem, there is much more risk when you use any kind of sleeping pill or antianxiety medication. The medications can easily end up reinforcing other drug-related behavior. There is also the risk that the medication will be seen as a way of adapting to a situation that should be considered intolerable. To take an extreme situation, a medication can be damaging if it helps a person to stay in a relationship where he or she is being physically abused, but it may be very useful if it gives a person the strength to leave or change an abusive relationship. The medication is not the cure, but it may still be useful.

What can you expect from an antianxiety medication when used for stress-related anxiety?

Medication can decrease some of the anxiety, hopefully enough so that you can cope more effectively with the real-life stresses that are causing the problem. Medication will rarely take away all of the anxiety. The goal is to decrease the anxiety to manageable levels, not to take so much medication that you are left drugged and numb. Medication is like a Band-Aid that can temporarily help you to heal. The real healing happens when you address the real-world problems underlying the anxiety. While the benzodiazepines tend to be well tolerated, they can all cause tiredness, may impact memory, and definitely can affect driving.

ANXIETY DISORDERS

Anxiety disorders refer to a pattern and level of anxiety that is
more than just a reaction to stress. At times, anxiety does not
make rational sense to either the anxious person or to those
around him or her. There are times when anxiety is not a reaction to the stress of the world but is a biological phenomenon
connected to either learned or genetic biological triggers that
cause anxiety even when there is no actual stress or danger. A
person can have real stress and also have an anxiety disorder
that seems unconnected to the stress. In academic books, these
various syndromes seem easily distinguished from each other.
For real people in the real world, who may have several different sources of real stress as well as several different kinds of
anxiety disorders, separating their cases with distinct diagnoses
can be much more difficult.

In the past, all kinds of anxiety were lumped together. The
current belief is that anxiety disorders can be separated into six
distinct diagnoses, each involving different brain pathways and
each having a different treatment. The six diagnoses include
(1) panic disorder, (2) phobias (extreme fears, such as social
phobia), (3) obsessive-compulsive disorder, (4) posttraumatic
stress disorder, (5) generalized anxiety disorder, and (6) adjustment disorder with anxiety. These anxiety disorders cause different kinds of distress and problems, and they can interfere
with someone's ability to function in various ways. A person
may have only one of these disorders and not any of the others
(e.g., panic disorder and nothing else). A person may also have
several of these different anxiety disorders at the same time, and
it may be difficult to come up with a simple connection between
specific symptoms and a specific disorder.

Panic Disorder

A *panic attack* is a sudden overwhelming sense of fear that
comes on without any clear reason. Common symptoms of
panic attacks include shortness of breath; pounding or racing

heart; chest pain; sweating; hot flashes or chills; nausea or GI upset; feelings of choking, dizziness, unsteadiness, and tingling numbness; and a fear of dying. A person having a panic attack often feels as though he or she are is having a heart attack. In addition to these describable feelings, there is often a sense of dread that makes the panic attack feel much more terrible than just the listing of symptoms would suggest. It is often difficult for the person to describe why it feels so bad. Not all panic attacks are equally severe. Some can be fairly mild, and others are completely overwhelming. Most panic attacks only last 10 or 15 minutes at the most, but they can feel much longer.

When you think about our evolutionary biology, panic attacks make some sense. We are wired to respond very rapidly if we suddenly come across a saber-toothed tiger that is about to pounce. Before we could consciously process what was happening, our heart would start to race, we would start to breathe rapidly, and there would be an outpouring of epinephrine to give us the burst of energy that we need to run away. The "button" for this cascade is still wired into our brain, and it can go off as a false alarm even when there is nothing to be afraid of and nothing in our environment to trigger it. Some of us are more genetically prone to having this panic button go off. Because the trigger is a chance firing in our brain, it usually is not connected to what we are doing and there is no reason why we would have a panic attack at a particular moment. All of this starts in the deep, older part of our brain that does not have language or logical thought. We become conscious of what is happening only when the activity stimulates our cortex and the cascade is already underway. The cortex then tries to make sense of the rush of feelings and emotions that seems to come out of nowhere and has no objective cause.

Occasional panic attacks are fairly common. Many people have a panic attack and then never have another, or they may have them so infrequently that they do not become a significant problem. They can occur when a person is relaxed and sitting at home or when a person is under specific stress. In short, an attack can occur any place and at any time.

Panic disorder is diagnosed when someone has frequent panic attacks and when the person becomes more and more anxious about the possibility of having yet another attack. This anticipatory anxiety, the anxiety about having another attack, is often more disabling than the attacks themselves. Over time, a person may become more and more fearful about when and where the next panic attack will come, and she may even start avoiding situations where she may not be able to find safety if she did have an attack. A person with panic disorder may avoid shopping centers, crowded places, or buses. She may even stay in her house as much as possible. This fear of going out is called *agoraphobia,* and it is a common problem associated with panic disorder. While it might seem reasonable for the person with panic disorder to just "tough it out" and go through the panic attack and wait for it to be over, the attacks can be overwhelming and terrible in ways that are difficult to describe. There is often pressure to "do something," and this often means taking a medication.

For someone with an occasional panic attack, no treatment may be needed. If the panic attacks are not frequent and the anticipatory anxiety can be managed in other ways, medication may not be necessary or recommended. In extreme situations, severe panic disorder and the accompanying agoraphobia can cause major disability and make a normal life impossible. Going to a store, taking a bus, and visiting a friend can all become impossible. A person may feel an overwhelming need to leave work in the midst of a panic attack, even if this results in being fired. Some people make repeated visits to an ER because they are convinced that they are having a heart attack, even after multiple negative medical assessments. One person I worked with had been an active bicycle rider until he developed such a severe panic disorder that being out in the open on a bike became impossible. Medication decreased the frequency and intensity of his attacks enough that he could get back on his bike and get over his fear of being outside.

Alcohol is a significant problem for people with panic disorder. Often people will use alcohol as a way of trying to prevent the next attack and to decrease anxiety about a future attack. However, alcohol does not work and in fact makes things worse. It can make treatment of the panic disorder more difficult, increase the person's disability, and increase the risk of suicide. Alcohol abuse is more common in people with panic disorder than in the general public, and people who suffer from panic disorder need to be very careful about trying to use alcohol to treat their anxiety.

General approach to treatment. Treatment of severe panic disorder has two components. It is important to decrease the frequency and severity of the panic attacks. It is then necessary to work on decreasing the anticipatory anxiety and associated agoraphobia that can leave the person afraid to go outside or engage in normal activities. Panic attacks respond well both to medication and to behavioral therapy. If the panic attacks are frequent and their interference into one's life is significant, medication can often decrease both the frequency and intensity of attacks. Behavioral treatment is also effective, and severe panic disorder responds better to a combination of the two than to either one alone. Medications can decrease the frequency of panic attacks, but they are less directly useful in decreasing the anticipatory anxiety and agoraphobia. For this part of the problem, behavioral treatment is likely to be much more effective. I generally first focus on the use of both medication and behavioral treatment for the panic attacks, and then once the panic attacks have gotten under control I focus on treating the agoraphobia.

Medications for panic disorder. There are no medications that work fast enough to stop a panic attack that has already begun. Most of the commonly used antidepressants and the benzodiazepine-type antianxiety medications are effective in decreasing the frequency of panic attacks. To be effective, the medication has to be taken regularly, not just in response to when an attack happens. While all of the medications listed below have some side effects, for the most part they are safe and relatively well tolerated and can work within a few days.

Antidepressant medications. Antidepressant medications, primarily SSRI (selective serotonin reuptake inhibitors) antidepressants such as fluoxetine (Prozac) or sertraline (Zoloft) can be very useful in decreasing the frequency and intensity of panic attacks. The antianxiety and antipanic effect is separate from the antidepressant effect; these medications can help decrease panic attacks even for people who are not depressed. These medications are generally safe, well tolerated, and nonaddictive, but they may have significant side effects for some people, including weight gain and sexual problems such as decreased libido and delayed orgasm.

Benzodiazepines. Benzodiazepines are Valium-type drugs, including clonazepam (Klonopin) and alprazolam (Xanax), that can also be useful in decreasing the frequency and intensity of panic attacks. Although one might think that taking a pill as soon as the attack starts would be effective, in reality the panic attack will be over before the pill has any chance of taking effect. One of the problems with benzodiazapines is that they are potentially abusable and addictive. They also can interfere with safe driving, and as the dose gets higher it can leave someone feeling and behaving as though he or she were drunk.

These medications are also used to treat the anticipatory anxiety and agoraphobia that are connected to panic disorder. Benzodiazepines can help decrease anticipatory anxiety, but the underlying fear will continue as long as the person is so afraid that she never goes out and experiences that the world is okay. Even if the panic attacks are well controlled, the fear of having another attack can be incapacitating. Medications may help the person feel a bit less distress, but medication alone will not help a person learn to feel that it is safe to go out into the world. Only the experience of actually going out into the world will change this emotional conditioning.

Behavioral treatment for panic attacks. Cognitive behavioral therapy (CBT) can be very effective for people with panic disorder. Initially, many people report that their panic attacks begin abruptly with no warning. When people pay attention to the very beginning of an attack, they find that there is often a short period of a few minutes of "wind-up" where the panic attack builds before it completely takes control. Once someone has learned to recognize these signs, it is possible to learn to actively distract oneself, decrease the intensity of the panic attack, or even abort it altogether. There are several good self-help books about learning how to distract oneself during the period before the full force of the panic attack takes hold (please see the Resource List).

The cascade of a panic attack often begins when the person starts feeling that he might be having a panic attack and he becomes more and more anxious about that possibility. The more anxious he becomes, and the more he attempts to try to stop it, the more he inevitably focuses on the anxiety, which just makes everything worse. It is virtually impossible to decide *not* to focus on something or *not* to think about something. The more you try not to, the more you just think about whatever it is you are trying to avoid. The more effective approach is to actively think about something else, something that will allow you to focus your attention completely. Once the panic attack begins, it is too late. It rapidly escalates out of control and becomes a biological cascade that just runs its course no matter what you try to do. The most effective approach is to prepare ahead of time. Decide what to focus on, and actively practice this focus so that it becomes automatic. Different people will find different kinds of focus more effective. Depending on one's interest, this could mean focusing on memories of positive events, such as a picnic or a vacation, or remembering a favorite piece of music or even a favorite novel. The more someone can learn to focus on something preplanned and specific, the more he or she can focus on something other than the panic attack.

Behavioral treatment of agoraphobia and anticipatory anx-

iety. Unfortunately, in someone with well-established panic disorder, decreasing or even eliminating future panic attacks does not necessarily eliminate the fear of having another attack. Agoraphobia is the fear of going out and being someplace when another panic attack could occur. Even when medication is effective in decreasing the frequency of panic attacks, the anticipatory anxiety and agoraphobia will continue until the person forces herself to return to feared situations. The only way to learn to get out of the house and return to a full range of normal activities is to force oneself to leave the house and engage in those activities. The standard approach, once the panic attacks themselves are under reasonable control, is to construct an "anxiety hierarchy." The person is instructed to list those things that cause some anxiety, and then other activities that cause more, all the way up to activities that cause the most anxiety. The person is then helped to get comfortable with each step of the hierarchy as a way of learning to overcome the fear that had become conditioned.

Medication for agoraphobia and anticipatory anxiety from panic attacks. While behavioral treatment of anticipatory anxiety and agoraphobia is very effective, medications are usually not. Medications may help some people, and they are often used, whether they are helpful or not. Antidepressants have antianxiety properties and may help, but the most important treatment is when the person goes out and engages in regular activities. A benzodiazepine such as diazepam (Valium) may help decrease anxiety enough to make normal activities less threatening, but there is at least theoretical concern that these medications could interfere with learning new response sets that allow behavioral treatment to be effective (Churchill & Furukawa, 2009).

Summary. Medications, whether benzodiazepines (Valium-type medications) or SSRIs and other antidepressants, can help to decrease the frequency and intensity of panic attacks. They are safe, effective, and commonly used. There are nonmedication approaches that also work well, but they take longer and take more effort than just taking a medication. For someone with severe and frequent panic attacks, CBT alone is unlikely to be completely effective. On the positive side, CBT does not have side effects and may lead to more permanent improvement. Often, medications and CBT are more effective when used together than when either is used alone.

Medications alone will provide little help for the anticipatory anxiety and agoraphobia that are commonly connected to panic disorder. The goal of the treatment of panic disorder is to encourage someone to get back to a full range of normal activities. If a person has been afraid to leave her home because of the fear of another attack, part of the treatment has to include helping her to get back to doing these activities. If she takes a medication that decreases the frequency of panic attacks, then it will be much easier to work on forcing herself to engage in normal activities. At the same time, if she does not force herself to go out into the world, the fear will continue, even after the panic attacks themselves are stopped or decreased.

Phobias

A phobia is an intense, irrational, persistent fear that interferes with one's normal life. Most of us are frightened of certain things. There are many different kinds of phobia. *Claustrophobia*, fear of enclosed spaces; *arachnophobia*, fear of spiders; and *acrophobia*, fear of heights, are well known. The long list of possible phobias also includes *alliumphobia*, fear of garlic, and *liticaphobia*, fear of lawsuits. A person can develop a phobia for any kind of object or action, although some are much more common than others. We may be afraid of spiders or snakes or high places. Phobias are an exaggeration of a natural fear response, or it is a fear response directed toward something that most of us would not find fearful. Most of us would be unlikely to voluntarily put a hand into a box containing a poisonous spider or walk on a steel beam 10 stories above the ground. The person with a phobia of spiders will have this same level of fear, the same feeling we would have if we were sticking our hands in a box with a poisonous spider, even in a situation where the actual risk of being bitten by a spider is so low as to be nonexistent. The person with a fear of heights will feel the same fear when inside a tall building that someone else might feel when walking along a narrow ledge outside of the building.

Many of us would avoid walking through woods that are known to have many poisonous snakes. At the same time we might be willing to walk through a forest where snakes were infrequent and we would be even more willing to walk through a grass lawn where snakes were theoretically possible, but very, very unlikely. Most of us with a normal fear of snakes would be even more willing to walk on the ground when it is winter and below freezing, and the possibility of a snake being active is so remote as to be almost impossible. The person with the phobia of snakes might avoid going onto the frozen ground just because of the remote possibility that a snake could be there, or going into a garage just because it is remotely possible that a snake could have crawled in. In the same way somebody with a phobia of small spaces may find that he cannot go into an elevator without feeling that he is suffocating and drowning.

Usually the person with phobia knows that his or her fear is irrational. The person with a phobia of spiders is aware that there are unlikely to be spiders in the garage, and even if there were spiders they would be very unlikely to be dangerous. At the same time, there *could* be spiders and they *could* be dangerous, so the real danger cannot be completely 100% ignored. The person who is afraid of heights is aware that it is very, very unlikely that anyone could fall out of a building when the windows are shut, but it is possible for the building to collapse or for some kind of explosion to throw her out of the window. The person with claustrophobia is very aware that there is no real risk of suffocating in an elevator, but that is how it feels to him. The person with a phobia feels as though a poisonous spider has dropped into his hair, as though he is on a steel beam hanging 10 stories over the ground, or as if he were in a closed box without any air.

Even though the person usually knows that the danger is

extremely remote, the subjective experience is so overwhelming that it is very difficult to overcome it. It is as if that part of the brain that signals "be afraid" is triggered by some common and not very dangerous stimuli. This part of the brain is primitive and powerful—it is instinct-driven rather than rational—and "knowing" that the fear does not make sense does not help. The person is still very afraid and acts as all of us would if we were in a situation that made us that afraid. We would try our best to avoid those things that scare us that much, and we would escape from those things as rapidly as possible when encountered.

A person with a phobia has a specific set of objects or situations that are so frightening that they need to be avoided at all cost. The person may be aware that these fears are irrational and do not make much sense, but they are so strong and powerful that they cannot be overcome. Often, people are so embarrassed by their irrational fears that they hide the fact that they are afraid, which makes their avoidant behavior even more confusing and odd. The person with a phobic disorder is not afraid of everything, and outside of his or her specific phobias may not even be a terribly anxious person.

Social phobia, or social anxiety disorder. Social phobia is the fear of people, primarily new people that someone does not know well. The person with a social phobia often would like to be with people and would like to be more social and have more friends, but meeting people causes overwhelming anxiety. A person may be so afraid of embarrassing herself that meeting people or talking to people can be painful. Social phobia is not the same as shyness. Shy people may have trouble with strangers or being in crowds, but this typically does not interfere with their lives. People with a social phobia find that even normal social interactions such as going to the store, going to work, or going to class provoke overwhelming anxiety.

For someone with social phobia, casually meeting a new neighbor next door may evoke the same level of anxiety that you might feel when giving a lecture to a thousand people when you are unprepared. Because of this, people with social phobia tend to be reclusive and isolated. This is not what a person with social phobia wants. A person who has a schizoid personality or avoidant personality may not want much contact with other people, but a person with social phobia wants friends and wants to be with people. Once a person with social phobia gets to know somebody and gets through the phobic period, he or she can often do very well with other people. It is the "getting to know" phase that presents an overwhelming barrier.

As with other anxiety disorders, alcohol can be a major problem. A person may start drinking as a way to calm himself or decrease his fear, and while this can help in the short run this rarely works in the long term and is best avoided.

Principles of treatment. The primary treatment for phobias is behavioral. The idea is that if you become afraid of something and then run away, this reinforces the fear. As you leave the fearful scene the decrease in anxiety feels good. The decrease in anxiety is reinforcing, and you learn to associate the leaving of the scene, the avoiding of the fearful situation, with feeling better. Every time you leave a situation where you are afraid, the fear becomes stronger. On the other hand, if you stay in the fearful situation long enough the anxiety will first get worse and worse, and then after a period of time the anxiety will decrease and you will start feeling better. If you can stay in the fearful situation long enough, the anxiety will decrease and the connection between the stimulus and the fear will become less intense. The old saying that you should get back on the horse after it throws you is based on this commonsense principle.

Behavioral therapy starts with setting up a hierarchy of situations or objects, starting with those that are a bit fearful but not so much as to be overwhelming, up to those so fearful that even thinking about them is difficult. Treatment then involves forcing yourself to stay in the presence of the least fearful situation on your hierarchy list until you get used to it and it is not as scary. Then you take on the next situation on your hierarchy, then the next, taking whatever time is needed to get used to each situation in turn. The fancy term for this is called hierarchical desensitization, and if you are willing to go along with this kind of program it is usually very effective. For example, if the fear is one of spiders, the hierarchy may start with looking at pictures of spiders until this does not cause too much anxiety, then moving on to a video of living spiders, then perhaps looking at a cage of living and moving spiders, then finally picking up a (nonpoisonous) spider. The problem is that it requires you to be willing to tolerate uncomfortable anxiety long enough for the connection between the object and the feeling of anxiety to begin to decrease.

Effective treatment requires that you work through your hierarchy one step and one item at a time, until the level of anxiety at each level becomes manageable and you go to the next level. Most people with a phobic disorder are afraid of more than one situation, and treatment requires that they need to go through this same process for each specific phobia. The good news is that this process usually gets faster and easier as you work through your second fear, and then your third and fourth.

Medications for treatment of phobias. Medications typically have a limited role in the treatment of most phobias. Benzodiazepines (antianxiety medications such as diazepam [Valium] or alprazolam [Xanax]) may help a bit, but they are abusable and addictive, and it is often tempting to try and take enough to numb yourself. Despite these concerns, antianxiety medications are very commonly prescribed and the majority of people with a phobic disorder will end up taking them at some point, whether or not they really help to overcome the specific phobic fear. There is a commonsense feeling that if you are really anxious and scared, then an antianxiety medication should be able to help. In the short term, these medications may help the person to feel less anxious, but there is some concern that they can also interfere with the relearning of connections, which is at the core of behavioral treatment (Bouton, Kenney, & Rosengard, 1990). On balance, if a small dose of an antianxiety medication really allows you to better confront what you are phobic about and go out and live in the world with less distress, then it may be worth trying.

Antidepressants are also often prescribed in the treatment for phobias. There is little research support for their effectiveness except for social phobia. At the same time, there is a lot of anecdotal experience that they probably help people feel less anxious and less overwhelmed by their phobic fears. Antidepressant medications are clearly indicated if you are depressed or have severe general anxiety, both of which are common problems for people with a phobic disorder. Antidepressants do not have a formal FDA indication for phobias other than social phobia, but their use is very common and they often seem somewhat helpful.

Social phobias do respond to a number of different medications, including SSRI antidepressants, benzodiazepines, gabapentin (Neurontin), and pregabalin (Lyrica). Behavioral treatment, by forcing oneself to be more social and starting with social interactions that are relatively easy, is still the core of treatment. Medications can be useful as part of this process and can make it easier for people to force themselves to go into fearful social situations.

Summary about phobias. Many people with phobias are prescribed either antidepressants or antianxiety medications. Because many people with phobias are also depressed or anxious, these medications can be helpful. If the person has social phobia, medications can clearly help, and if the social phobia is severe enough a medication may be worth trying. For other phobias the role of medication is less clear. While medications may help somewhat, it is the behavioral treatment that is most effective in helping someone to decrease disabling fear.

Performance anxiety. Performance anxiety refers to overwhelming anxiety that is specifically connected to some kind of performance: either giving a talk, making a presentation at work or at school, playing music in front of other people, or taking an exam. For some people, just thinking about a public performance is enough to elicit the anxiety. It typically does not show up during practice or in other situations, only when there is a real performance or the person is actively thinking about a real performance.

It is a common problem, even though it is not included as a formal diagnosis in the *DSM-IV* (Diagnostic and Statistical Manual of Mental Disorders TR). One study showed that 33% of adolescent musicians reported a negative impact on their performance because of their anxiety, and 10% reported that their anxiety was having a negative impact on their careers (Fehm & Schmidt, 2006). It is common for people with performance anxiety to change jobs, avoid giving presentations even if this would help their careers, or stop activities that they would otherwise enjoy. The person may have little anxiety in other situations, may have no problem meeting new people, and not have other phobias or fears. A person with performance anxiety often has significant "somatic" symptoms. Somatic symptoms refer to physical symptoms, including increased heart rate, sweating, and tremors, in addition to being overly self-critical and having other feelings of anxiety. Performance anxiety is probably related to an increased release of norepinephrine, the "fight or flight" hormone that gets us prepared for some emergent physical activity. Common ways of coping with performance anxiety include overpractice, but it often continues to be a problem.

Medications for performance anxiety. If your performance anxiety is severe enough to cause you to avoid or significantly interfere with a performance, then some kind of intervention is worth considering. Over-practice can help, as can "practice performances" in front of friends, although these strategies do not always help in people with a more severe problem. A benzodiazepine such as diazepam (Valium) or alprazolam (Xanax) is often prescribed for performance anxiety. The problem is that while this can decrease the anxiety, it also interferes with cognitive performance. One would lose a certain "edge," either a lot or a little, from taking any of these medications during a performance or before an exam. It would be like using alcohol to calm down before a performance. It is commonly done but is not recommended.

Beta blockers such as propranolol (Inderal) or atenolol (Tenormin) are often more effective than antianxiety medications in the treatment of performance anxiety. These medications do not affect the brain or the mental sense of "anxiety." Rather, they block beta-receptors outside of the brain that are all over the body. Epinephrine stimulates two kinds of receptors: alpha-receptors and beta-receptors. Stimulating epinephrine beta-receptors causes many of the body's reactions to anxiety, such as increased heart rate, tremors, and sweating. Blocking these beta-receptors blocks the body's response to anxiety, including racing heartbeat, tremors, sweating, and agitation, which all amplify the brain's sense of anxiety. By blocking the body's response, the sense of anxiety tends to markedly decrease without interfering with brain function that is required for the effective performance of the music or speech or taking an exam. Alpha-adrenergic receptors affect relaxation of smooth muscles throughout the body. Blocking these alpha-receptors can help to lower blood pressure and decrease urinary retention, and have other effects throughout the body.

Propranolol is a short-acting medication that works rapidly and lasts for several hours. Its effect is often dramatic, even at low doses. It will not help the anticipatory anxiety that precedes the performance, but it can be very effective in decreasing the feelings of anxiety during the performance itself. It is safe to use it every day and is neither addictive nor subject to being abused, but daily use is generally not required. Propranolol can easily be used symptomatically only as needed, taken an hour or two before the performance or exam without the need that it be taken at other times. It should initially be taken as a "test dose" when the person is not driving and is not required to perform anything, just to see the person's individual reaction. While it can cause tiredness and dizziness, at the relatively low dose use for performance anxiety, these side effects are uncommon.

Unfortunately, unless someone has significant somatic symptoms connected to his or her anxiety, other kinds of anxiety disorder do not usually respond to propranolol. Because it is safe and works rapidly, if a person with other kinds of anxiety does complain of rapid heart rate, sweating, tremor, or a sense of motor agitation, propranolol may be worth trying at least for a dose or two to see if it may help.

Obsessive-compulsive disorder

Obsessive-compulsive disorder (OCD) refers to obsessive thoughts that go round and round in your head, enough to cause significant distress or compulsive behaviors, behaviors that "must" be repeated over and over. Many of us have minor little quirks or behaviors that we tend to repeat. We go back and check the light switch a second time, or go back to check to make sure the door is really locked, or go back after we left the house to make sure the gas is off. Children commonly have these rituals and even we, as adults, often have some lingering rituals. When these rituals become intrusive and get in the way of how we would like to live our lives we call them a disorder. Going back to check your hair in front of the mirror once or twice is not usually considered a problem. It becomes a disorder when you *need* to go back and look at yourself 13 times or 23 times, when you *need* to spend more and more time having to do it, and when you feel increasingly anxious or terrible if you are prevented from doing it.

Almost any behavior that can be repeated can become a part of OCD. A person with OCD may need to dress and then undress many times before leaving the house, or she may require that lights or faucets be checked many times, over and over. Often, people with OCD are too embarrassed to give a clear explanation of their bizarre behaviors. Often, they do not understand it themselves. People with OCD will usually get very upset and very anxious if the behavior is interrupted or if they are prevented from completing it. Over time the behaviors can become more intrusive, and can take longer and longer amounts of time. It may take hours of repetitive dressing and undressing before the person can leave the house. A person may need to count every light switch in the house before leaving the house, or he may need to go up and down the stairs 13 times before sitting down to eat a meal, or he may need to open and close a door nine times before finally going out the door.

Behaviors often migrate, going from one kind of repetitive behavior to another. OCD can be a minor annoyance or completely incapacitating, making it impossible for the person to live a normal life because of the intrusiveness and time required by the rituals. The person with OCD feels that she "must" do these behaviors until it feels right or until the right number of repetitions has occurred. It is unclear what would happen if she did not follow out her rituals, only that she "must" and she will feel increasingly anxious until she can complete the required behavior.

Most people with OCD know that this is all irrational. Like the other anxiety disorders, OCD occurs when a normal part of our biological brain wiring is triggered inappropriately. As a "thought experiment," think how you would feel if you were forced to pick up some human feces with your bare hands. You would feel dirty, contaminated, and would want to wash your hands as soon as possible. If you were prevented from washing your hands, you would probably be focused on wanting to get your hands clean as soon as possible. If you were supposed to be listening to a lecture or doing some other activity, knowing that you had human feces on your hands would likely interfere with your ability to focus and concentrate on whatever else you were supposed to be doing. This is the kind of anxiety experienced by someone with OCD.

Once you were able to wash your hands you would feel a sense of relief, a decrease in that anxiety. But if you washed your hands and they did not feel clean, if you felt that there could still be some feces under your fingernails or in a crevice, you would want to wash your hands again until you felt that they were really clean, until you had that sense of relief from knowing that your contaminated hands were now clean. And if your hands still did not feel clean you would wash them a third or a fourth time, until you get the sense that they are finally clean. Again, this is the feeling experienced by someone with OCD. Somebody with obsessive hand washing might wash them many, many times until the skin becomes raw and cracked.

The obsessive part of OCD involves intrusive, recurrent, end-less thoughts that are the thinking counterpart of compulsive behaviors. An obsessive thought is thinking the same thing over and over again without being able to stop. Many of us have had the experience of having a jingle go round and round in our heads and not being able to stop it. Some people have obses-sive thoughts about doing something bad or embarrassing, which is out of character with the person's normal thoughts. It is bad enough to have obsessive thoughts, but it is even more upsetting if the intrusive thoughts involve something violent or immoral or illegal. At times, people with obsessive thoughts become very frightened that they will actually do whatever the obsessive thought requires. This may cause further problems with their ability to function normally.

Obsessive thoughts are not voices or hallucinations. While the person may feel that he is under some pressure to do what the thoughts command, it is clear to him that these are his own thoughts. At the same time, they are often disturbing and difficult to ignore. At times the thoughts have content that is deeply disturbing. Most people with OCD do not act out on these thoughts, but just the idea that they might is often deeply disturbing to the person involved.

Most people with OCD feel embarrassed, upset, anxious, and confused by their own need to repeat their behaviors. They do not understand it, and they know they cannot stop it and it does not make any sense. Many people with OCD try their best to hide their compulsive behaviors from others, doing the required rituals in secret, which can add to the sense of isolation from others. At the same time, the need to complete the rituals can completely control how the person behaves in the world. People with OCD who try to stop or interrupt their compulsive behaviors will become more and more anxious and feel increasingly forced to do whatever they are obsessed about.

OCD is often associated with other compulsive behaviors, including trichotillomania (compulsive hair pulling) and hoarding behavior. Like other forms of OCD, these are often embarrassing and irrational, even to the person who is doing them.

Management and treatment of OCD. Treatment of OCD can be very difficult, and at times OCD can be as disabling as any major mental illness. The primary treatment is behavioral. Again you establish a hierarchy of behaviors starting with those that are relatively easy to stop doing, and if necessary you get some help to stop doing them. As with phobias, the anxiety will initially mount and get higher and higher but over a period of time, if you are able to stop doing the particular behaviors, the anxiety will decrease. Behavioral treatment starts by developing a hierarchy of repetitive rituals that go from easy to those that are very hard or impossible to stop doing.

Medications in the treatment of OCD. Medications can have an important role in the treatment of OCD, but it is a secondary rather than a primary role. Medications may help a person learn to resist the compulsion, but the medications do not work if there is not very active effort from the person to change his own behaviors. The antidepressant medications that work through the serotonin system in the brain, the SSRIs, such as fluoxetine (Prozac) or sertraline (Zoloft), are the medications commonly used. Most of the OCD research has been with fluvoxamine (Luvox), which is an SSRI antidepressant similar to the other SSRIs, although it is not clear if any one of these medications is any more effective than the others.

If an SSRI does not work, clomipramine (Anafranil) can be tried. It is an older tricyclic-type antidepressant, which also has a strong effect on the serotonin system of the brain. It has more potential side effects than do the SSRIs, including more risk of death if taken as an overdose and more risk if taken by someone with an already damaged heart. Clomipramine can also cause a wide variety of other side effects, including dry mouth, constipation, and tiredness, but it is effective in some people who do not find the SSRIs effective.

A small dose of an antipsychotic medication, taken along with one of the SSRI antidepressants, can sometimes be more effective than the antidepressant alone, even for people who have no psychotic symptoms. Risperidone (Risperdal) has the most research support and is most commonly used for this, although it is likely that all of the antipsychotic medications would work equally well.

There is some recent research that suggests that D-cycloserine, an amino acid that one can purchase in health food stores, may make behavioral treatment more effective. D-cycloserine has no effect by itself. It is only useful in combination with behavioral treatment. It seems to help some of the relearning, and specifically seems to help extinguish fear, which is the core of behavioral treatment.

Summary about OCD. OCD can be a terribly disabling condition that is often difficult to treat. In its mild form, it causes some distress and perhaps some embarrassment. In its more severe form, it can interfere with almost all normal activities. Medications alone are not effective. A medication can sometimes help a person fight her obsessive behavior or thoughts more effectively, but medication cannot replace the need for her to force a change in her own behavior. A therapist can greatly assist in this, as can self-help books. Change in OCD behavior requires that the person actively work to decrease her ritual behavior in some organized fashion. If a person with more severe OCD wants to try a medication, it may help and is probably worth a trial.

Posttraumatic stress disorder (PTSD)

After we suffer trauma, such as being in a car accident or having a near death experience or being robbed, we all will go through a period of adjustment. We will typically obsess about the event, relive it over and over again in our minds for a while, perhaps go through a period of having trouble sleeping or having nightmares, and then go back to normal. This kind of stress reaction is a normal adaptive way of dealing with a bad situation.

We all have a limit as to how much stress we can deal with. When this limit is exceeded, when we are under more stress than we are designed to tolerate, it can cause permanent changes in our brains and in our behaviors. This permanent alteration is called posttraumatic stress disorder (PTSD). Common symptoms of PTSD include difficulty falling or staying asleep, irritability and anger outbursts, difficulty concentrating, hypervigilance, being overly sensitive to what is going on around oneself, and exaggerated startle response. There is often a persistent re-experiencing of the traumatic event, with the person reliving it over and over again as though it just happened yesterday even though it may have been years before. Intrusive nightmares are common. People with PTSD are both hypersensitive to noise, people, events, as well as being generally numb to normal human emotion and connection.

It appears that some kinds of stresses are more likely to produce PTSD than others. Data suggest that recurrent sexual abuse in children, especially by a trusted adult, is more likely to cause PTSD than something equally horrific such as one-time rape by a stranger (Manigilio, 2009). We know that people who are exposed to war combat over a longer period of time are more likely to develop PTSD than if the combat exposure is more time limited. It seems that there are biological or genetic predispositions to developing PTSD, but this is not connected to IQ or psychological health. While normal stress reactions eventually dissipate and go away, posttraumatic stress disorder can endure forever.

People with PTSD often have flashbacks, during which they can feel that they are back in the midst of the trauma, even years later. This is often accompanied by nightmares, increased arousal, and hypervigilance with the constant sense that they need to be on guard. Situations that can trigger memories or flashbacks are often avoided, which sometimes involves avoiding crowds, noisy places, or other situations that have some element that can be connected to the traumatic event. Anger and irritation are common. There is often an associated emotional numbness. People with PTSD often have problems feeling connected to others. These symptoms often cause difficulty in intimate relationships and may cause problems at work. Alcohol or drug abuse is a common complication of living with PTSD.

In its pure form, PTSD is easy to recognize. When it is combined with other problems, it can be much more difficult to decide what part of the problem is from PTSD. If somebody with schizophrenia, depression, or chronic substance abuse develops PTSD, the symptoms of the PTSD can be confused with the symptoms of the other mental illness. A person with schizophrenia may have intrusive nightmares and have an excessive startle response, recurrently relive old childhood experiences, and even talk about terrible things that have happened, and yet all of this can be written off as just being part of the psychotic illness. A person who is alcohol dependent can have a range of PTSD symptoms that may be assumed to be related just to the alcohol use.

PTSD can appear in many different guises. A person can look depressed, have trouble sleeping, avoid people, be overly sensitive to noise or to people moving too rapidly, and at the same time have trouble maintaining normal loving relationships. Alcohol and other drug use is common as the person tries to self-medicate. People with PTSD often have trouble understanding why they react so strongly to things that seem pretty innocuous, and at the same time they have trouble connecting to people in a normal way. They are aware of the flashbacks to the traumatic event and the intrusive nightmares, and they realize that their response to the world is very different from other people's responses. This sense of "differentness" can increase the sense of isolation.

If the initial trauma was childhood sexual abuse, the specific memory of the events may be either repressed or so embarrassing that it is not discussed. Other people with PTSD become emotionally out of control when they try to talk about the traumatic event. Some people with PTSD are so anxious and sensitive that they are in a perpetual state of crisis. Depression and anxiety are frequent components of PTSD, and suicide can be a concern. Some people with PTSD have pushed away their friends and family and are left with a limited natural support system. All of this adds to the distress and disability connected to the condition.

General treatment approaches for PTSD. Psychosocial support is the cornerstone of effective treatment for PTSD. The main approach is to support the person's feelings as normal and appropriate after such a traumatic situation and help this person to focus on problem solving and learning adaptive behavior. Effective treatment often includes supportive group therapy where people with similar life experiences can share and normalize their feelings. It can be helpful to allow the person to talk about the traumatic event, especially how he feels about the event, as long as it is not the therapist or others who are pushing this agenda. Pushing the person to graphically retell and relive the traumatic event can lead to re-traumatization and make the PTSD worse. Rather, the goal is to help people to feel safe, feel that they are not alone, and know that their reactions and feelings are normal feelings to an abnormal situation. The focus of either group or individual therapy is to let people realize that whatever they are feeling is shared and normal and not unique to them alone. Cognitive behavioral therapy can also help the person to recognize and interrupt automatic thoughts that have become associated with the traumatic incident.

Role of medications in PTSD treatment. Medications can help some people with PTSD tolerate some of their symptoms with less distress. There are no medications that are officially approved for treatment of PTSD, and medication use is focused on symptoms rather than on treatment of PTSD itself. For a person who is depressed, anxious, or hyperreactive, an antidepressant, such as an SSRI-type antidepressant, might be useful. For a person with significant problems with mood swings, a mood stabilizer, such as valproic acid (Depakote) or carbamazepine (Tegretol), might be useful. For a person with intrusive nightmares, sleep disturbance, and hypervigilance, prazosin (Minipress) or guanfacine (Tenex) can be useful. Both of these medications were developed for the treatment of high blood pressure and to decrease the effect of the norepinephrine system on the brain. For people who are extremely reactive, startle easily, are very anxious, and are hypersensitive, a very low dose of an antipsychotic medication may help decrease some of this extreme sensitivity.

All of these medications have significant side effects, and for each person the risks and side effects need to be weighed against the positive effects from each medication. SSRI antidepressants can cause decreased sexual function and weight gain, and can increase the sense of being emotionally disconnected from others. Prazosin and guanfacine can cause sedation and dizziness. Antipsychotic medications, even the newer second-generation ones, and even at low doses, come with at least some risk of causing tardive dyskinesia, a potentially permanent movement disorder. For the most part, these side effects are not severe and are not very likely, but they are all part of the decision about whether the medication is worth it.

Because anxiety is a prominent part of PTSD, it makes sense that antianxiety medications such as diazepam (Valium) or clonazepam (Klonopin) are often used in its treatment. Unfortunately, they tend to be less effective than one might expect, and there seems to be a significant risk of abuse and dependency. Many people with PTSD already have problems with alcohol or other drug abuse. People with PTSD are often in such distress and are so anxious that it is very easy to start taking higher and higher doses of diazepam or clonazepam or one of the other similar medications in this class in an attempt to get some relief. Unfortunately this can easily lead to dependence or abuse of the antianxiety medication. If this occurs in a person who is already abusing alcohol or other medications, then the person ends up with a double dependence. As a result, most physicians are appropriately cautious about prescribing these medications for people with PTSD; when I prescribe them I tend to be careful about the dose and the amount of medication actually being used. Benzodiazepines can cause problems driving, some sedation, and problems with thinking clearly.

Summary about PTSD. PTSD is often unrecognized and can lead to multiple problems that may not be connected to the PTSD. Substance abuse, problems getting along with people, and a general level of distress are all common parts of PTSD, and such factors can make it confusing to figure out what parts of a person's problems are connected to the specific PTSD diagnosis. In many ways, it does not matter. What does matter is to help the person get more control over his or her own life. There is no medication for PTSD and no medication will have much effect on the core problems caused by the trauma, but medications can help to decrease some of the symptoms associated with the disorder. Medication can help decrease some of the intrusive nightmares that are often a prominent part of PTSD. Other medications can help decrease the startle response and overreactivity of the disorder. Antidepressants can help with general anxiety and depression. The biggest issue is to avoid doing things that make the PTSD and its associated symptoms worse. This means paying attention and minimizing alcohol and other drug use, and making sure that one does not use prescribed antianxiety medications in ways that can increase abuse and dependence.

General anxiety disorder

Generalized anxiety disorder (GAD) is not just anxiety about "something," it is anxiety about everything. While GAD may be accompanied by other specific kinds of anxiety, such as panic disorder or phobias, the generalized anxiety is not limited to specific situations and is severe enough to cause major life problems. People are not just anxious in reaction to a particular fear or event, but they are very, very anxious most of the time. All of us are on a continuum of how much baseline anxiety we feel. Anxiety is an internal signal that helps us pay attention to events or stimuli that are most important. If we are not anxious at all, then it is hard to focus, stay alert, or be interested. Too much anxiety can interfere with being able to concentrate or enjoy things. It is likely that GAD has a significant genetic basis (Cerdá, Sagdeo, Johnson, & Galea, 2010). While life events can cause us to be more or less anxious, the extreme anxiety of someone with GAD is part of their biology. Not all extreme anxiety is from GAD. It can be part of another illness, like depression or schizophrenia. It can be caused by a medical illness or from a prescription medication. A common problem in people with GAD is alcohol and other substance abuse. One can understand why a person who is desperately anxious may try to use alcohol or other drugs in an effort to feel better. The problem is that it often requires more and more alcohol or drugs in order to have the desired effect. While alcohol can help decrease anxiety in the short run, over time it stops working and can cause other problems.

Treatment approaches for GAD. There are a number of treatments that can help, although none of them will "cure" the underlying condition. Meditation, mindfulness training, regular exercise, yoga, and other kinds of body work all help. Psychotherapy can help, especially psychotherapy that focuses on "automatic thoughts" and how the anxiety impacts the person's life. Group and individual therapy can help someone understand his anxiety and cope with it. Generally it makes sense to stop doing those things that can make anxiety worse, such as drinking coffee or abusing alcohol, and do things that can lessen anxiety, such as regular exercise and paying attention to things that cause life stress.

The role of medication in GAD. A variety of medications can also help. Antianxiety medications, such as diazepam (Valium), clonazepam (Klonopin), or alprazolam (Xanax), can all help and can be taken for long periods of time. Most people can take these medications over time and never get addicted to them. They stay on a stable dose that is helpful, and their lives are better because of the medication. The risk is that some people do fall into abusive or addictive behaviors with these medications, needing a higher and higher dose to achieve a smaller and smaller effect. The use of Valium-type drugs must be approached with some caution, especially if the person has had a history of abusing alcohol or other drugs.

Most of the antidepressant medications can also help with anxiety, even if the person is not depressed. SSRIs, such as fluoxetine (Prozac) or sertraline (Zoloft), are often useful for GAD.

Summary about GAD. Generally, it makes sense to stop doing things that can make anxiety worse, such as drinking coffee, and do things that lessen anxiety, such as regular exercise and paying attention to things that cause life stress. It is also important to avoid using alcohol or other drugs as a way of coping with anxiety. For people whose anxiety is so severe that it causes a major problem, a medication, either an antidepressant or an antianxiety medication, may help. The goal is to take enough medication to decrease the anxiety enough so that the person's distress is a bit less and he or she can function a bit better. The goal is *not* to completely eliminate all anxiety. Using medication to block all anxiety is likely to require such a high dose of medication that the person will end up feeling drugged and intoxicated, and even then some anxiety is likely to persist. A person who tries to take enough medication to eliminate all anxiety often seeks a higher and higher dose, which can easily lead to dependency.

Adjustment disorder with anxiety

Bad and stressful things happen to people. We react to these events with anxiety or depression or other feelings. This is natural and normal. The expectation is that when the event is over and when things are better, we will then feel better. At times, the stress is over and the danger has passed but the person continues to feel extremely anxious. As this anxiety continues and interferes with the person's life, this overreaction is labeled as an adjustment disorder. Adjustment disorders are not lifelong occurrences. They start with a real event, but then trigger a reaction that seems out of proportion to what has happened.

At the beginning, an adjustment disorder may look like a normal reaction to a bad situation. As the reaction continues, and as the anxiety does not decrease, it begins to look more abnormal. The type of reaction can be anxiety or depression or any other feeling. It can become chronic, but more commonly it eventually dissipates. Often the person may readily acknowledge that he or she is overreacting to the situation, but the feeling of anxiety or depression is real and cannot easily be shaken off.

General approaches to treatment. Usually, an adjustment disorder is a temporary condition. Emotional support, psychotherapy, and encouragement to keep active can all help. If sleep is a problem, the use of sleeping pills may be helpful. In general, prescription sleeping pills are both more effective and safer than those bought without a prescription. In rare cases, an antidepressant medication may be useful, but for the most part medication is not needed and is not the core of treatment.

An important treatment consideration is to avoid things that make the condition worse. It is most important that the person not respond to the stress with an increased use of alcohol or other drugs.

Overview of Medications Used for Treatment of Anxiety[*]

As discussed in the introduction, medications are a tool that can be helpful in decreasing anxiety or coping with it more effectively. Understand the problem first, think about what might be causing it, consider things that you might be doing that could be making anxiety worse, and think about things you could be doing that might lessen the anxiety. Then consider whether a medication is likely to be a useful tool to treat your problem, as you now understand it.

This is intended to be a book about how to think about the

---

[*] Please refer to Instant Psychopharmacology (3rd ed.) for more detailed information about these medications.

use of medications, rather than a book that goes into details about the medications themselves. There are many psychopharmacology books available that can provide much more information about specific medications (Diamond 2009). At the same time, it does seem useful to provide a brief overview of the major classes of medications used to treat the various anxiety disorders, with a listing of the most commonly used medications in each class.

Benzodiazepine antianxiety medications (anxiolytics)

Benzodiazepines (e.g., diazepam [Valium], clonazepam [Klonopin], and alprazolam [Xanax]) are medications that decrease general anxiety. For the most part, they can decrease anxiety no matter what the cause, although they are generally not helpful for OCD and can decrease the effectiveness of some behavioral treatments. They are useful for panic disorder and can also be used to help with sleep disorders. They have some potential for dependence and can be abused. This potential for abuse is of most concern for people who currently abuse alcohol or other drugs or have a history of such abuse. People who are dependent on a benzodiazepine can have a medically dangerous withdrawal if it is stopped abruptly. The other concern is that a benzodiazepine can impair driving, similar to the effects of alcohol.

Generic/Brand name	Dose = 10 mg of Valium	Speed of Onset	Peak Level	Duration of Action
alprazolam/Xanax	0.5 mg	fast	1–2 hr	3–5 hr
chlordiazepoxide/Librium	25 mg	medium	1–4 hr	10 + hr*
clonazepam/Klonopin	0.5 mg	medium	1–4 hr	10–12 hr
diazepam/Valium	10 mg	fast	1–2 hr	4–6 hr*
estazolam	1–2 mg	slow	0.5–5 hr	6–8 hr
flurazepam/Dalmane	15–30 mg	fast	1–1.5 hr	7–10 hr*
lorazepam/Ativan	1 mg	fast	1–1.5 hr	4–6 hr
oxazepam/Serax	20 mg	slow	1–5 hr	6 hr
temazepam	15–20 mg	medium	0.5–3 hr	5–6 hr
triazolam/Halcion	0.25–0.5 mg	fast	0.8–1.2 hr	0.5–1 hr

* (Cloos, J.M 2010)

Buspirone (Buspar)

Buspirone (Buspar) is in a class of medication all to itself. It is not addictive and has no potential to be abused. Unlike the benzodiazepines, which work within hours, buspirone takes 1 to 3 weeks to be effective. It can be useful for general anxiety but is not useful for panic disorder and does not help with sleep disorders. While it is effective in decreasing anxiety, there is no subjective "feeling" that it is doing anything and as a result it is often less satisfying than something that works more rapidly and has a more apparent subjective impact.

Antidepressant medications

Most of the commonly used antidepressants, with the exception of bupropion (Wellbutrin), are also useful in the treatment of anxiety disorders, even for people who are not depressed. The antianxiety effect seems separate from any antidepressant effect. They can be useful for generalized anxiety disorder and panic disorder. The SSRIs and SNRIs (selective serotonin and norepinephrine receptor inhibitors) are also useful in the treatment of OCD. These medications take 1 to 3 weeks or even longer to be effective. Some are sedating and can help sleep disorders, while others do not cause sedation.

These medications have the advantage of being effective and of not being subject to abuse. They are not addictive, and for the most part they are safe even when taken over long periods of time. They are generally well tolerated and most people take them with few side effects. They can cause various side effects in some people, including some risk for weight gain, sexual dysfunction, and increased mood instability.

The following is a list of antidepressants that are useful in the treatment of anxiety disorders (whether or not the person is depressed):

- SSRIs (e.g., fluoxetine [Prozac] and sertraline [Zoloft])
- SNRIs (e.g., venlafaxine [Effexor] and duloxetine [Cymbalta])
- Mirtazapine (Remeron)

Beta blockers

These medications are most commonly used to decrease blood pressure, and they work to block the effect of anxiety on the body rather than working on the brain. Anxiety is typically accompanied by somatic symptoms, or changes in the body, such as increased heart rate, sweating, or tremors. These body changes are picked up by the brain and felt as anxiety. These peripheral symptoms are caused by the release of a chemical messenger called epinephrine. Epinephrine has alpha effects and beta effects. When the beta effects of epinephrine are blocked by a beta blocker, the person's body reaction to anxiety is also blocked. There is less of an increase in heart rate and decreased sweating and tremors, and this can decrease the feeling of anxiety in some people.

Beta blockers are particularly useful for people who have performance anxiety. A person can become extremely anxious when required to give a talk at work, take an exam, or give a musical performance, but may not particularly be anxious at other times. A beta blocker can block the sweating and racing heartbeat that increases the feeling of anxiety. A beta blocker has the advantage of causing little sedation or problems with thinking in the way that benzodiazepines can cause.

Antipsychotic medications

Antipsychotic medications used to be called "major tranquilizers." They are effective, but they have more potential risks and side effects than other medications that can be used for the treatment of anxiety. Most people prefer how they feel on other antianxiety medications, and there is a risk for more serious side effects. Antipsychotic medications can treat severe anxiety that has not responded to other treatment, and anxiety that is so severe that it causes someone's thinking to become disorganized. When used for the treatment of anxiety, antipsychotic medications are typically used at a much lower dose than is typical when they are used in the treatment of schizophrenia.

While these medications can be used safely for long periods of time, there are long-term risks that must be considered. All of these medications have some risk for causing tardive dyskinesia, a potentially permanent movement disorder that is usually reversible if recognized early. Many of these medications can cause weight gain in some people, and some are associated with an increased risk of diabetes if taken over time. The following is a list of common antipsychotic medications used for anxiety disorders:

- Second-generation antipsychotic medications (e.g., quetiapine [Seroquel] or risperidone [Risperdal])
- First-generation antipsychotic medications (e.g., haloperidol [Haldol])

Alpha1-adrenergic agonists and Alpha2-adrenergic antagonists

These medications are commonly used to help control high blood pressure. They work through the alpha side of the epinephrine system that was discussed above. They can decrease some of the symptoms of PTSD, specifically intrusive nightmares and hyperactivity. Examples of these medications are prazosin (Minipress) and guanfacine (Tenex).

D-cycloserine

D-cycloserine is an amino acid that can be purchased at health food stores. It is not effective by itself, but it does seem to increase the effectiveness of behavioral treatment of OCD.

GABA-agonists

These medications are primarily used as anticonvulsant medications. They also seem to help some kinds of pain that is related to nerve irritation, such as the pain caused by diabetic neuropathy. These medications also appear to be useful in the treatment of generalized anxiety and social anxiety. Examples of these medications include gabapentin (Neurontin) and pregabalin (Lyrica).

Topirimate (Topamax)

Topirimate is another anticonvulsant medication that appears to have some effectiveness in PTSD, although it has significant side effects on thinking and word finding.

2

Depression

> It is a positive and active anguish, a sort of psychical
> neuralgia wholly unknown to normal life.
>> —William James, *The Varieties*
>> *of Religious Experience*

Everyone has had the experience of sadness. Bad things happen to all of us. We are disappointed, we become frightened, we feel overwhelmed by stress, or we just go through a period of feeling "down." Sadness is a transient sense of feeling unhappy or gloomy. A depressive disorder or a clinical depression is more than just a brief or fleeting feeling. Sadness that is continuous and pervasive; that lasts for weeks or months, that is accompanied by other symptoms, such as changes in sleep patterns, appetite, or concentration; that blocks the ability to enjoy normal pleasures; and that interferes with day-to-day function is usually called a clinical depression or a depressive disorder.

The distinction is not always clear-cut, and the words we use can add to the confusion. The term "depression" can refer to the feeling of being depressed, normal periods of sadness that get better on their own, or a clinical disorder that is associated with significant distress and dysfunction and that without treatment can last for months or years. In general, as a feeling of sadness lasts longer and is accompanied by other symptoms and more ongoing distress, a person passes from being "sad" to having a depressive disorder. This distinction is easy to understand in more extreme situations. It is clear that there is a difference between a person who feels sad for a couple of hours and then "snaps out of it," and a person who is so profoundly depressed that for months he cannot get out of bed or care for himself.

Unfortunately, there is often no clear line for when a person passes from being temporarily sad to having a depressive disorder. Some experiences of depression seem to be a normal part of life, at least for most of us. Most of us go through some periods in our lives when our sadness lasts longer than just an hour or a day, and it is embedded with other symptoms that suggest the syndrome that is called "depression." It may be connected to some obvious loss or problem or disappointment, or it may seem unconnected to life events. In the past, many psychiatric textbooks made a distinction between "biological depressions," which are those that seem to be based on some biological abnormality, and "reactive depressions," which seem to be primarily connected to life events. It now seems that this distinction is rarely clear-cut. Everyone experiences losses and disappointments, some much more profound than others to be sure, but everyone has experiences that could potentially lead to depression. Not everyone develops a depressive disorder, however.

FACTORS IN THE DEVELOPMENT OF DEPRESSION

The current thinking is that stress interacts with both our genetic makeup and our own history of life events. Whether we develop a depressive disorder is the result of this complicated interaction. For example, research has demonstrated that people with certain genetic patterns are much more likely to become depressed if they are exposed to stress, but if there is no significant stress, then the rates of depression are not influenced by the gene (Caspi et al., 2003). One can probably become depressed just from biological factors or from stress, but often depression is the outcome of a complicated interaction between genes and stress. Stress, of course, does not mean just current life events but our personal history of stress and our history of how we have learned to cope with stress.

All depressions have a biological component—a biological predisposition that may be larger or smaller but is always a factor—and virtually all have some psychological component as well. The issue is not whether a depression is biological or psychological, but rather how bad is it, how much of a problem it is causing, and what the best way is to treat it. *Supports, coping style,* and *biology* all interact with these life events, either in positive or negative ways. These factors can make the development of a depressive disorder less likely or more likely.

Supports include outside connections, including friends and family and even activities that can help to buffer the effects of life events. Friends and family and other personal connections can help prevent a problem from being quite so overwhelming. An enjoyable job or regular pleasurable activities can help to keep a person stable and resilient. Regular contacts and structure can help keep us from withdrawing into a deeper depression, even if something bad happens. If you start veering too far off your normal path, your supports can notice and help you to reset your course. On the other hand, the lack of supports can make a depression more likely to occur.

Coping style refers to the way that people have learned to deal with problems in the past. How someone has learned to cope with bad situations or bad feelings in the past can help or hurt when similar bad things happen again. People who have a history of being upbeat and thinking of the positives in life get in the habit of this orientation, which helps when bad feelings threaten to take over. People who respond to depression by taking care of themselves, staying active, reaching out, and focusing their attention on positives learn to be more resilient. People who have a long history of disparaging themselves, withdrawing when depressed, and using alcohol or other drugs to ward off bad feelings are likely to be much less resilient when bad things happen.

Biology also influences how likely we are to experience a serious depression. Some of us are genetically more likely to feel happy, and others are more likely to feel sad (Kimberly, 2005). Some people can experience pleasure more easily and more intensely, while others are less enthusiastic in their reactions to positive events. While some of this behavior is clearly learned from parents or previous life experiences, much of it is also based in biology. Some people can have a biology that will cause them to go through periods of depression, no matter what kinds of supports and coping styles they develop. More commonly, biology can be an influence on how likely a person is to become depressed and how severe the depression is likely to be. Biology can always be modified, within some people more than others.

Biology is often equated with genetics, but there are actually a number of ways that biology can be modified outside of someone's genetic makeup. Certain kinds of brain damage and some medical problems such as decreased thyroid or too little vitamin B12 can cause people to feel depressed, as can some medications such as interferon (most commonly used for treatment of hepatitis C and other illnesses). At times, biology can be protective and help people ward off a depression despite a terrible life circumstance. At other times, the biological push toward depression is so strong that the person is going to become depressed no matter what supports and resiliency the person has in his or her life. Often, our biological tendency toward depression, different within each of us, interacts with life circumstances, learned resiliency, and coping mechanisms. For most people, depression is not caused just by biology or just by life events but is the product of some interaction between them.

What does depression look like?

We have all had the experience of feeling sad at some time in our life, so some parts of having a depressive disorder are easily understandable. As already discussed, a depressive disorder is more than just the normal transient feeling of sadness. It lasts longer, is more severe, and interferes more with how we would like to live our life. Even transient depressions are associated with feeling sad, losing the ability to enjoy normally enjoyable activities, feeling tired, and having decreased energy and decreased concentration. We often become more pessimistic when we are feeling sad and have a harder time seeing that we are doing a good job at work or at home. While we have all had some experience with sadness, most of us have been able to pull ourselves out of the feeling or can wait until it passes on its own. In the meantime, even when depressed we may have been able to function more or less normally, even if things were not as much fun and it took more effort to go to work or take care of daily requirements.

About 10% of the population has had the experience of a much more severe depression, called major depressive disorder. People can get so depressed that it is impossible for them to just "pull themselves out of it." When people have major depression they cannot function or even get out of bed, and they will spend much of their time thinking about being dead or even about killing themselves. Energy plummets, concentration becomes so impaired that it can be difficult to read a book or follow a TV show, and there is a loss of interest in doing anything, even things that used to be pleasurable. People who are significantly depressed often feel guilty, even over things that they have not been responsible for or that may have happened many years before. There is often a feeling of worthlessness and helplessness that the mood and the situation will ever change. A person who is significantly depressed will often feel hopeless and often becomes suicidal because he or she cannot imagine ever feeling better.

Not everyone who develops a depressive disorder experiences it the same way. One person may find it impossible to get out of bed, while another may become quite agitated. One person may become very tearful all of the time, while another may feel numb and dead inside and have no tears at all. Some people with a depressive disorder become actively suicidal and will kill themselves, while others have little thoughts of suicide even when profoundly despondent. Physical symptoms can also vary from one person to another, with one person gaining weight and another losing a considerable amount; one person may complain of physical pain and another may pay little attention to his own body. Not everyone who has a depressive disorder acknowledges the feeling in the same way. A person may look and act depressed, seem depressed to everyone around him or her, but call the problem something different than depression. People who are older, male, or from non-Western cultures will sometimes attribute the problem to a medical issue or a super-natural-based problem, rather than immediately think that they may be depressed.

Depression is often accompanied by feeling decreased energy, concentration, and motivation. Sleep disruption is common, and it becomes hard to enjoy normal activities. As the depres-sion becomes more severe, it often includes feelings of helpless-ness and hopelessness; it feels like it will go on forever. As the depression worsens, going to work, reading a book, or having a conversation with friends all become more and more difficult. Thoughts of death or even suicide become a solution to the pain of the depression.

What does it feel like?

Depression feels terrible. All of us have had some hint of feeling sad, down, or "depressed," but the anguish and hopelessness of a clinical depression is hard for someone who has never had it to fully understand.

> Instead of pleasure I was feeling in my mind a sensation close to, but indescribably different from actual pain. . . . If the pain were readily describable the countless sufferers from this ancient afflic-tion would have been able to confidently depict for their friend and loved ones (even their physicians) some of the actual dimen-sions of their torment. For myself, the pain is most closely con-nected to drowning or suffocation—but even these images are off the mark. (William Styron, *Darkness Visible*)

Many people with clinical depression describe a pervasive hopelessness that depicts a bleak future and makes it impossible to even attempt a change. There is a pain that very depressed people describe that is akin to physical pain, just as terrible to live with and just as disabling, but is harder to describe or to locate. People with both physical illness and depressive disorder describe the depression as being more difficult to live with, even if the physical illness is terminal or painful.

KINDS OF DEPRESSION: DIAGNOSIS

Not all extreme cases of sadness indicate a disorder. The first consideration is whether the change in mood is more severe, or more prolonged, than the situation warrants. Would most people feel similarly in the same situation? This is very clearly a value judgment. One person's view on this may be very different from another's. With less severe depressions there is more likely to be disagreement about "normal sadness" and "disorder." However, with more severe depression it becomes obvious that most people would agree that something is wrong. Calling something a "disorder" does not mean that medication is necessarily indicated. It only means that this mood seems more extreme than what most of us would label as normal variation.

Depressive disorders have been separated into a number of different diagnoses or kinds of depression. In real life, one kind of depression can overlap with another, and the same person can have different kinds of depression at the same time. For example, a person can have both dysthymia and a major depressive episode or have SAD (seasonal affective disorder) as well as bipolar disorder. At the same time, the different diagnostic criteria for the different kinds of depression can help to structure a treatment approach. Each of the disorders will be discussed in turn, with discussions of when and how medication might be helpful.

Sadness

Sadness is a normal feeling that can be helped by support and positive coping from both the person experiencing it and the friends and family of the person. The issue is how to distinguish the normal feeling of sadness from a disorder of depression. At both ends of the continuum the distinction is easy. If a person is a bit down for a day or so and then "snaps out of it," few people would label this a clinical depression. If a person spends weeks or months tearful, despondent, unable to function, hopeless, and suicidal, almost everyone would say this is more than a normal mood variation and falls into some different kind of category. Deciding when a mood is "sadness" and when it is part of a "clinical depression" can be much more difficult in the middle of the severity spectrum. How do we label or categorize a person who is able to function but who for weeks or months thinks that everything is less enjoyable, or a person who goes through brief but intense periods of sadness, hopelessness, and even suicidal feelings? When is a reaction to a loss or a stressful event "normal" and when is it an indication that something is wrong outside of the norm? Some part of this depends on our own personal values, how we see the world and what we consider to be normal or abnormal. Some of us will worry about a friend being depressed, while someone else might feel it is still on part of the continuum of "normal sadness." Whether a sad mood would be best thought of as a period of normal sadness or the beginning of a depressive disorder is based on the person's own history. A person who has had previous episodes of serious depression is at high risk for becoming clinically depressed again, and it is normal that friends and family will be aware of this risk and have more of a tendency to label a period of sadness as the possible beginning of another depression. A person whose sadness seems "understandable" is less likely to be thought of as clinically depressed by family or friends, or even by himself or herself. Another way to think about the distinction is to consider whether the person's normal coping mechanisms continue to work. Is the person able to do those things that are likely to help feelings improve, or does the person seem "stuck"? Despite all of the formal criteria in the diagnostic manuals, there is no absolutely clear line to indicate where "normal sadness" turns into "clinical depression." Even if we are not able to draw an exact line where it starts, we do know that some people have a kind of depression that is outside of normal sadness. A "depressive disorder" is more than just a normal feeling of being "down" or "sad" or "having the blues."

Major depressive disorder

Major depressive disorder is just what the name implies: it is a depression that is severe enough to significantly interfere with the person's ability to function. Major depressive disorder can be a one-time event, although more commonly it is recurrent. Most people with major depressive disorder will eventually stop being depressed, or at least become much less depressed. Most people with a major depressive disorder do not stay severely depressed forever, although the person who is feeling depressed may feel that he will never get better. On the other hand, most people with a major depressive episode will have other periods of depression at some time in the future, which is why it is commonly considered a recurrent disorder. Most people who say they are now depressed can identify a time in the past when they have been depressed, even if that depression is not as bad as the current one.

In its mildest case, having a major depressive disorder may block the person's ability to feel pleasure even when doing a pleasurable activity or it may decrease concentration so that reading or even watching TV are difficult. Sleep and appetite are often disrupted, libido is decreased, and the person often feels tired. In more severe depressions the person may be unable to function at work or at home, become tearful, stop many normal activities, and start thinking about death. At times, people can start thinking about suicide or even plan how they would kill themselves. In even more severe depression the person may stop taking care of himself, stop bathing, or stop eating or changing clothes. Suicide may become a preoccupation and could be a very real risk. Not taking care of a medical illness or not taking needed medications can become a problem. In some cases a person can become so depressed that she loses touch with reality and becomes psychotic. A person with a depression-related psychosis may start believing that she is the devil and needs to die or that she is personally responsible for deaths around the world.

One of the most difficult parts of depression is that it can be infectious. The depressed person often feels that the depression will last forever, that it will never get better, that there is no use to even try. This sense of hopelessness and helplessness can infect support people, and family and friends can also become discouraged and feel like giving up.

Dysthymic disorder

Some people stay depressed for years, or even for their entire lives. Often these depressions are not as severe and do not cause the same degree of dysfunction as major depressive disorder, but they can still cause significant distress. An ongoing chronic depression is called dysthymia. People with dysthymia can usually function well, but they have trouble enjoying activities, roses do not smell as sweet, energy levels may be low, there may not be much of a sense of personal optimism, and the normal ups and downs of life can be more burdensome. While there can be some confusion between a normally somber mood and a dysthymic disorder, the person with dysthymia is more than just somber. The diagnostic criteria for dysthymia include changes in sleep and appetite, poor self-esteem, poor concentration, difficulty making decisions, and a feeling of hopelessness.

Seasonal affective disorder (SAD)

SAD is often called "winter depression." It is a depression caused by a shortening of the day, or a decreased photoperiod. Some people get depressed every winter, beginning around the same time that days begin to get shorter. The person may attribute this to the cold of winter or decreased activity, but the depression is actually caused by the shorter day. Our brain is very sensitive to the photoperiod, or the length of the day, and people can get depressed as the period of light becomes shorter. The increased amount of time that people spend indoors during the winter will exacerbate the problem. Even on a very overcast day, the outdoors has a higher light intensity than even the most brightly lit room would have.

Bright light therapy is not a medication but it is a biological treatment that is both safe and effective. It causes changes in the brain that are similar to what a medication can do. For SAD and "winter depression," bright lights can be helpful. The brain is very sensitive to the length of daylight and the amount of light. Even a very bright room, or the kind of bright light that you would normally have around the house is not bright enough to be effective. The lights used in SAD treatment are much brighter than any normal light, and they have UV rays screened out so that they do not cause a dangerous tan or eye cataracts in the course of treatment. The lights are typically used for around 30 minutes a day, during most days of the week from early fall through spring.

Like other effective treatments for depression, light therapy for SAD can increase mood instability and in a few cases can even precipitate a manic or hypo-manic episode in susceptible people.

Depression associated with medical illness or chronic pain

Many medical illnesses, including some cancers, anemia, thyroid disorder, and others, can cause a person to feel depressed. People can develop a depression after a stroke or brain injury. Chronic pain often causes fatigue and depression, which can lead to a feeling of hopelessness and "giving up." Certain kinds of medical treatments can also cause depression, as can many common medications. Interferon, commonly used in the treatment of hepatitis C, is well known to increase feelings of depression in many people who take it (Sockalingam, W., & Abbey, S.E., 2009). People can become depressed in reaction to other mental illnesses, from anxiety disorders to schizophrenia. Life events, including grieving, can cause depression. And substance use and abuse, including alcohol use, can cause depression or make it worse.

Bipolar disorder and bipolar depression

Major depressive disorder, dysthymia, and SAD are all "unipolar depressions." People with one of these disorders have periods of depression or "downs," but they do not have periods of abnormal "ups" or mania. In contrast, people with a bipolar disorder have periods of both "downs" (depression) and "ups" (mania). While the manic periods are more dramatic and cause more life disruption, most people with bipolar disorder spend much more of their lives being depressed than being manic.

Many people have some degree of mood variation. Many people have weeks or months of time when they are relatively more "up," during which they feel particularly good, have more energy, require less sleep, have more ideas, and have a more optimistic attitude about the world. These same people typically go through other periods when they are a bit "down," when they do not feel quite so good, have a bit less energy, and are a bit more pessimistic about themselves and the future. Most people with these mood variations learn to recognize that they occur but do not consider them to be a problem or something that needs to be treated.

The essential feature of bipolar disorder (or manic depressive disorder as it used to be called) are extreme mood swings that are both severe and cause major problems for the person having them. In bipolar disorder, these mood swings typically last weeks or months rather than hours or days. A person can have recurrent depressions without ever becoming manic, but people do not typically have recurrent manic or hypo-manic periods without also having periods of depression.

Bipolar I: Mania. A person who has had at least one full manic episode has a bipolar I disorder. Mania is much more than a normal mood variation or a period of feeling exceptionally good. A person in the midst of a manic episode may believe and act as though he or she is the smartest or richest or most important person in the world. Judgment is often impaired, and the person can become so impulsive as to become truly dangerous. One manic person drove through downtown Madison, Wisconsin, at almost 100 miles an hour. Another borrowed many thousands of dollars on credit cards in order to buy junk at garage sales that he was convinced he could sell for vast profits. Another burned down his girlfriend's porch as part of performance art to demonstrate how much he loved her. A woman who normally was personally cautious became hypersexual and picked up strange men at bars during manic episodes. A person who is in a manic episode is often thinking and talking so fast that he may stop making sense, even when he feels that he is being perfectly articulate. He may also be irritable, argumentative, require very little sleep, and may be very hard to reason with. A person in a full manic episode can become psychotic, believing that he is receiving special messages or that he has special powers, hearing voices, and acting on beliefs that are irrational.

Bipolar II: Hypo-mania. A person who has had one or more hypo-manic episodes but no full manic episodes is considered to have a bipolar II disorder. Hypo-mania refers to a mood state that is elevated enough to be a significant problem, but less elevated than full mania. The distinction between bipolar I and bipolar II often influences treatment decisions: both about what medications to consider using and what the relevant dose should be. A person who is hypo-manic may have enough grandiosity, impulsivity, or impaired judgment to be a real problem, but she may not be psychotic and is not as out of control as someone who is manic. A person who is hypo-manic may become impulsive and quit his job over a disagreement with a boss, gamble more than he can afford, or drive much faster than is safe. As with mania, a person who is hypo-manic typically feels extra energetic and often requires less than a normal amount of sleep. A person can have recurrent hypo-manic episodes but never progress to a full manic period, while for other people the hypo-mania is a stage toward even more out-of-control behavior. The depression associated with bipolar I and bipolar II can be equally severe and long-lasting. The difference is in the severity of past manic episodes.

Bipolar depression. A person with bipolar depression is now depressed but has a history of having been manic or hypo-manic in the past. Calling a depression "bipolar" does not indicate how severe it is, how connected it may be to life stress, or whether it is recurrent. It only refers to depression in someone who has a history of mania. A person can be recurrently depressed without ever becoming manic, but a person who has been manic or hypo-manic virtually always also has periods of depression. The treatment of a person with bipolar depression is somewhat different than the treatment of one of the unipolar depressions discussed earlier. While some treatment principles overlap, many are different. Both the focus of psychotherapy and the decision about which medication to use will differ between unipolar depression and bipolar depression.

While the "high" part of bipolar is dramatic, most people with bipolar disorder spend more time being depressed than being "up." For their friends and families, the "high" is a much bigger and intrusive problem, but for the person himself or herself the "lows" are often much more difficult to live with. Given the havoc that the person has done to her life and relationships during a manic episode, it can be difficult to know how much of the depression is connected to real-life events and real losses, and what part may be due to the biology of the bipolar illness. The reality is that both the biology and the social environment must be considered. The life instability of bipolar illness often leads to real stress, and the biological potential for depression is also real.

GENERAL APPROACH TO THE
TREATMENT OF DEPRESSION

While there are some general principles that apply to the treatment of all depressions, there are also specific treatment issues for each of the different depressive disorders. Effective treatment for any depression requires assessment of the various stressors and life events that may be connected to the depression and also the identification of the specific depressive disorder.

A person who is responding to the death or loss of someone close may need someone willing to listen and to provide support for the grieving process. A person who is depressed because she has just been fired or is about to be evicted from housing may need concrete help in managing these life changes, in addition to treatment for the depression. If a person becomes "stuck" in his grieving, or so overwhelmed by life issues that normal resiliency is lost, additional help beyond normal support may be useful. The stress may precipitate a depressive disorder, and either psychotherapy or medication or both may be effective in helping the person regain the capacity to cope with the world more effectively.

In general, there are five broad approaches that can be helpful to a person who is depressed.

1. Spend time on activities that promote wellness and healthy coping. These can be extremely effective in helping anyone to improve his or her mood.
2. Do as much as possible to deal with those real-life problems that are causing the stress, which is in turn causing the depression, or making the depression worse.
3. Stop doing those activities that may be making the depression worse.
4. Use specific psychotherapies, such as "talk therapies," to help learn new skills, change automatic thoughts, and improve mood.
5. Consider the use of biological interventions that can help overcome a depression and that may allow the other approaches listed above to be more effective. Most people think of medications as the primary biological intervention, but there are others as well. For example, both SAD lights (special very bright lights used in the treatment of SAD) and exercise will change biology without the use of medi-

cation. Some of the distinctions between these categories are less clear than commonly thought.

Wellness and healthy coping activities

Wellness will be discussed much more in Chapter 11 because it can be a significant part of the treatment of any mental illness. Wellness includes activities that promote health and well-being help someone to engage with a support system that can help him or her to feel connected to other people and avoid the use of alcohol and other drugs in ways that interfere with how one wants to live life. For example, many people who feel depressed drop out of normal activities, often tend to isolate themselves, and stop doing those activities that used to give them joy. Working to keep to some kind of structure, staying involved in normal activities, forcing oneself to stay connected to other people, and continuing to do those activities that promote health can all help with depression. Doing the activities that one would normally do if one were not depressed can be very helpful. All areas of wellness are important, but exercise has a special role in the treatment of depression.

Exercise as treatment of depression. Regular aerobic exercise is a reasonably effective treatment for depression. Aerobic exercise three to four times a week for 30 minutes or more is safe, effective, inexpensive, and typically has few side effects. The problem is with getting someone to do it, especially if he or she is depressed. It is often very difficult for someone who is more seriously depressed to follow any kind of regular exercise program. Starting slowly with a walk or easier exercise can help. Exercising with a friend or family member can make it easier. Asking a person to record exercise on a calendar can help increase its frequency.

Work to decrease the life problems that are causing or increasing the depression

Depressions can be caused by stress, the time of year, past life experiences and habits of thought, and biology. The loss of a job or spouse, a medical illness, an eviction, financial problems, or chronic pain can all cause or exacerbate a depression. Some of these stresses may be difficult to decrease. It may not be possible to eliminate all of life's real woes. The idea of trying to work on a marriage, reconnect with friends, or look for a new job may seem hopeless. Trying to figure out what, if anything, can be changed to make the world a bit easier can be very difficult to even think about. In the midst of a depression it may feel that no change is possible and everything is overwhelming. On the other hand, there may be some stresses that one can try to do something about.

Try to make a list of those life problems that bother you the most, whether you feel that you can do anything about them or not. Think about whom you can get to help you rethink what you can do about the problems on this list. Are there any friends, counselors, family members, or ministers that may be able to help you rethink anything you could do about any of the stresses? Some of the problems may truly be beyond anyone's ability to do much about. Some of the problems that seem fixed and unchangeable may actually be more open to change than one thinks. We all get stuck thinking about problems in a fixed way, and it can be very difficult to step back and really examine options. It may be possible to work on a marriage or connect with friends and family members with whom you have been arguing. It may be possible to figure out a new budget or a new job. It may be that some things are unchangeable, but it also may be that some things can be changed.

Stop doing things that make the depression worse

It may not be treatment, but stopping the abusive use of alcohol or other drugs is often a very important part of treatment of a depression. People often drink because they are depressed, but the alcohol makes the depression worse rather than better. It is also important to make sure that there is no medical illness that is causing the depression or making it worse. Thyroid disease, anemia, vitamin B12 deficiency, and even some cancers can cause depression. Many medications prescribed for other illnesses can make depression worse, including medications such as interferon used for treatment of hepatitis C, steroids used for a wide variety of medical illnesses, or even some blood pressure medications. If you are taking a prescribed medication, you may want to ask your physician if it could be making your depression worse.

Psychotherapy

A number of psychotherapies such as cognitive behavioral therapy (CBT), interpersonal psychotherapy, and problem-focused therapy have been demonstrated to be useful to people with depression. The focus of the therapy can vary depending on the needs of the person, but there are several common approaches to modern psychotherapy. Therapy can help someone to problem solve, receive emotional support, rethink and learn new skills to improve relationships with friends and families, and work to change habitual ways of thinking that keep him or her in the rut of depression.

CBT: Cognitive behavioral therapy. The basic idea of CBT is that it is almost impossible for any of us to directly change our own moods. We cannot force ourselves to change our feelings. We cannot will ourselves to be less depressed or happier, or even less anxious for that matter. On the other hand, we all know that if we think about a really happy event our moods will improve. If we think about a really nice day, or a wonderful event, if we let ourselves go back to it and immerse ourselves in the memory, we will feel better. If we focus on a terrible event, our fears, or what we are most worried about, our moods will worsen. When a person is depressed he tends to focus on just those things that make him more depressed. Even if you cannot directly change your mood, you can learn to attend more to positive thoughts and dwell less on negative thoughts. This is the essence of CBT, and although it sounds very simple it actually works pretty well. There are a number of good self-help books that teach this approach.

Interpersonal psychotherapy and problem-focused therapy. Interpersonal therapy and problem-focused therapy can also be very useful. Interpersonal therapy focuses on relationships and how one can improve current relationships and establish new ones. If a person's depression is related to the stress of a relationship, or the lack of a relationship, focusing on relationships is an obvious part of treatment. Interpersonal therapy can help us better connect with and get support from those around us.

Problem-focused therapy can help someone explore his problem in new ways, so that he can re-examine the entire range of possible options on how to approach problems. Most of us make automatic assumptions about people and problems that can make it very difficult to think about new kinds of solutions. Problem-focused therapy helps us to look at problems from a fresh perspective and to come up with solutions that our own assumptions may have kept us from seeing.

Therapy can also help a person learn the early warning signs of sliding into another depression or another manic episode. It is important to learn ways to cope with these mood changes before they get out of control. People can actually learn ways to better stabilize their own moods. Many of these techniques are also available in self-help books for people with depression and with bipolar disorder.

Biological treatments

Medication is commonly thought of as the major biological treatment for depression. While medication is the most discussed and researched type of treatment, many other biological treatments can also be useful. For example, some research suggests that folic acid and Omega 3 fatty acids (fish oil) might help people with depression (Freeman, Fava, Lake, Trivedi, Wisner, & Mischoulon, 2010; Schonfeldt-Lecuona, Cardenas-Morales, Freudenmann, Kammer, & Herwig, 2010). Regular aerobic exercise has clear antidepressant and mood-stabilizing effects. Electroconvulsive therapy (ECT) has a bad reputation and has been misused in the past, but as it is currently used it is very safe and can be extremely effective (Baghai & Moller, 2008). Other biological treatments, including vagal nerve stimulation and transcortical magnetic stimulation (TMS), may be useful in some kinds of more severe depression (Rush & Siefert, 2009). Medications are not the only biological treatment, but they are the most common type and will be the focus of this chapter.

MEDICATION FOR UNIPOLAR DEPRESSION

There are a number of different kinds of medication for depression. While these are called antidepressants, most of them are useful in the treatment of a variety of other problems completely apart from their roles as antidepressants and even for people who are not depressed. Medications labeled as antidepressants are often used for anxiety, panic disorder, fibromyalgia, and chronic pain. None of the antidepressants are addictive, although they can cause uncomfortable withdrawal symptoms if they are stopped suddenly. None of these medications are "happy pills." None will force a person to be happy or overcome the sadness of real-life events and stresses. At the same time, if a person is overwhelmed to the point where his or her brain is not working properly, antidepressant medication may allow the person to cope more effectively.

All medications have side effects, and all take from a week to a few weeks to work. They are only useful when taken consistently, and they will not start working right away. Not all people and not all depressions will respond to antidepressants, and medication is not always useful. *The most difficult question is not which medication to use, but rather whether to use a medication at all.* In general, medication is most likely to be helpful if the depression is more severe. With mild depressions, the effect of medication may be marginal or nonexistent. As a very general rule, the more severe the depression is, the more it is recurrent, and the stronger the family history of depression, the more likely that a medication will be an effective part of the solution. The more the depression is mild, does not interfere with function, and seems clearly related to real-life stress, the less likely that the medication will be an important component of treatment.

What can you expect from an antidepressant medication?

The effects of antidepressant medications are subtle. They are not happy pills and except for side effects, it often feels as though the medications are not doing much of anything. They take a week or multiple weeks, perhaps longer, before there is any response at all and to be fully effective. A week or so after starting an antidepressant, you may find that you are sleeping better or eating more normally, but you may not initially feel less depressed. You may find that you can start to push yourself to be more active and engage in activities that before were just too hard to do. Family and friends may note that you look better before you feel different. It may be that some favorite activities start being at least somewhat enjoyable again. Crying may decrease or stop, and some of the negative thoughts that things will never change may be easier to push out of mind. Suicidal feelings may decrease. The last part of the improvement is a change in the subjective sense of feeling "good." It would not be unusual for you to be looking much better to friends, doing more things that are enjoyable, feeling less suicidal, but still not feeling that the medications are helping very much. Only after multiple weeks might you be able to reflect that you are feeling better more of the time, enjoying activities more than before, spending more time with friends, being more productive at work, and feeling more hopeful about the future.

There is a big difference between feeling better and feeling good. Many people notice some improvement from antidepressants but are still feeling depressed. Feeling less depressed is very different from not being depressed. "Improvement" is different from "remission." Remission, essentially a "cure," refers to the absence of all symptoms of depression. Improvement is easy, but full remission can be very difficult. Different antidepressant medications work differently for different people.

There is no way to predict who will respond to what. It may not be elegant, but if you are depressed you may need to try two or three different medications, alone and in combination, before finding the medication that works the best for you.

At times, going from "less depressed" to "not depressed" requires trying different medications; sometimes it requires combining medications. Almost always, this requires some active participation from you, the person trying to recover from the depression. Antidepressant medication is less likely to be effective if the person taking it is passive and just waits for the medication to work. Medication is more likely to be effective if the person taking it is actively trying to change his negative thought patterns, is actively engaged in interacting with friends and families, and is pushing himself to be more active and to exercise.

When is it worth trying an antidepressant medication?

So when is it worth trying a medication? In many ads on TV and in magazines, it appears that an antidepressant can help almost everyone feel great. After looking at some of these ads full of happy, ecstatic people, it is easy to think that all of us should try taking one of these medications. On the other hand, a recent research paper in the medical literature that has been widely publicized has suggested that in mild to moderate depression, medications do not work any better than a placebo (Fournier et al., 2010). The methodology of the paper is very complicated and based on what is called a "meta-analysis," which clumps together results from previous studies using very complicated statistics. Only two of the many available antidepressants were included in this analysis, and there are many problems in trying to predict the results of this study for depressed people in the real world. The reality is somewhere between these two extremes. An antidepressant will not cause someone to feel happy. The most a medication will do is to remove biological barriers that may have partially interfered with the person's feelings of happiness. If depression is severe, interfering with function and leading to thoughts of suicide, then a trial of an antidepressant medication is probably worth trying. If your depression is relatively mild and seems clearly related to real-life stress, then trying to make other life changes first may make sense before trying an antidepressant.

If after trying to make other life changes, perhaps trying psychotherapy if available, you continue to feel sad, have no sense of joy, think that life is a drag, and feel hopeless that things will get better in the future, then an antidepressant may be well worth trying. The problem is not in deciding to try an antidepressant with a mild depression, but in trying a medication before trying to make other life changes that may be more effective and less risky. It may be worth trying an antidepressant even for a mild depression, if that depression is causing significant problems or distress in your life, and after you have tried other nonmedication solutions first. In mild depression, a medication may have a useful role but it is not the place to start.

Medications for unipolar depression

Note that the discussion below is focused on the use of medication for unipolar depressions, or depressions where there is no history of mania or hypo-mania. The treatment of *bipolar depression* will be discussed later in this chapter. Standard antidepressants may be less effective and may have special risks when used by people with bipolar depression.

Five major classes of antidepressants
commonly used for unipolar depressions

1. SSRIs and SNRIs. SSRIs (selective serotonin reuptake inhibitors, including Prozac, Celexa, and Zoloft) are the most commonly used antidepressants. They work at the synapses, or gaps, between nerve cells. Nerve cells communicate by releasing a chemical messenger, a neurotransmitter, that then triggers a receptor on the nerve cell at the other side of the very small gap. There are many different neurotransmitters used in the brain, but the three that have been most associated with depression are serotonin, norepinephrine, and dopamine. After a neurotransmitter is released, it is very rapidly deactivated by a number of different mechanisms in the brain. One of these deactivation mechanisms is to suck the just-released neurotransmitter back into the releasing nerve cell. The SSRIs block the reuptake of serotonin back into this releasing nerve cell, so that it stays active a bit longer and has a bit more time to act on the receptor of the next cell.

SNRIs (selective serotonin and norepinephrine reuptake inhibitors, including Effexor and Cymbalta) are very similar to SSRIs, except that they block the reuptake of norepinephrine in addition to blocking the reuptake of serotonin. They are much more similar to SSRIs than they are different. For a group of people who have never tried any antidepressants, the SNRIs are no more effective than the SSRIs. They are different enough that if an SSRI does not work, then switching to an SNRI makes sense. The side-effect profiles of SNRIs are similar to the SSRIs except that they are more likely to increase blood pressure.

All of these SSRI and SNRI medications are also effective in the treatment of panic disorder, OCD, and generalized anxiety disorder in addition to depression. For the most part, they are well tolerated and are very safe, even if taken as an overdose. All can cause side effects, including decreased sex drive and delayed time to orgasm. They can all cause some weight gain, although this is usually fairly modest, and all can cause a sense of emotional numbing. They can cause increased risk of bleeding in some people, and occasionally they can cause nausea or headaches that typically go away after a few days of use. Abruptly stopping one of these medications can cause an uncomfortable but not medically dangerous withdrawal syndrome of irritability, sleep disruption, and general malaise.

For a group of people, SSRIs and SNRIs seem equally effective, and currently there is no way to predict who will respond better to one over another. However, the medications are different enough that one may work better than another for a particular person. This means that if the first SSRI is not effective, it may still be worth trying a second or even a third.

There are some minor differences between the various medications. For example, venlafaxine (Effexor) seems more likely to cause withdrawal symptoms than most of the other antidepressants. The one area where SNRIs are more effective than the SSRIs is in the treatment of people with neuropathic pain and fibromyalgia.

2. Presynaptic antidepressants. Mirtazapine (Remeron) influences the amount of serotonin and norepinephrine released by a nerve cell, and therefore it influences that amount that is available to stimulate the nerve cell at the other side of the synaptic gap. It works by influencing the nerve cell that releases chemical transmitters into the synapse, rather than influencing the receiving cell. Mirtazapine is very effective and can be used along with an SSRI or SNRI. It is very sedating, which can be good if a person is having problems sleeping and bad if it causes the person to be more tired the next morning. Like the SSRIs and SNRIs, it is also useful in the treatment of anxiety and panic disorder. It may be less useful than an SSRI in the treatment of OCD. Mirtazapine can cause significant weight gain, which is its most common problem. There is some suggestion that it is less likely to cause sexual side effects than an SSRI or SNRI, which is a potential advantage.

3. Bupropion (Wellbutrin). Bupropion seems to increase the activity of the dopamine system. It has advantages and some disadvantages over the other antidepressants. It usually does not cause weight gain or sexual side effects, and it is usually activating rather than sedating. While most people like the sense of increased energy often connected with bupropion, some people feel a bit agitated, like they have taken in too much caffeine. Bupropion is not helpful in promoting sleep or in the treatment of anxiety or OCD. It is very effective as an antidepressant and can be safely and effectively used along with the SSRIs and SNRIs if one medication is not enough to completely treat the depression. It is also unique in that it can help decrease the urge to smoke. Other antidepressants do not seem to help control smoking urges in the same way. The original form of bupropion was a short-acting medication that needed to be taken two or even three times a day, so longer acting, timed-release versions of the medication have been developed called either bupropion SR (sustained release) for twice-a-day use and bupropion XL (extended release) for once-a-day use, typically in the morning.

   4. *Tricyclic antidepressants.* Tricyclic antidepressants are older medications that are currently used for a variety of conditions having little to do with depression, including neuropathic pain and some kinds of headaches. They are less commonly used to treat depression. Examples are amitriptyline (Elavil), nortriptyline, imipramine, and desipramine. They work at least as well as the newer medications and sometimes work when the newer medications do not. The problem is that they have many side effects, especially in the higher doses needed to effectively treat depression, including weight gain and feelings of being drugged and tired. The biggest problem with the tricyclic antidepressants is that they are very dangerous when taken as an overdose. A month's prescription of any of these medications can be fatal if taken all at once.

   5. *MAOIs.* *MAOIs work by blocking monoamine-oxidase, one of the enzymes that breaks apart both norepinephrine and dopamine.* This is a very effective type of antidepressant that often works for people who do not respond to other antidepressants. Examples include tranylcypromine (Parnate) and phenelzine (Nardil). Unfortunately, these medications have significant risks and side effects, and they cause potentially dangerous interactions with other medications and with some foods. Many foods contain tyramine, which is rapidly broken apart and causes no problem. Unfortunately, MAOIs block the breakdown of tyramine, and as a result tyramine can rapidly build up and cause very dangerous elevations in blood pressure. As a result, anyone taking an MAOI has a list of foods that they cannot eat. There is also a long list of medications that are dangerous when taken along with an MAOI, including any of the other SSRI or SNRI antidepressants, Demerol, and many of the opiates used for pain control, and even dextromethorphan, commonly found in many cough medicines. Because of all of these complications, MAOIs are now rarely used.

There is an MAOI in the form of a skin patch (called Emsam) rather than a pill. This avoids most of the problems with certain foods, because the medication is not absorbed in the gut. While this is a major advantage and makes it easier to use, the drug-drug interactions continue to be a risk.

General Approaches to the Treatment of Bipolar Disorder

As previously discussed, the treatment of bipolar disorder and bipolar depression is somewhat different than the treatment of unipolar depression. For a person with bipolar depression, there must be concern about the treatment of the current depression as well as the risk of a manic episode. A person with a bipolar depression can switch rapidly from being depressed to being manic, or from being in a normal mood state to being manic. The medications commonly used in the treatment of unipolar depression may not be as effective in the treatment of bipolar depression and may increase the risk of precipitating a manic episode. Treatment of a person who is currently manic must consider the current manic episode, and then think about how to support future mood stability.

Just as the medications used in bipolar disorder are different than the medications used for unipolar depression, so, too, are some of the psychosocial interventions. It is very important for a person with bipolar disorder to learn his or her own early signs of mood instability and to have planned how to respond in order to decrease the risk of a full manic or depressive episode. It is also important to learn what can increase the risk of a manic or depressive episode and what life changes can increase or decrease mood stability. This discussion of bipolar disorder will start with life changes that can help stabilize mood, before discussing the use of mood-stabilizing medication for bipolar disorder and then medications specific for the treatment of bipolar depression.

Life change that can support mood stability

While medications are the mainstay in the treatment of bipolar disorder, there are a number of life changes that can also be an important part of increased mood stability. While the specific life changes are different for each person, for most people they include learning early signs of relapse so that they can intervene early, maintaining a regular sleep pattern and a regular life structure, and stopping activities that make moods more unstable. There are a number of very good self-help books that focus on these issues, but the bottom line is that people can do things to help maintain mood stability (see the Resource List for a list of self-help books).

Know your early warning signs of a manic episode. If you and your family are aware of the early warning signs of a manic or depressive episode, with a list of signs written down, it becomes easier to intervene earlier. Early warning signs are different for each person, but they are typically behavioral changes such as decreased need for sleep, increased irritability and impulsivity, spending more money, and driving faster. Develop your own list of early warning signs, based on how your past episodes have developed. Write the list down, and share it with family and friends. Develop an "early warning network" that can help you recognize early signs, perhaps before you can recognize them yourself. Decide ahead of time what you can do if you were to start becoming manic again. What can help you slow yourself down, stabilize your life, and decrease your own impulsiveness if you are at the very beginning of an episode? Develop a plan and write that down as well. Your plan might include forcing yourself to go to sleep early, avoiding some high-risk activities such as gambling or going out to a bar, and learning how to slow your own thinking down. Each person will have a different response plan. A part of the plan should be to consider what medications have helped in the past. What medications do you want to use if you were to become manic or if you were to become depressed? It is often much easier to make these plans in a calm period when there is no pressure, rather than in the midst of a crisis with emotions running high and the risk of imminent catastrophe causing everyone to become emotional.

Maintain a regular sleep pattern. Most people sleep less as they become manic. Not sleeping can also trigger a manic episode in a susceptible person. It does not matter what causes the sleep disruption, whether it is a crying baby, a night shift, or an all-night party. It is not uncommon for a person to become manic after flying to a place with a different time zone and having her normal sleep cycle disrupted. A manic episode can develop if a person starts feeling that she does not need to sleep and has too much to do to bother sleeping. The mild hypo-mania can be pushed into a full manic episode by self-imposed sleep deprivation. If you have a bipolar history, it is important to understand the need for a regular night of sleep. This might mean avoiding all-night study sessions, trying to avoid shift work if possible, and forcing yourself into a regular sleep pattern. One person I worked with was a musician who traditionally participated in music jams all night, until he figured out that this made his mood instability much more out of control. He was able to continue with his music but found that he needed to go home and sleep by 1 a.m., no matter how good the music was. The need for regular sleep might require using sleeping pills more readily than someone without a bipolar disorder, just to maintain regular sleep.

Keep to a regular structure. Getting up at around the same time, exercising on a regular basis, and having a regular structure can all help maintain mood stability. Not everyone is equally sensitive to life chaos. Some people tolerate a life of little regular structure without any problem. For many people with significant mood instability, forcing themselves to live within some kind of life structure can be very useful. Having a regular life structure can help maintain consistent behavior even if your mood varies a bit. If you regularly exercise three days a week, it becomes easier to keep exercising even if you get a bit depressed or a bit hypo-manic. If you normally go to sleep and wake up around the same time every day, it becomes easier to keep to this sleep structure if your mood starts to vary so that you feel like sleeping more or less. If you normally have lunch with friends every Sunday you will tend to have this lunch, even if you are getting depressed or becoming hypo-manic. These kinds of structures can actually help you stabilize your mood. It keeps you in a regular pattern of sleep, activity, and social interaction, which are inherently stabilizing.

Stop doing things that make the mood instability worse. The most important thing to stop doing is to stop abusing alcohol or other drugs of abuse. A person may use alcohol to help get to sleep, slow down, or deal with depression. People who are depressed may try cocaine or a similar drug to try to feel better. Drugs and alcohol tend to increase mood instability and almost always make the problem worse. Avoiding the use of drugs will not "cure" a bipolar disorder, but continuing drug use will make effective treatment much more difficult.

There may be other things that you need to avoid, in addition to drugs and alcohol, based on what you know about what have caused mood episodes in the past. One man figured out that trying to start his own business was the stress that led to another manic episode. He was very successful working for someone else, but on each occasion he tried to work for himself he became ill. Another man figured out that too much business travel seemed to make his mood instability worse. An occasional business trip was okay, but if he traveled too often the stress would build up, his sleep would inevitably get disrupted, and he would start having a problem controlling his mood, even though he stayed on medication throughout the episode.

Mood Stabilizers for Bipolar Disorder

Most people with bipolar disorder will need medications to maintain mood stability. Psychosocial interventions can help, but for most people they will not be enough. Mood stabilizers help to decrease the severity and the intensity of episodes. Without treatment, bipolar episodes tend to become more severe and more frequent over time. Treatment stops this progression. Unfortunately, all of the available mood stabilizers have significant side effects, and most of them are more effective in treating the "highs" than the depressive part of the illness. Not all possible medications are discussed in this section, only those that are most commonly used.

Lithium. Lithium is a mineral that is mined, purified and put into a pill. Lithium is naturally present in the water supply in some parts of the United States. It is very effective in treating manic episodes, especially in decreasing the frequency and intensity of the episodes. It can also be useful in treating the depressive side of the illness, although it may be more effective in preventing the next depressive period than in treating a current depression. Lithium has been shown to decrease the suicide risk associated with bipolar illness. Lithium is also used along with an antidepressant to treat unipolar depressions that have not responded to an antidepressant alone.

Lithium has a number of common side effects, including weight gain, increased urination, tremor, and a metallic taste. It can cause nausea and diarrhea, especially if the blood level gets too high. If the blood level gets too high, it can become dangerous with muscle twitches and, in extreme cases, convulsions and damage to the brain and kidneys. There is a relatively narrow gap between an effective level and a dangerous level, and it can be hard to determine when the level is getting too high. This is why regular blood tests to measure lithium levels are needed, more often at the beginning of the medication trial and then every 6 to 12 months. Lithium can also cause damage to the kidneys, another reason for regular blood tests every 6 months. At times, kidney problems develop after years or even decades on lithium. Lithium can also cause birth defects in the first trimester, and women who are of child-bearing age should be aware of this risk. Finally, it can interfere with thyroid function, though this is easily treated with thyroid hormone replacement. If a person starts gaining weight, feeling sluggish, or having trouble with cold temperatures or dry skin, then a simple blood test to monitor thyroid function would make sense.

Lithium has been found to effectively augment or increase the effectiveness of other antidepressants, even in people who have unipolar depression. While the research on this is still a bit unclear, it seems that lithium can decrease the risk that another antidepressant will precipitate a manic episode in someone with a bipolar depression and therefore will make the use of an antidepressant safer.

Valproic acid, sodium valproate, and divalproex sodium (Depakote) (note that these are different names for the same active medication).Many medications originally developed for treatment of epilepsy are very good mood stabilizers. Valproic acid is very effective and generally well tolerated. It is very effective for mania, but it is not clear how effective it is as a treatment for bipolar depression. The biggest side effect is weight gain. It can also cause other problems, including tremor or movement disorder, nausea, polycystic kidney disease in young women, and rarely liver or pancreas problems. It interacts with many other medications. It is also damaging to a developing fetus; women who are pregnant should avoid it if at all possible, and women who are of childbearing age should make sure that they do not become pregnant while taking valproic acid.

The dose of valproic acid is adjusted according to blood levels, so, as with lithium, a person taking this medication needs to get a blood level test after each dose adjustment, and then every 6 or 12 months afterward. It is also useful to get a blood test to monitor liver function at the same time. There is some concern that valproic acid can cause or at least be associated with polycystic ovarian syndrome (PCOS) when it is taken by young women, especially women in their teens or perhaps even early twenties. This is a hormonal problem associated with an increase in testosterone, weight gain, irregular menstrual periods, high blood pressure, acne, and a change in distribution of body hair to a more typically male pattern.

Carbamazepine (Tegretol, Carbatrol). Carbamazepine is another anticonvulsant medication that, like divalproex sodium, is an effective mood stabilizer. It has the advantage of not causing significant weight gain. It has the disadvantage of having a number of other side effects, including feeling sedated or a bit "drugged." It can affect the liver and can interfere with the formation of white blood cells. It also interacts with many other medications, usually by lowering the other medication's serum level. For example, it can lower the serum level of birth control pills enough so that they may not be effective. This is a particular problem since carbamazepine can cause birth defects. Like the other mood stabilizers it is more effective for the treatment of mania than for the treatment of depression. Also like the other mood stabilizers, it requires a blood test to monitor both the serum level of the medication, as well as liver function and white blood counts. Carbamazepine can also cause a decrease in serum sodium, so this too must be monitored with a simple blood test.

A rare but dangerous side effect of carbamazepine is called Stephens–Johnson syndrome, which causes a rash that becomes very widespread and can affect internal organs as well as the skin. While virtually any medication can cause this on very rare occasions, it is somewhat more common with carbamazepine, occurring approximately five times for every 10,000 Caucasian people who take it. It is much more common within people from Asia, especially people of Chinese, Thai, Malaysian or Filipino ancestry who have a specific type of gene. There is a special blood test that can detect this risk and is recommended for anyone with Asian ancestry who is starting carbamazepine.

Antipsychotic medications. All of the antipsychotic medica-

tions can be useful to control an acute manic episode. Antipsychotic medications have been used in the treatment of acute
mania for many years, even before the introduction of the newer
antipsychotic medications. The second generation of antipsychotic medications, including risperidone (Risperdal), olanzapine (Zyprexa), quetiapine (Seroquel), ziprasidone (Geodon),
and aripiprazole (Abilify) are very effective mood stabilizers.
That is, in addition to helping to treat acute mania they all seem
to help stabilize moods over time. They can help control and
decrease the risk of mania and may be useful in the treatment
of bipolar depression.

Medication for bipolar depression

Treatment of bipolar depression presents a number of special
problems. People who have bipolar depression, who are now
depressed but who have a history of mania or hypo-mania,
respond differently to antidepressants. Antidepressants can
increase the chance that the person will "switch" from being
depressed to being manic. Antidepressant medications can also
increase the chance that the person will become more labile,
having a mood that goes up and down rather than stabilizing
at a place of feeling good. There is also some suggestion that
antidepressants may not work as well for someone with bipolar depression. The bottom line is that the treatment of bipolar
depression is often complicated, is difficult, and often requires
more than one medication.

Lamotrigine (Lamictal). Lamotrigine is an anticonvul-
sant/mood stabilizer that is more effective for treating bipolar
depression than it is for treating mania. It has few side effects,
once a person has been on it for a few months, and it causes
no weight gain. The problem is that it has a much higher risk
of causing the Stephens–Johnson syndrome (discussed above
with carbamazepine). For people who start taking a full dose of
lamotrigine, 1–2% will develop this very dangerous condition.
The problem is only at the beginning of treatment, and the risk

decreases after 2–3 months. However, if a person starts at a very low dose and increases slowly, the risk decreases to about 1 out of 2,000, and a serious reaction is much rarer than this. Anyone taking lamotrigine must start at a low dose, and it takes more than a month to get onto a dose that is clinically effective. If a person stops his or her medication for 4 to 5 days, he or she would need to start all over again. Anyone taking lamotrigine who develops a rash on the mucous membranes (mouth, lips), a rash on the palms or bottoms of the feet, or a rash that spreads over the face and upper torso should see a doctor. Anyone with a rash that is associated with fever and enlarged lymph glands should see a doctor. Rashes are very common, and for people on lamotrigine even a few rashes are dangerous. The risk of a dangerous rash is a concern that needs to be discussed with your physician before starting this medication.

Antipsychotic medications (e.g., quetiapine [Seroquel]). All of the second-generation antipsychotic medications have true mood-stabilizing and antidepressant effects, even for people who have no psychotic symptoms. That is, these medications help to decrease a person's chance of a future manic episode. They are also useful in the treatment of bipolar depression, again even if the person has no psychotic symptoms. The data are best for quetiapine (Seroquel), which has been clearly established as an effective treatment for bipolar depression. The data for effectiveness in bipolar depression are more limited for the other second-generation antipsychotic medications, but they are all commonly used for this purpose. The second-generation antipsychotic medications are effective in treating both ends of the bipolar continuum. You can be on a full dose of the medication within days, without needing to wait the 4 to 6 weeks that it takes to get to a full dose of lamotrigine. At the same time, all medications have risks and side effects. Many of the second-generation antipsychotic medications cause weight gain, increase the risk of diabetes, and are associated with at least some risk of tardive dyskinesia, a potentially irreversible movement disorder. Despite these risks, the second-generation antipsychotic medications, especially quetiapine, can be an important part of helping someone with bipolar depression reestablish control over his or her life.

Antidepressant medications. The problems of using a traditional antidepressant in the treatment of bipolar depression have already been discussed. All of the traditional antidepressants can increase mood instability in someone who has a bipolar disorder, and they all have the risk, small but real, of switching a person who is susceptible from being depressed to being manic. For someone who has a history of having full, out-of-control manic episodes, this risk, even if small, is likely to raise a real concern. There are also some data that indicate that standard antidepressants may not work as well for people with bipolar depression as they do for people with unipolar depression. The research in this area is both complicated and inconsistent. Some studies show that antidepressants are not helpful for bipolar depression, but a recent study shows that antidepressants are both safe and effective in bipolar II depression, which is a depression where the person has a history of past hypo-mania (Amsterdam & Shults, 2010). Despite these concerns, antidepressants are often used by people who have bipolar depression. Usually they are prescribed along with a mood stabilizer, with the expectation that this will decrease the chance of precipitating a manic episode.

What can you expect from a mood-stabilizing medication?

The goal of a mood stabilizer is to decrease the frequency and the intensity of mood swings. Mood swings may not completely disappear, but hopefully medication can help them become more manageable. One problem with many mood stabilizers is that the manic periods decrease, but the depression remains. The use of lamotrigine, quetiapine, and other medications can help decrease the severity and the duration of these depressed episodes. Most people with a bipolar disorder end up on multiple medications. While there is realistic concern about the risk of interactions between the various medications, the benefits of the careful combination of medication can outweigh the risk.

CRISIS RESPONSE AND SUICIDE

Before leaving the topic of depression, it is important to consider the issues of crisis response and the risk of suicide. People can get so depressed that they are unable to function. They can stop eating, bathing, or doing even the most basic self-care activities. People can also give up and become helpless and hopeless. This can be infectious. Anyone around the depressed person can also feel hopeless and helpless. It is important for anyone who has a history of recurrent depressions and for family and friends to understand this, so that they can be aware of it and not fall into this trap. Problems with self-care can also extend to not taking care of medical problems and not taking important medications or following through with required medical therapy. It might also mean not going to appointments required for a job, or housing or disability determination.

Depression is also associated with a risk for suicide. Men are at more risk than women; people who have tried to kill themselves in the past are at more risk than those who have not. People with alcohol or other substance abuse problems are at even greater risk. In particular, a person who is alone and has experienced losses, either from medical illness or social losses, is at risk. Anyone who is feeling hopeless or feeling that things will never get better, is of very real concern. If you are worried about a friend or family member, *ask about suicide directly.* Ask if the person has thoughts about suicide, has ideas of how he or she would do it, and if he or she has made any preparations. A person with a definite plan and who has gone out and bought a bottle of pills or thought about where he or she could buy a gun is at most risk.

ANTIDEPRESSANT MEDICATIONS

Generic Name	Brand Name	Class of Medication	Common Indication
amitriptyline	Elavil	tricyclic	commonly used for headaches
amoxapine	Ascendin	tricyclic	
bupropion	Wellbutrin/ Budeprion		also used for smoking cessation
citalopram	Celexa	SSRI	
clomipramine	Anafranil	tricyclic	primarily used for OCD
desipramine	Norpramin	tricyclic	
desvenlafaxine	Pristiq	SNRI	similar to venlafaxine
doxepin	Sinequan	tricyclic	very sedating; can be used in very low doses as a sleeping medication
duloxetine	Cymbalta	SNRI	effective with some kinds of pain
escitalopram	Lexapro	SSRI	similar to citalopram
fluoxetine	Prozac	SSRI	very long-acting
fluvoxamine	Luvox	SSRI	often used for OCD
imipramine	Tofranil	tricyclic	
isocarboxazid	Marplan	MAOI	interactions with common foods
mirtazapine	Remeron		very sedating
nortriptyline	Pamelor	tricyclic	often used for headaches and other pain
paroxetine	Paxil	SSRI	
phenelzine	Nardil	MAOI	interactions with common foods
protriptyline	Vivactil	tricyclic	
selegiline patch	Emsam	MAOI	
sertraline	Zoloft	SSRI	
tranylcypromine	Parnate	MAOI	interactions with common foods

Generic Name	Brand Name	Class of Medication	Common Indication
trazodone			used primarily as a sleeping pill
trimipramine	Surmontil	tricyclic	
venlafaxine	Effexor	SNRI	effective with some kinds of pain

MOOD-STABILIZING MEDICATIONS

Generic Name	Brand Name	Notes on Use	Common Concerns
carbamazepine	Tegretol, Carbatrol	may be effective when other mood stabilizers are not	no weight gain; significant risk of birth defects; many drug-drug interactions; small risk of life-threatening rash
lamotrigine	Lamictal	most effective for bipolar depression	risk of life-threatening rash if not started very slowly; no weight gain
lithium carbonate	Eskalith, Lithobid	mood stabilizer with longest history of use	requires blood tests every 6–12 months
valproic acid/ sodium valproate	Depakote	rapidly effective as mood stabilizer; more effective for mania than depression	weight gain; requires blood test every 12 months; significant risk of birth defects; many drug-drug interactions

3

Problems with Concentration: ADD and ADHD

PROBLEMS WITH CONCENTRATION

Concentration is the process of paying exclusive attention to one thought or object. Concentration requires narrowing the range of stimuli being considered. Attention deficit disorder (ADD) is an inability to maintain or focus attention. Attention deficit hyperactivity disorder (ADHD) is the inability to pay attention combined with hyperactivity and impulsivity. A diagnosis of ADD or ADHD requires that the concentration deficit causes significant problems. The diagnosis of ADD or ADHD should not be made if the problem is mild or transient. Attention deficit is appropriately diagnosed when the person's inability to maintain attention significantly interferes with his or her ability to go to school, hold a job, or maintain social relationships.

The ability to concentrate is a "more or less" quality rather than an "all or none" category. Like other biological variables such as height or weight, the ability to concentrate is an issue of "more" or "less" rather than one of "I can" or "I cannot." No one can fully concentrate all of the time, and if he could it would mean that he would not be aware of activity happening outside of his focus of attention. A complete focus on what you are reading means that you will find it much harder to notice if someone walks into the room. Alternatively, everyone can concentrate some of the time. Someone who complains of poor concentration can follow the last few minutes of an exciting football game, especially if he is interested in football. The question is whether you have a problem concentrating in situations where concentration seems needed and important. Do you feel that you have more problems concentrating than most other people would in a similar situation?

You will concentrate much better if you are interested in a topic, and you will have more trouble concentrating if you are bored. Some material is harder to concentrate on than others. Concentrating for an hour is more difficult than concentrating for 15 minutes. The environment, interest, light level of the room, noise level, and many other variables can all influence whether you can concentrate or how well you can concentrate. As people mature, they tend to be able to concentrate better and longer. Most adults can hold their attention on a topic much better than most children can. Most 10-year-olds can concentrate better than they could when they were 6.

Many people worry about whether they may have ADD or ADHD. There are many reasons why a person may find it difficult to concentrate. Concentration problems are nonspecific. That is, many different factors can interfere with concentration. Being tired, not having a good night's sleep, being depressed, or being worried about something can all cause problems with concentration. A number of medical problems can interfere with concentration. Something as simple as a cold or an allergy can interfere with concentration, as can a significant infection or anything causing pain or discomfort. Many medications, both prescribed and over-the-counter versions, interfere with concentration. Drug and alcohol abuse as well as withdrawal can cause concentration problems.

There are also significant biological differences in one's ability to concentrate. Some people are born to be better concentrators than others. There is a range in the natural or inherent ability to concentrate that is part of a person's biology. While much of this individual biological difference is genetic, many nongenetic biological factors occur between the fertilization of the human egg and the growth and development of an adult.

A person's biological predisposition can be influenced by

environment. A person who was well nourished as a child will tend to be taller than a person with the same genetic background but who was chronically malnourished. There are genes related to height, but a person's actual height is caused by an interaction of genes with other environmental factors. Similarly, a stimulating environment will tend to enhance a person's IQ, within her biological limits. Thus, a person's natural inclination to be relatively better able to or relatively less able to concentrate can be influenced by training and environment. Stories read from a book tend to hold one's thought or idea for a somewhat longer period of time than a TV cartoon. If young children are frequently read to, they learn to increase their attention span. TV cartoons have a new frame or scene shift every few seconds, designed to easily grab a child's attention. Children who spend most of their time watching TV cartoons will not have the training experience that comes from reading, and they will not have the chance to increase their innate ability to hold attention (Christakis, Zimmerman, DiGiuseppe, & McCarty, 2004).

Finally, some situations are more boring than others. Many people who would not normally have symptoms of ADD will complain of concentration problems if they are forced to listen to a boring lecture. If a person is in a school filled with boring lectures, or in a job with many boring meetings, there is an intersection between that person's ability to concentrate and the level of concentration needed for the situation. Much of the debate about whether stimulants are overused in children is in relationship to this intersection between a boring environment and a mild concentration deficit. If schools were more interesting, if classes were smaller, and if there was more individual attention, then many children with mild ADD who are now placed on medication might be better treated with behavioral interventions without the need to use a medication.

Unfortunately, schools are unlikely to make these major changes, classes are not going to get smaller, and children are forced to accommodate to the schools as they exist or else get extruded from the school system with life-changing repercussions. Using medication may not be ideal, but in many cases it may be better than the alternatives that are realistically available. In the same way, an adult with mild ADD who has an active job may be able to adapt to his relative concentration difficulty without the use of a medication, while someone else with the same degree of concentration difficulty may require a medication if her job requires more intense and prolonged attention.

ADHD AND ADD

ADHD and ADD is more than just a minor problem with concentration. The formal diagnosis requires that the problem with attention be persistent and that it causes impairment in more than one setting. Someone who just has a problem only at work or at school would not meet the formal criteria for the diagnosis. ADD is in part a problem of concentration and inattention. It is also a problem of executive function, being able to organize tasks, inhibit impulses, manage frustration, and pay attention to details. It is difficult for most people with ADD to finish tasks, and many projects are left incomplete. ADHD includes problems with hyperactivity in addition to those of inattention. The formal diagnostic system was focused on its use with children rather than adults. There is considerable controversy about whether ADD and ADHD are being overdiagnosed and about whether the stimulant medications used in the treatment of these conditions are also being overused. Concentration problems are very common, and the symptoms listed as being connected to ADD are also very common. Virtually everyone has some degree of concentration difficulty. On the other hand, some people are not just slightly worse than average but have such a severe problem with concentration that it becomes a real impairment. People appropriately diagnosed with ADD have problems with concentration that are not just worse than others but are so seriously aberrant that they interfere with work, school, relationships, and life.

While concentration difficulties are at the center of a diagnosis of ADD, problems with executive function seem to be a part of the syndrome (Brown, 2005). Executive function refers to a variety of thinking capacities involved in focusing and regulating attention, and includes being able to organize and prioritize tasks, being able to focus attention and then appropriately shift attention to a new task, being able to regulate alertness, and being able to sustain effort and manage frustration. Impairment in these capacities may not completely correlate with just an inability to concentrate. Some of the problems that people with ADHD experience can be better understood in terms of these executive function deficits.

ADD is both overdiagnosed and underdiagnosed. That is, some children and some adults given a diagnosis of ADD may have behavioral or concentration problems that are not so severe as to warrant a diagnosis. In other cases there may be a better way to account for a concentration problem than ADD. There are many adults whose ADD presents in complicated ways that may be confounded by substance abuse or another illness, which may make the diagnosis easy to miss. A person may have had persistent problems with school and jobs going back to childhood, with interpersonal relationships and impulse control all complicated by substance abuse, and a doctor may never have considered the possibility of ADD.

The treatment of ADD can significantly improve a person's quality of life. However, when there are other reasons for the concentration problem or when the concentration problem is not all that severe, the use of medication can unnecessarily expose the person to risks and side effects. Most of the medications used in the treatment of ADD are potentially abusable. On the other hand, effective treatment of ADD can decrease the risk of substance abuse. Diagnoses of adult ADD or ADHD requires a history of attention problems going back to childhood. The problem may not have been diagnosed or treated in childhood, but childhood behavior in terms of school performance or parent observation is an important part of making a diagnosis in adults. Most children with attention problems have symptoms of hyperactivity in addition to problems with concentration. Over time, as children mature, the hyperactivity often drops out, leaving the attention deficit as the primary concern. Boys are diagnosed with ADHD more frequently. Some of this difference in diagnostic rates is probably related to real differences in prevalence, and some may be an artifact of ADHD diagnoses being more commonly overlooked in girls (Ramtekkar, Reiersen, Todorov, & Todd, 2010).

Symptoms of adult ADD include frequent problems with the following:

- Making careless mistakes;
- Problems concentrating when reading or engaging in other tasks;
- Not listening even when spoken to directly;
- Not following through with tasks at home or work;
- Difficulty organizing activities;
- Avoiding tasks that require sustained mental effort (such as reading or some work assignments);
- Frequently losing keys or wallet or other objects;
- Being easily distracted; and
- Being very forgetful in normal day-to-day activities.

Another way to think about adult ADD is to think of the various kinds of activities that require maintenance and shifting of attention. These include the following:

- Organizing and prioritizing tasks;
- Focusing, sustaining, and shifting attention to tasks;
- Regulating alertness and sustaining effort;
- Managing frustration and modulating emotion;
- Focusing memory and accessing recall; and
- Monitoring one's own activities (adapted from Brown, 2005).

ADHD is very different in adults than in children, and adults become hyperactive in different ways than kids. Hyperactive children squirm and fidget; they run around excessively and cannot play quietly. Hyperactive adults often complain of an inner restlessness. They often choose active jobs and may engage in a variety of impulsive behaviors from frequent job changes to driving too fast. For example, the Adult ADHD Self-Report Scale (ASRS) is a 17-question scale that includes the following questions:

1. How often do you have trouble wrapping up the final details of a project, once the challenging parts have been done? . . .
3. How often do you have problems remembering appointments or obligations? . . .
9. How often do you have difficulty concentrating on what people say to you, even when they are speaking to you directly? . . .
17. How often do you have difficulty waiting your turn in situations when turn taking is required? (Kessler, 2005)

A formal ADD or ADHD diagnosis requires that problems must have started in childhood, must cause significant impairment in multiple life areas (not just at work or just at home), and cannot be better accounted for by substance use or abuse, other mental illness, or physical illness. A person can have ADD along with substance abuse or another mental illness, and disentangling the intersecting problems to determine which disorder is causing the concentration problem can become difficult.

Adults can also have hyperactivity as well as concentration problems, although often adults have learned to inhibit some of the behavioral problems more frequently demonstrated by children.

When to Use a Medication for a Concentration Problem

Because concentration problems are so common and can be caused by so many things, and because they are part of the normal range of human experience, it can be confusing to know when (and when not) to use a medication. The fact that a person's concentration improves with medication does not necessarily mean that a person has ADD or that medication is necessarily indicated.

The common medications used for ADD are stimulants. Either very mild stimulants, such as caffeine, or more powerful stimulants will increase concentration in most people. Stimulants will help improve concentration if a person is bored, tired, or just having normal problems with concentration. It will not improve concentration if the basic problem is too much anxiety. In a wide variety of situations a stimulant will improve concentration, at least for a while. Many people use caffeine for just this purpose, and college students and truck drivers and others who need to stay awake and concentrate for long periods of time use stimulants on a regular basis; however, the risks of stimulants have been recognized and they are now regulated.

- Consider all of the other issues that may cause the problem with concentration. Lack of sleep, depression, and boredom are common causes of concentration problems, and they should be addressed before any other treatment is even considered.
- Consider substance abuse and withdrawal. Stimulants are drugs that make people feel good and they are common drugs of abuse.
- Consider the pattern of the concentration problems. ADD and ADHD are concentration problems that go back to childhood. It may not have been diagnosed in childhood, but a history should demonstrate problems in school and in other settings at that time.
- Consider how serious the concentration problems are and how much functional impairment they cause. Some people are inherently better at concentrating than others. A diagnosis of ADD and the use of medication should be reserved for those with severe problems and who have significant functional impairment.

- Consider non-medication ways to help improve your ability to concentrate. A good night of sleep, taking mental breaks, and structuring activities with clear goals can all help. There are a number of self-help books that provide techniques and exercises to improve concentration. These techniques will not eliminate problems but for someone with a more mild disorder these techniques can help.
- Consider the risks and problems that could be caused by a medication, and then balance out the size of the seriousness of the problem and the use of alternatives with the risks and side effects in order to decide if a medication trial is worth it.
- If you decide to try medication, monitor your behavior and your ability to concentrate to see if it really makes your life better. If the medication does not clearly help and if it does not help you function better, then either change it or stop it. Do not continue to take a medication if it is not clearly helping.

Medications for ADD

Medications for ADD fall into one of two categories: stimulants and "everything else." The stimulants themselves fall into two large categories: amphetamines and methylphenidate. Each of these categories has different salts and various formulations, with differences in how long they are effective and in their potential for abuse. The "everything else" primarily refers to atomoxetine (Strattera), bupropion (Wellbutrin), and guanfacine (Intuniv, Tenex), although other medications such as modafinil (Provigil) are sometimes used without FDA authorization.

Stimulants. All of the stimulants work through similar mechanisms. Some people may respond better to one than to another—a person may respond better to an amphetamine or better to a methylphenidate or have fewer side effects to one over the other—but the primary differences between the medications have to do with how many hours it is before they start to work, how long they continue to work, and how likely they are to be abused. Both amphetamines and the methylphenidates are available in relatively short-acting and longer-acting forms; some are only effective for a few hours and others are effective all day. They all work on the first day they are initially taken, without the need for any prolonged trial period to see if they will be effective.

Methylphenidate-related compounds.

- Methylphenidate (Concerta, Ritalin, Methylin): all available in short-acting and long-acting forms
- Dexmethylphenidate (Focalin)

Amphetamine-related compounds (available in short- and long-acting forms).

- Dextroamphetamine (Dexadrine)
- Methamphetamine (Desoxyn)
- Mixed amphetamine salts (Adderall)
- Lisdexamfetamine (Vyvanse)

Atomoxetine (Strattera). Atomoxetine blocks the reuptake of norepinephrine back into nerve cells after it has been released. This is less effective than a stimulant, but it has the advantage of not being subject to abuse. It also has the disadvantage of taking multiple days to weeks to be effective, which means that people often stop taking it before it has a chance of working.

Antidepressants used for ADD. A number of antidepressants are useful for ADHD. They are generally less effective than one of the stimulants, but they are safe and are not subject to abuse. Bupropion (Wellbutrin) is the most effective and the best studied of the antidepressants, but a number of other antidepressants can be useful as well.

Miscellaneous medications. A variety of other medications, each with different mechanisms of action, can also be useful and are not subject to abuse. Guanfacine (Tenex), which is commonly used to treat high blood pressure and posttraumatic stress disorder, has recently been approved by the FDA for ADD and ADHD.

Other medications are sometimes used for ADD and ADHD (without FDA approval), including modafanil (Provigil), which is approved for narcolepsy and sleep apnea; r-modafanil (Nuvigil), which is approved for excessive sleepiness from shift work disorder and narcolepsy; and clonidine (Catapres).

How these medications work

What these medications all have in common is their ability to "wake up" the attention-focusing part of the brain. When you are tired, it is hard to concentrate. If you are doing something that is very stimulating or you only need to concentrate for a short period of time, you can overcome your lethargy for a while but it is difficult. If you get some sleep, your concentration improves. These medications all stimulate the part of the brain that keeps the rest of the brain awake.

All of these medications have side effects and risks. Both the stimulants and atomoxetine can increase heart rate and blood pressure. They can all interfere with sleep. They can all make symptoms of anxiety, OCD, or psychosis worse. And there is a very small reported risk of sudden death—this is much more common if the medication is misused or if the person has a preexisting heart defect. For every 1,000,000 people who take one of these medications for a year, there will be 2 to 5 sudden deaths, or people who just fall down dead for no clear reason. This is very close to the incidence of sudden death in the general population who are not taking these medications. The risk seems to be a bit higher in adolescents, perhaps 3 to 10 people per million. There is a higher risk if the person has a family history of sudden death or if the person has complaints of shortness of breath, fainting spells, or chest pain.

All of the stimulants can be abused. Many people with ADD and ADHD already abuse substances, and there is legitimate concern about prescribing an abusable medication for someone who is already abusing other drugs. There is also concern that these medications can be sold or diverted to others. The available data suggest that using these medications as prescribed will not lead to later drug abuse. On the contrary, current data suggest that the effective treatment of ADD with stimulant medications can decrease substance abuse (Katusic et al., 2005). If someone has a history of substance abuse, I will often require collateral information from family or from a substance abuse counselor about current drug use and medication use before I am willing to prescribe a stimulant. If the person is currently abusing drugs or alcohol, I may require participation in a drug or alcohol treatment program before I am willing to prescribe a stimulant. I am also very prepared to stop prescribing if substance use continues. At the same time, some people with severe ADD are much more likely to stop using illicit drugs and stabilize their lives if their ADD is effectively treated. The decision to prescribe a stimulant to someone with a known drug use history is difficult, and it often requires that family, friends, and a drug counselor be part of the decision-making and monitoring process.

How do you know if the medication is working?

Stimulants work rapidly. If the medication is going to be effective, it will probably be effective within the first day or so of use, often within an hour or two of taking the first pill. Given the various risks of the medications, I feel that they should be continued only if they make a significant functional improvement in the person's life. If the person "feels a bit better" or feels he can "concentrate a bit more," I am usually unimpressed. If the person reports he can now sit down and read a book, or finish a project at work, or has a partner who reports that he now listens much better and can participate in a conversation without interrupting, then those are clear functional improvements. These behavioral changes tend to be much more concrete and easier to follow than more subjective feelings that "things are a bit better."

Before starting any medication, it is useful to develop a list of "target symptoms." What are you hoping will get better when taking this medication, and how would you know that it is working? This list will be somewhat different for each person. Think about whether there have been similar periods of improvement even before starting the medication. Think about whether there are other changes that may also account for the improvement. For example, if a person has both started a stimulant and also stopped using marijuana, it may be difficult to determine which change was the cause of the improvement. It may require going off the medication for a day or two, then restarting it, to see the effect of the medication alone.

The stimulants are generally short-acting medications. They work rapidly, and they stop working rapidly. Some people find they do better when these medications are taken all of the time, but others find that they need the medication when at school or when they have a big problem at work, but can take a break from the medication over the weekend or at other times.

*How would you know if the
medication is making things worse?*

All medications have risks and side effects, and the medications used for ADD are no exception. If the medications are not clearly helping, they should be stopped. Problems caused by stimulants, in addition to those already mentioned, commonly include increases in anxiety and problems with sleep.

Summary

Stimulants and other medications used in the treatment of ADD and ADHD are very effective but there are drawbacks. Most people with complaints of decreased concentration do not have ADD or ADHD, but they may have some other problem or set of problems that should be addressed before starting another medication. Many people with ADD have some degree of difficulty when concentrating, but the problem may not cause enough distress or dysfunction to warrant the use of a medication. For a person with severe ADD, who has looked into all of the other issues involved, a medication can help significantly improve function, stability, and quality of life.

COMMONLY USED AMPHETAMINE PREPARATIONS

	Average Duration
Dextroamphetamine (Dexedrine, Dextrostat)	4–9 hr
Dextroamphetamine + amphetamine salts (Adderall)	5–7 hr
Dextroamphetamine + amphetamine salts, delayed release (Adderall XR)	10–12 hr
Dextroamphetamine spansules (Dexedrine spansules)	4–9 hr
Lisdexamfetamine (Vyvanse)	12 + hours

COMMONLY USED METHYLPHENIDATE PREPARATIONS

	Duration of Action
Methylphenidate (Ritalin, Methylin)	3–5 hr
Methylphenidate, sustained release (Ritalin LA)	6–8 hr
Methylphenidate, sustained release (Ritalin SR)	4–6 hr
Methylphenidate, sustained release (Concerta)	10–12 hr
Methylphenidate, sustained release (Metadate CD)	8 hr
Methylphenidate, sustained release (Metadate ER)	4–8 hr
Methylphenidate patch (Daytrana)	Wear time not to exceed 9 hrs

NONSTIMULANT MEDICATIONS

atomoxetine (Strattera)	Approx. 24 hrs
guanfacine (Tenex/Intuniv)	Approx. 24 hrs
bupropion (Wellbutrin)	Approx. 24 hr for extended release
modafanil (Provigil)	Approx. 15 hrs

4

Sleep Disorders

Sleep that knits up the raveled sleeve of care
The death of each day's life, sore labor's bath
Balm of hurt minds, great nature's second course,
Chief nourisher in life's feast.
—William Shakespeare, *Macbeth*

Sleep is a requirement for life. A human being will die if he or she is completely prevented from sleeping over a long period of time. Even minor disruptions in sleep can cause significant medical as well as psychological problems. Everyone has had some problem getting to sleep or staying asleep. Problems with sleep can be an occasional annoyance or can interfere with a person's ability to function. Even an occasional problem with sleep can cause difficulty if it comes right before an important event such as an exam or an important meeting requiring rest and concentration. Most sleep problems can be categorized as a problem getting to sleep, a problem staying asleep, or a problem with circadian rhythms, making someone want to sleep at the wrong time of the 24-hour period.

Sleep disruption causes next-day fatigue and excessive daytime sleepiness. Fatigue and sleepiness are often confused with each other. Fatigue refers to feeling weak, lethargic, and exhausted. A person can feel fatigued and will just want to sit and not do anything, without necessarily feeling the need to sleep. While lack of sleep can lead to fatigue, so, too, can boredom, worry, the flu, or overwork. Sleepiness refers to the desire or pressure to go to sleep. As a person stays awake, pressure to sleep tends to increase until over time it becomes irresistible.

Sleepiness increases from the last time you woke up, until you go to sleep again. Sleepiness is also influenced by the quality and quantity of your most recent periods of sleep and by your circadian rhythm, when you are on your normal sleep/wake cycle. Some sleep disorders, such as narcolepsy, can also increase sleepiness, sometimes dramatically. One measure of current sleepiness is the Epsworth sleepiness scale, which asks a person to rate on a 1–4 scale how likely he is to go to sleep in a number of common situations, for example while reading, or watching TV, or sitting and talking to someone, or in a car stopped for a few minutes in traffic (Johns, 1994).

Excessive sleepiness causes a number of problems. It is difficult to think clearly or to concentrate if you are sleep-deprived. Many people become irritable if they are sleepy and prevented from going to sleep. Sleep problems can impair judgment and can significantly impair driving much more than most people would realize (Philip et al., 2010). Sleep deprivation can build up over days, and it can take a number of days of good sleep for concentration to completely return to normal. Chronic sleep problems can also lead to medical problems and are associated with increased risks for diabetes, obesity, and heart disease (Barone & Menna-Barreto, 2010; Budhiraja, Budhiraja, & Quan, 2010).

A number of conditions other than poor sleep can lead to both fatigue and decreased concentration, including decreased thyroid function (hypothyroidism), too little hemoglobin in the blood (anemia), and a variety of other endocrine and cardiovascular problems. Depression is a common cause of both sleep problems and fatigue. That is, depression can both disrupt normal sleep leading to excessive daytime sleepiness, and it also can cause fatigue. While sleep problems are a common cause of daytime fatigue, a person can be tired during the day even when she has had adequate sleep.

Some people who complain of insomnia actually have little problem with their sleep. Rather they have an idea of how

much a person "should" sleep or how much they want to sleep
(such as 9 hours), and they label it as a problem if their sleep
pattern is different (if they only sleep for 7 hours). The problem caused by sleep disruption is fatigue during the day, and
an important issue is not how much sleep a person gets, but
whether a person feels refreshed the next day. Some people
who complain of "insomnia" are really sleeping as much as
their body needs, but they expect to be able to sleep more.
One of my patients complained of "insomnia" because she
could not get to sleep when she wanted. What she wanted
was to go to sleep after dinner, around 6 P.M., and sleep until
the next morning, around 7 A.M. The real problem was that
there was little for her to do in the evening, and she responded
to her boredom by wanting to sleep through it. Older people
normally have more disrupted sleep at night, with more naps
during the day. While this can be a problem, this change in
sleep pattern is a normal part of the aging process. It becomes
a problem when the older person takes medication or uses
alcohol in an attempt to continue the same sleep schedule he
or she had at a younger age.

Other people become so anxious about not sleeping that their
own anxiety interferes with sleep. The fear of not sleeping has
the effect of causing the problem. After a period of insomnia,
many people will become anxious about whether they will be
able to sleep regularly again, and in some cases this can make
an otherwise temporary or occasional problem much more
chronic.

Another problem is in what people do to try to get to sleep.
People use alcohol, when actually alcohol disrupts normal sleep
architecture and makes good sleep less likely. Many of the over-
the-counter medications sold as sleep aids contain sedating
antihistamines, either diphenhydramine (Benadryl) or a close
relative. They can make you tired, which may help promote
sleep, but they are not generally very effective and can cause
side effects, including drowsiness the next day, dry mouth, con-

stipation, and even confusion. In men who have an enlarged prostate, non-prescription sleep aids can increase problems with urinary retention (not being able to urinate).

COMMON CAUSES OF INSOMNIA

Before trying to use a medication to force yourself to go to sleep, it is useful to try and determine the cause of the problem. A full description of everything that can interfere with sleep would be a book in itself. It is important to think through the common causes, however, because understanding the cause can often point the way toward a better solution.

1. **Stress and worry** can certainly interfere with sleep. While negative worries are an obvious cause of insomnia, an exciting, positive upcoming event can also make sleep difficult. What is going on in our life, whether good or bad, will influence how well we are able to settle into sleep and how well we will sleep once we get to sleep.
2. **Poor sleep hygiene** is a common cause of sleep problems. Sleep hygiene refers to your personal habits, your sleep environment, and what you can do to promote a good night of sleep. Is there noise in the background when you are trying to sleep? Is there bright light? A dark, quiet room will promote sleep much better than a room that contains noise and light. While some people can sleep well with a TV on in the background, TV tends to be very engaging, which makes sleep difficult. For some people, the noise from the TV and the flickering light of the screen can significantly interfere with sleep. Taking naps during the day may make sleep much more difficult at night. A person may feel so tired that he needs to take naps during the day, and then he will complain that he is unable to sleep at night. Since he cannot sleep at night, he wakes up tired the next morning and the cycle continues. Daytime

naps are not necessarily a problem, and many people find that they increase alertness and concentration without interfering with nighttime sleep. A nap is a problem only if it causes other problems, and if sleep at night is poor the nap may be part of the cause. Settling down into quiet activity for an hour or two is more likely to promote sleep than trying to sleep immediately after an activity that is very stimulating.

3. **Mental illness** of almost all varieties can cause insomnia. Depression almost always impacts sleep, either by making sleep more difficult or by increasing a person's need for sleep. All of the anxiety disorders can make sleep difficult. Generalized anxiety can make it difficult to relax enough to allow sleep to happen, PTSD can cause nightmares that interfere with sleep, and OCD can leave someone so focused on something that still needs to be finished that sleep becomes impossible. Schizophrenia can cause significant sleep disruption, either through its impact on causing anxiety and depression, because the person may become afraid to sleep, or just from the disruption in the normal circadian rhythm. Mania can cause the person to feel he or she does not need to sleep. Identifying and treating an underlying mental illness is an important step to treating insomnia.

4. **Medical illnesses**, including those that cause pain or discomfort, can interfere with sleep. Chronic pain and breathing difficulties will cause insomnia. Severe breathing problems, diabetes, severe renal disease, thyroid disease, and others can all interfere with sleep. Alzheimer's disease and Parkinson's disease can also interfere with sleep. Many commonly prescribed medications for various conditions can interfere with sleep patterns, with the list being way too long to begin to list.

5. **Substance use and abuse** commonly interferes with sleep. Substance use is such a common cause of sleep

disruption that it should be assessed and dealt with before even considering the use of a sleeping medication. Even a couple of cups of coffee at dinner or a few alcoholic drinks before bed can cause a problem. Caffeine is used to promote wakefulness, so it makes sense that caffeine can interfere with sleep. Nicotine is a stimulant, so a cigarette before going to bed or by habit after waking up in the middle of the night can make going to sleep or back to sleep more difficult. Heavy smokers, especially those smoking two or more packs a day, can wake up partway through the night because of the body's response to nicotine withdrawal. Alcohol can cause some initial sedation and it is relatively common to take a drink to help get to sleep. Unfortunately, alcohol can cause a person to wake up in the middle of the night or to awaken with less than a fully restful sleep. Finally, withdrawal from alcohol or a number of other sedative drugs can make sleep much more difficult.

6. **Circadian rhythm disruption** can be a source of insomnia. We are designed to get to sleep when it gets dark and wake up when it gets light. Unfortunately, we now live in an artificial world of light and dark, and our sleep patterns do not fit the requirements of the outside world. We may have a job that requires us to wake up when our body wants to go to sleep, we may travel to a different time zone that causes our internal sleep rhythm to be out of step with the day and night cycle, or our body may just get out of sync with the world around us. The problem may not be that a person sleeps too much or too little but that the sleep cycle causes sleepiness when the person wants to be awake, and alertness when the person wants to go to sleep. Delayed sleep disorder refers to people whose circadian rhythm is thrown off so that they become drowsy much later in the night than they would like. Advanced sleep phase disorder refers to people whose circadian rhythm is set to cause them to

become drowsy too early, when they would still like to be awake.

7. **Specific sleep disorders** are relatively rare, but they can cause significant medical and psychiatric problems when they are present. Sleep apnea and restless legs syndrome are the two most common sleep disorders that cause insomnia.

Sleep apnea

People who have sleep apnea stop breathing when they go to sleep. The lack of breathing causes people with sleep apnea to wake up enough to breathe, and they then go back to sleep without ever being fully conscious that they were ever awake. This cycle of going to sleep, having breathing blocked, and then waking up can repeat itself many times during the night (as many as 50 times a night), leaving sleep so disrupted that people become chronically exhausted and sleep-deprived, no matter how many hours of apparent sleep they had. A mechanical block in breathing causes the most common kind of sleep apnea. The person's throat and tongue are relaxed enough to block the free movement of air in and out of the lungs. This is almost always accompanied by loud snoring as the person drops into sleep, interspersed with periods of awakening when the snoring briefly stops. Obesity can cause or make this kind of sleep apnea much worse. In addition to problems with concentration, depression, and all of the other issues associated with sleep deprivation, this mechanical block increases pressure in the blood vessels in the lung, and it can lead to very serious heart and lung problems. A pattern of loud snoring interspersed with grunting and awakening is the chief diagnostic clue to obstructive sleep apnea, and asking the person's bed partner may be the fastest way to screen for it. A much less common kind of sleep apnea is caused by the brain having stopped sending signals to breathe during sleep. The same sleep/wake/sleep cycle occurs but without the snoring that is characteristic of obstructive sleep apnea.

Restless legs syndrome

Restless legs syndrome is a neurological condition that causes one's legs to move around during sleep. Someone can thrash herself awake, as well as make things very difficult for any potential bed partner. Some people with severe restless legs may find their legs moving even when they are trying to relax; for others it is associated with sleep or trying to sleep. The problem is that the chronic interference with sleep can cause all of the problems associated with sleep deprivation.

TREATMENT OF INSOMNIA

The treatment of insomnia starts with understanding the cause. It is tempting to just "pop a sleeping pill" and in some cases this may be a good solution. In other cases a sleeping pill may not help very much and may make the problem worse.

1. **Start by stopping those things that may interfere with normal sleep.** Stop the evening caffeine, heavy alcohol use, or midday naps. Assess what medications may be making sleep worse. Avoid activities right before sleep that are stimulating, such as watching an exciting TV program. Exercise earlier in the day instead of right before bedtime.

2. **Change your nighttime "going to bed routine" to promote sleep**. Darken your bedroom, decrease noise in the room, and turn off the TV. Develop a "going to sleep" pattern that helps you relax even before you lie down to sleep, either by your choice in music or reading material, relaxation exercises, meditation, or other relaxing activities. Focus your mind on thoughts that are calming. Try to think of things other than the problems of the day or the problems coming up tomorrow. Try cooling off the room a bit. Make sure the bed is comfortable. If you cannot sleep, get out of bed so that you do not associate the bed with fretting about going to sleep. If you cannot sleep, rather than tossing and turning get up and read, or listen to quiet music in

a different room, with lights turned low in a way that will promote sleepiness. If you cannot sleep, do not start playing computer games or engaging in other activities that will be engrossing.

3. **Treat those medical and mental illness conditions that may interfere with sleep.** If you are regularly waking up to go to the bathroom, try to drink less fluid before going to bed, and talk to your doctor about medical options. Make sure that pain, depression, anxiety, psychosis, and breathing problems have all been addressed as much as possible.

Consider the use of medications for promoting sleep

Currently, there are five major classes of medication that are commonly used to promote sleep, although not all are approved by the FDA as hypnotics (sleeping agents). There are also some herbal remedies that commonly are used, although they are not FDA approved and research on them is very limited. The issues you must consider when deciding on a sleeping pill include (1) effectiveness (will it work?), (2) morning sedation (will it lead to problems the next day?), (3) quality of the sleep (will it promote a normal night of sleep as well as just help getting to sleep?), (4) tolerance and dependence (how likely am I to need more and more of the medication just to get to sleep, and will I have problems with withdrawal if I try to stop it?), and (5) risk, including side effects and risk of death. Many of the older medications, no longer routinely used, had many more problems in these areas than the medications now in more common use. For example, secobarbital (Seconal) was very addictive and was very dangerous if taken with alcohol or in too high a dose even by accident. Chloral hydrate rapidly led to tolerance and after a few days was no longer effective.

Sedating antihistamines (e.g., diphenhydramine [Benadryl]). These are present in many of the over-the-counter sleep medications. They can help make a person tired but can also cause confusion and memory problems and dry mouth, and they may not be that effective in promoting sleep. There are no studies on the long-term use of these medications, even though they are often used for long periods of time.

Sedating antidepressants (e.g., trazodone, doxepin). There are few sleep studies demonstrating that these medications work or what they do to sleep architecture, but they are widely used as first-line treatments for insomnia. For example, trazodone is not addictive and is safe even when taken as an overdose, has relatively few clinically dangerous interactions with other drugs, and is inexpensive. It does have the very rare risk of priapism (prolonged, painful erection of a man's penis), but this is unusual enough that if a man is warned it should not be a major problem. When used in the much higher dose required to be an effective antidepressant, day-time sedating and weight gain can be a problem, but in the smaller doses used to promote sleep this is less of an issue.

Other sedating antidepressants can also be used as sleeping agents. Recent research suggests that an extremely small dose of doxepin, 3 or 6 mg a night, can be a safe and effective sleeping agent (Owen, 2009). This compares to the 150–300 mg/day dose required when doxepin is used as an antidepressant. Amitriptyline (Elavil) and other sedating antidepressants can also be used, but these have more potential risk and are less often used unless they are also treating some other condition in addition to sleep.

Benzodiazepines (e.g., lorazepam [Ativan] or temazepam [Restoril]). These benzodiazepines increase the activity of a specific brain chemical called GABA. GABA is an inhibitory neurotransmitter, which means that increasing its activity inhibits or decreases other kinds of brain activity. As a result, these medications are general antianxiety agents and anticonvulsants and they also promote sleep. When taken in a small dose, they can cause some sedation but have more of an effect on anxiety. In a somewhat larger dose they can be used as sleeping pills. As a group, they are safe and well tolerated, but they can all be at least somewhat habit-forming and all can be abused. The abuse potential is less than that of alcohol. Like alcohol, most people can use these medications without any problem of abuse or dependency, but for some people abuse can be a significant problem. These medications also can increase the effect of alcohol, and while an overdose of these medications when taken alone is relatively safe, when combined with alcohol an overdose of benzodiazepines can be dangerous. Some of these medications are FDA approved only for anxiety (diazepam [Valium]) while others are approved only as a sleeping pill (flurazepam [Dalmane]), but this is more of a marketing decision than because of any differences inherent in the medications themselves. They typically work rapidly and can be used when needed, for a night or two or three, without having to be used every night.

Selective GABA A receptor agonists (e.g., zolpidem [Ambien]) These also increase GABA, but these medications only affect those specific GABA receptors that are involved in sleep. As a result, these medications are not very effective for treating anxiety and are not anticonvulsants, but they are very effective in promoting sleep. They are reportedly less likely to be abused and less likely to lead to dependence than the benzodiazepines that affect all of the GABA receptors in the brain. These medications are generally very safe and effective. There is some concern about reports of sleepwalking and other complicated behaviors associated with their use. Like the benzodiazepines, these medications work rapidly. Often, they can be used for a few nights only. Even when taken every night, they seem to continue to be safe and effective.

Melatonin receptor agonists (e.g., remelteon [Rozerem]) These work by stimulating that part of the brain that regulates the sleep/wake cycle. Melatonin, which has long been available in health food stores, triggers the brain to go into a sleep cycle. Melatonin itself also stimulates other parts of the brain and there is concern that it could trigger depression in some susceptible individuals. Remelteon is more specific to that part of the brain that is connected to sleep. These medications need to be taken regularly for at least 7 to 10 days to be fully effective. It has no potentiwal for abuse or dependence.

Brand Name	Generic Name	Comments	Time to Onset	Half-Life
Ambien	zolpidem	generic/inexpensive GABA A agonist	30 min	2.5–2.6 hrs
Ambien CR	zolpidem, controlled release	slightly longer action than Ambien; much more expensive GABA A agonist	30 min	2.8 hrs
Atarax/ Vistaril	hydroxyzine	sedating antihistamine	15–30 min	8–20 hrs
Ativan	lorazepam	benzodiazepine	30 min	8–24 hrs
Benadryl	diphen-hydramine	sedating antihistamine	15–60 min	1–3 hrs
Noctec	chloral hydrate	rarely used/more dangerous and more addicting	30 min	4–12 hrs
Dalmane	flurazepam	accumulates over days—higher likelihood of next-day sedation	30 min	40–250 hrs
Halcion	triazolam	benzodiazpine that has more risk/not used often	20 min	1.5–5 hrs
Lunesta	eszopiclone	GABA A agonist	1 hr	5–7 hrs
	melatonin	available from health food stores		
Restoril	temazepam	benzodiazpine	1 hr	3–25 hrs

Brand Name	Generic Name	Comments	Time to Onset	Half-Life
Rozerem	ramelteon	melatonin receptor agonist	30 min	1–2 hrs
Sinequan	doxepin	sedating antidepressant: use in very low dose of 3–6 mg before bed	1 hr	15 hrs
Sonata	zalepion	GABA A agonist	30 min	6 + hr
	trazodone	sedating antidepressant	30 min	7 hrs
Valium	diazepam	benzodiazepine	30 min	14–80 hrs

Herbs. There are a number of herbs that have been used to promote sleep. There has been little research on how well each works or on what risks or side effects each may have. "Natural" or "herbal" does not necessarily mean safe. For many years L-tryptophan, a food supplement, was promoted as a natural sleep agent. Unfortunately, hundreds of people who took L-tryptophan developed a disease called eosinophilia, which caused very high levels of a particular type of white blood cell called eosinophils. Thirty-eight people died and a large number of others were left with permanent disabilities. The presumptive problem was not with the L-tryptophan but with a contaminant in the manufacturing process. Herbs are not regulated by the FDA, which means that there is little oversight over how they are made, whether the label of an herb accurately reflects how much of the active ingredient is actually in the tablet, and whether the herb is safe and effective as suggested in the label and in popular press. At the same time, herbs are widely used and some seem to work better than others. (Information on specific herbs can be obtained from the NIH National Center for Complementary and Alternative Medicine, http://ods.

od.nih.gov/health_information/information_about_individual_
dietary_supplements.aspx.)

Valerian root (*Valeriana officinalis*) is mildly sedating and
has been used as a medicinal herb for thousands of years. Dried
roots are most commonly prepared into a tea or are made into
extracts that are put into capsules or tablets. Valerian root was
described by Hippocrates, and the Greek physician Galen recommended it for insomnia. Despite the very long history of its
use, there are only a few small scientific studies with somewhat
mixed results. There seem to be few problems associated with
its use.

Lavender (*Lavandula angustifolia*) is promoted as an herb
that encourages a feeling of relaxation. It is most commonly
used in aromatherapy, with a few drops of lavender oil put into
water, which is boiled and inhaled. It can also be used to make
tea or it can be put into an extract that can be taken by mouth.
Lavender oil may be poisonous if too much is congested. Lavender tea can cause headaches, and applying the oil to the skin
can cause irritation. There are some small research studies
showing mixed results when used in the treatment of anxiety.

Chamomile (*Matricaria recutita, Chamomilla recutita*) has
been used for thousands of years for insomnia, anxiety, upset
stomach, and diarrhea. The plant can be used to make tea, liq-
uid extracts, pills or capsules, or an ointment. There are few
scientific studies on the effectiveness of chamomile. People can
have an allergic reaction to the herb, but other side effects seem
rare.

Passionflower (*Passiflora incarnata*) has been used by
Native Americans for insomnia and anxiety. Side effects are
rare but can include rapid heartbeat and nausea. There are no
scientific studies of passionflower, and it is not listed by the NIH
National Center for Complementary and Alternative Medicine.

How to use a hypnotic (sleep medication)

People who have had trouble sleeping become so anxious about
not sleeping that this anxiety adds to the initial problem. Some-

one may get to sleep by taking a sleeping pill, but then if he does not take a pill he again becomes anxious about not sleeping and cannot sleep without taking another pill. This can easily reinforce the idea that the sleeping pills are necessary to sleep and will lead to the idea that a sleeping pill must be taken every night.

While some people with chronic insomnia may need a sleeping pill nightly on an ongoing basis, for most people taking a sleeping pill for a night or a few nights to reestablish a sleep rhythm, combined with other parts of good sleep hygiene, will be enough. With stress, a sleeping pill may be needed for a night or two but not necessarily on an ongoing basis. The "trick" is to avoid the habit of thinking that the sleeping pill is required, because this will reinforce the anxiety of not taking the pill and will be a self-fulfilling prophecy. If you need a sleeping pill, take it for a night or two or three, and then assume that your normal sleep cycle and normal tiredness will return and will be enough.

GENERAL APPROACH TO INSOMNIA

The use of sleeping pills is very common. They can be useful and are generally safe and effective. They are also not the first solution to the problem of not sleeping. Start by thinking about why you are having trouble sleeping. What are you doing or taking that could be making it more difficult for you to sleep? Think about any medical problems that could be contributing. Are you in pain, or uncomfortable, or having trouble breathing? Think about your use of alcohol and caffeine and even prescription medications. Then think about potentially more specific causes for insomnia. Do you have sleep apnea, restless legs, depression, or an anxiety disorder? Are you suffering from recent grief, or are you under particular stress? What could you do to sleep better? Is your nighttime ritual helpful for sleep? Is your room dark and quiet, and do you prepare yourself to go to bed in a useful way? Can you focus your thoughts on meditation or something that will not raise your anxiety?

If, after this thinking process, you decide to try a sleeping pill, think about what you want it to do and for how long. Do you intend to take it for a day or two or three, or have you had such chronic insomnia that if a medication helps you get to sleep you will be afraid to stop taking it? Do you want to try an over-the-counter sleeping pill, or might it be worth it to get a prescription for a medication that is likely to be more effective?

Sleep is very helpful and very necessary. When used as part of a more comprehensive approach, sleeping pills can be part of an effective treatment approach. When used without more careful consideration, they can end up doing little good and will complicate the problem.

5

Substance Abuse

Alcohol has been a part of human society from the beginning of civilization, and it may have preceded the making of bread as a staple (Patrick, 1970). Drug and alcohol abuse has probably been a problem for almost as long. Any brief discussion about drug abuse is difficult because of the wide range of drugs that is subject to abuse, the wide range of patterns of abuse, and the effect of those different drugs on different people. A drug that is enjoyable and not an apparent problem for one person can become a drug of abuse leading to loss of control and behavioral problems for another person. Some drugs, such as alcohol, do not seem to cause medical problems when used infrequently in a low dose, while other drugs such as tobacco seem to increase risks of health problems even at a low dose and frequency. Some drugs, such as alcohol or tobacco, lead to physiological dependence, while other drugs, such as marijuana, can lead to major life disruptions without dependence being an issue. Some people are very public about their drug use, while other people try very hard to hide their drug or alcohol use from their closest friends and family. While medication is not the primary treatment for any substance abuse, medications are available that can be useful as part of comprehensive treatment for some people struggling with substance abuse.

Medications have three potential roles in drug and alcohol abuse treatment. (1) Medication can be part of an effective, integrated treatment strategy for people with co-existing mental illness and substance abuse. Medication can be effective in treating the underlying mental illness and can therefore make drug or alcohol treatment more effective. (2) Medication can have a role in treating withdrawal from alcohol and other drugs, decreasing some of the discomfort associated with the withdrawal. In some cases, such as when someone is withdrawing from alcohol, benzodiazepines, or barbiturates, a medication may make the withdrawal less medically dangerous. (3) In addition to treating mental illness, medication can also have a direct role in the treatment of some substance abuse. There is now substantial research demonstrating that medication can be useful for the treatment of some people with both alcohol abuse and dependence, and for the treatment of people with opiate and nicotine dependence. There is currently little convincing research that medications have an effective role in the treatment of other drugs of abuse, including cocaine, amphetamines, marijuana, or hallucinogens. In many treatment settings, medications are probably underused even when they may be helpful. That is not to say that medication is enough for the treatment of abuse of these substances, but in some people the use of medication may add to the effectiveness of other treatment.

PSYCHOSOCIAL TREATMENT OF SUBSTANCE ABUSE

The primary treatment for substance abuse is psychosocial. Drug and alcohol treatment starts with assessing and enhancing motivation to stop using. It is also important to consider the needs of the person's support system, family, and friends. Effective intervention requires staging specific alcohol or drug abuse (AODA) treatment to fit the needs and interest of the person. Finally, it is important that AODA treatment be integrated with any needed mental health treatment. Medication can sometimes help in drug and alcohol treatment, but it is not a primary focus. Even though this book is about the role of medication, it is important to first understand at least a bit about some of the elements of drug and alcohol treatment.

Enhancing motivation

Not everyone who is abusing drugs is necessarily committed to stopping the abuse. The problem may be much more apparent to people around the person abusing the drugs than to the person using the drugs. Many people whose lives are being wrecked by substance abuse are unwilling to acknowledge it or to stop using. In the face of this kind of denial, it is very unlikely that the person will enter into drug or alcohol treatment, and it is very unlikely that he or she will be willing to take any medication that has the goal of decreasing substance use. Even if a person were willing to take a medication or was pushed into taking a medication, it is unlikely it would be very helpful if there was not a significant commitment to stopping the drug abuse. It is always worth a try to be direct with a family member or friend about your concerns about his substance use, but after one, or two, or five, or fifty attempts to suggest that he should stop using drugs, saying it yet again is unlikely to be useful.

An alternative approach is to invite someone to think about what she would like her life to be like, and to compare this to how her life is currently. Initially, it can be counterproductive to focus on the substance abuse; rather, just discuss the discrepancy between what kind of life the person wants and what kind of life the person currently has. This can sometimes lead to a more productive discussion about the role of substance abuse in causing this gap between what is and what is desired. It may then be possible to invite the person to consider what life would be like without the use of substances, what would be better, and what might be difficult. Once she can imagine a better life and begin to think about a life that is free of substances, then it may be much more productive to discuss treatment and other ways to actually achieve this change. Focusing on the need for treatment is unlikely to be very useful for someone who is strongly resisting any thought that she has a problem with substance abuse or is unable to consider how life could get better (Miller & Rollnick, 2002).

Support for family and friends

Treatment of substance abuse, whether psychosocial treatment or treatment with medication, requires that the person acknowledge at least to some extent that he or she has a problem that could get better with treatment. Not everyone with a substance abuse problem is ready or willing to acknowledge this. In the meantime, the person's family and friends can get support for themselves, either through Al-Anon, or one of the other organizations set up to provide education and to support the people around the person who has a substance abuse problem.

Integrated drug or alcohol and mental health treatment

The effective treatment of the underlying illness, where this is possible in the face of the substance abuse, is likely to help in both cases. An underlying principle is that treatment is likely to be much more effective if the treatment for the mental illness and the treatment for the substance abuse is integrated, conducted at the same time by the same clinicians who can focus on both and the interaction between them. This is very different from older models of care where people were told to get treatment for their drug or alcohol problems before they would be accepted for treatment of their mental illnesses, and they were then told that they needed to get treatment for their mental illnesses before they could get treatment for their substance abuse. Treatment is likely to be less effective if the treatments for mental illness and substance abuse are separated, and it is even worse if one problem must be treated before the other can even be addressed. Too often even today, a person is told that his mental illness cannot be treated until his substance abuse is under better control, and he is also told that his substance abuse cannot be treated until his mental illness is under better control.

STAGING DRUG AND ALCOHOL TREATMENT

The primary treatment of substance abuse is psychosocial, either with individual therapy, group therapy, or both. At times this requires intensive treatment within a residential setting that separates the person from drugs. At other times various intensities of outpatient treatment are effective. Drug and alcohol abuse can vary enormously from one clinic to another and from one person to another. Typical drug and alcohol treatment often has a number of steps that flow into each other. They can be organized in different ways by different treatment programs, and a particular person may go back and forth on his own journey toward sobriety.

1. Treatment often starts with information about alcohol and the different drugs of abuse, how those drugs affect a person, and information about how drug abuse, addiction, and dependence develop and are maintained. Many people who are abusing drugs or alcohol have little real information about the drugs they are using. It is useful to start treatment with a review of the psychological and medical effects of the drugs, how dependence develops, and what is known about the long-term impact of the use of the specific drug. For example, heavy alcohol use can cause depression. Heavy marijuana use can interfere with motivation, making it difficult for a person to pursue other life goals that were previously important. Knowing the risk of HIV and hepatitis may help discourage a person from trying IV drugs. Learning about fetal alcohol syndrome may help motivate a pregnant woman to stop drinking.

2. Treatment then typically includes exploration of how substance use fits into the person's life. Substance abuse helps the abusing person in some way. If the substance use were not doing something positive, it would be easy to stop it. It may be that the substance helps to pass time or decrease anxiety, feels good, or just helps to avoid withdrawal; in all cases the person who is abusing a drug feels it is helping in some way. For example, he may feel that using marijuana is the only way to avoid being nervous or to fit in with his friends who smoke pot.

3. A third step is often a discussion of the person's own life goals and how the person would like his or her life to be. For most of us, there is a gap between how life actually is and how we would like life to be. What is the gap for the substance abuser, and does the drug or alcohol add to this gap? How is the use of drugs interfering in very specific ways with how this person would like his or her life to be? For example, he may talk about how much he had wanted to finish college and go to graduate school, but that it now seems impossible. Maybe the marijuana is part of his problem. Or someone would like to be a good parent but is now unreliable and always broke. Perhaps her cocaine use is part of this problem.

4. Once the person is clear about how the drug use is interfering, it is possible that he will want to commit to making changes necessary to stop the use. A person can enter drug treatment without a commitment to stop using. Many people enter treatment because of outside pressure, because they are forced to or with considerable ambivalence about whether they really want to quit. At some point, if treatment is going to be effective, it will be because the person has decided that the drug use has to stop. Only after there is a commitment is it possible to get into a discussion of what life changes would be needed to make sobriety a reality. This commitment does not need to be in place before starting treatment; it can evolve as part of being in treatment. A decision to stop using drugs or alcohol often requires a decision to make major changes in one's life. It is hard to not use drugs if someone is still spending time with other people who are using, is engaged in activities associated with use, and is surrounded by cues that are connected to use.

5. Effective drug or alcohol treatment requires recognition of "triggers," or situations that can precipitate relapse, and strategies to help avoid or cope with such triggers must be developed. There is typically a strong group component to

treatment, either AA, 12-step, or professionally run groups. These can provide a sense of support and a sense that the person is not alone, and they can inspire shared ideas about how to effectively change one's life to achieve and support increased control over substances. Modern AODA treatment is effective for many people, but addiction is often a chronic condition and the way to getting control of substances can take many paths. Some people, even those with heavy drug-use patterns, can just stop and never use again. This is true for tobacco, alcohol, cocaine and other drugs of abuse. Other people find themselves going through multiple bouts of different kinds of AODA treatment before finally getting in control of their abuse patterns. Still others will achieve significant sobriety, only to relapse after some period of time. *Relapse is not a treatment failure but is only a misstep as people gain more control over their substance use and their lives.*

USE OF MEDICATIONS AS PART OF DRUG AND ALCOHOL TREATMENT

Historically, many AODA treatment programs have not considered that medications have any role in successful treatment; some have even been actively "anti-medication." The idea that a person who has a life history of drug abuse could be helped by another drug has been met with skepticism by the AODA treatment community. At times, this went so far that people who were taking medication for a serious mental illness were discouraged from continuing their medication by AODA counselors. The lack of good research on the appropriate role of medications for people with drug abuse problems justified the suspicion about the use of any medication. Finally, the reality that some prescribed psychiatric medications were themselves abusable and addictive also increased the confusion over the appropriate role of psychiatric medication.

This situation is now rapidly changing. There is better research that outlines the appropriate role of medication in the treatment of substance abuse, and the training of AODA counselors helps them to have a more sophisticated idea of what medications can help and what medications can make the AODA issues worse.

Integrated treatment strategy for people with co-existing mental illness and substance abuse

Many people with mental illnesses will also end up abusing drugs. Anyone who feels terrible will look for solutions to feel better. Drugs and alcohol are used in an attempt to feel less anxious or less depressed. Someone who feels socially awkward may use drugs or alcohol as a way of trying to fit in and feel more comfortable with other people. A person who cannot sleep may try alcohol as a way of getting to sleep. The reasons are endless, but the statistics are overwhelming. Studies suggest that 60% of people with a major mental illness also have a co-morbid problem with substance abuse.

Most mental illnesses can become more severe and problematic when combined with substance abuse. For example, heavy alcohol abuse may cause or make depression much worse. A person with schizophrenia who is already having problems with loss of motivation and suspiciousness may find these symptoms become much worse with regular marijuana use. A person with bipolar disorder who has rapid mood changes may find that this pattern is exaggerated when added to cocaine abuse. Many people with mental illnesses will find that the abuse of alcohol, cocaine, marijuana, or other substances will typically increase the difficulty in functioning connected to the mental illness. There is an apparent destructive feedback loop, where the mental illness for a variety of reasons can increase the likelihood that a person will engage in substance abuse, and the substance abuse will make the mental illness worse.

For example, a person with bipolar disease may also have some problems with alcohol abuse, but she may start drinking much more heavily when she becomes manic. The ongoing use of alcohol is likely to decrease her life stability and increase her chances of having more manic episodes. When she does have a manic episode, her use of alcohol is likely to make it much worse with much more out-of-control behavior. Mood-stabilizing medication can be safely used even in the face of chronic alcohol use. Training in the early recognition of mania, controlling issues that make a manic episode more likely such as sleep deprivation, and early intervention strategies such as learning to slow your mind down and forcing a more regular sleep pattern, can all help stabilize the mood disorder. Integrating this into the destabilizing role that alcohol plays is an important part of effective treatment. It is understandable that a person developing a manic episode may have a strong inclination to start using more alcohol as a way of trying to get to sleep and slow down. Working on recognizing the actual consequences of the alcohol use and coming up with alternatives to alcohol are both ways to solve the same problem.

General concerns about the use of psychotropic medication for someone with ongoing substance abuse

The treatment of an underlying mental illness can be an important part of effective AODA treatment. At the same time, there is a legitimate concern that it could be dangerous for a person to continue using psychotropic medication in the face of ongoing substance use. It is important to think about the specific medical dangers from interactions between specific medications and specific drugs of abuse. Most prescribed psychiatric medications, including antipsychotic medications, mood-stabilizing medications, and antidepressants, may be less effective when used by someone who continues to drink or use drugs, but with few exceptions they are relatively safe to use. In general, if a person clearly needs an antipsychotic medication, a mood stabilizer, or an antidepressant, it is almost always better to continue the medication even in the face of ongoing substance use than to just discontinue it. The exceptions are antianxiety medications and sleeping pills that do present specific risks when used along with ongoing alcohol or substance use.

Sometimes the concern about continuing psychiatric medication is not because of the risks from the medication but rather from the confusion about whether the purported mental illness is real or just part of the substance abuse. At times, the underlying mental illness is clearly a part of the AODA issues. Someone may have a significant history of serious depression, bipolar disorder, schizophrenia, or another major mental illness apart from the AODA issues. It becomes more confusing when the mental illness and substance abuse are more entangled. Someone may have had psychotic symptoms for a long time, but he has been using substances for a long time as well. This can become most complicated in someone who is depressed. Many people who drink heavily become depressed, and it can be unclear whether a person's current depression is caused by the alcohol use or whether the alcohol use could be a response to depression. Many people who are heavy drinkers will be much less depressed after 3 weeks of sobriety, even without the use of an antidepressant. This would suggest that, where the situation is unclear, it might be worth not starting an antidepressant medication for someone who is alcohol dependent until he has had 3 weeks or more of sobriety, to see if sobriety is enough to reverse the depression. The problem is that more depressed, alcohol-dependent people will achieve sobriety if they are started on an antidepressant at the beginning of active AODA treatment. This would expose some people to antidepressant medication when they probably do not need it, but it may allow other people to have a better chance of achieving sobriety. There is no simple answer to these issues, and individual decisions need to be made depending on the underlying mental illness, the specific drug of abuse, the specific medication that is prescribed, and the individual client.

Schizophrenia and other psychotic disorders. At times, it can be very confusing whether a person has schizophrenia or ongoing psychotic symptoms from chronic drug use. An antipsychotic medication is often useful in either case. There are few medically dangerous interactions between alcohol and other drugs of abuse and antipsychotic medications. If an anti-psychotic medication helps resolve an underlying psychosis, the substance abuse is usually easier to treat. There is legitimate concern that providing treatment for the psychotic symptoms can, at times, just allow the drug use to continue. While this is worth considering on a case-by-case basis, for the most part antipsychotic medications should be continued even in the face of ongoing substance use. If a person with a psychotic disorder is getting help from an antipsychotic medication, his quality of life and his likelihood of responding to AODA treatment will be better if the medication is continued.

Bipolar disorder. The most common mood-stabilizing medications used for bipolar disorder are lithium carbonate and sodium valproate (Depakote). Lithium carbonate, sodium valproate, and the other commonly used mood stabilizers are safe to use even in the presence of ongoing substance abuse.

Most people with bipolar disorder will have a more stable mood and have a better chance of controlling their substance use if their mood-stabilizing medication is continued, even in the face of ongoing substance use. There is some concern that a person taking lithium could develop a dangerously high serum lithium level if he were to become dehydrated as part of very heavy alcohol use over a period of time. While this is a theoretical risk, in reality a person drinking enough to become seriously dehydrated will almost always stop his lithium while on this kind of binge. There is a theoretical concern that sodium valproate could cause further liver damage in a person who already has liver damage from heavy alcohol use. This is unlikely to be a serious problem, especially if the sodium valproate is effective in helping someone to stabilize his mood and decrease his alcohol use.

Depression. There is ongoing controversy about the use of antidepressants in the treatment of depression when substance abuse is also present. If a person is depressed at the beginning of AODA treatment, especially if she has a history of depression, a trial of an antidepressant medication may be worth trying. On the other hand, if she continues to abuse substances and continues to be depressed, continuing the antidepressant may not make much sense. There are few medically dangerous interactions between most of the commonly used antidepressants and either alcohol or drugs of abuse, but the antidepressants are likely to be less effective as long as the drug abuse continues. SSRI-type antidepressants, like fluoxetine (Prozac) and citalopram (Celexa), and SNRI-type antidepressants, like duloxetine (Cymbalta), are generally safe even in the face of ongoing substance use, as is mirtazapine (Remeron) and bupropion (Wellbutrin). MAOIs (monoamine oxidase inhibitors) and tricyclic antidepressants, such as amitriptyline (Elavil) or nortriptyline (Pamalor), are now rarely used. There can be dangerous interactions with stimulants and other drugs of abuse and these older types of antidepressants. If someone continues to abuse alcohol or other drugs, it becomes more complicated to determine if the medications are really helping or if they are just enabling ongoing substance use.

Anxiety. Many substance abusers complain about anxiety. Panic disorder, PTSD, OCD, and generalized anxiety are all associated with an increased risk of alcohol and other substance abuse. People with anxiety disorders are more likely to abuse drugs, and drug abuse and the daily withdrawal from drugs can increase anxiety. Complaints about insomnia are also extremely common. The problem is that the benzodiazepines, such as diazepam (Valium) and lorazepam (Ativan), are themselves addictive and can be abused. While these medications are less addictive than alcohol, they are much more likely to be a problem for someone who already has a problem with alcohol or other drugs. They can also trigger a relapse in a person who has had problems with alcohol in the past, even if he is now sober. As a result, the use of benzodiazepines is generally not indicated in people with current or recent substance abuse, and they should be used somewhat cautiously by people with past histories of significant alcohol or other substance abuse.

This concern about the use of benzodiazepines is not an

absolute injunction never to provide them to people who abuse substances. Benzodiazepines have a role in acute withdrawal from alcohol and some other drugs. They can also have a limited role as part of active AODA treatment in a person who has achieved sobriety and where the use of the medication may keep the person in active AODA treatment. Many people with substance abuse are very anxious, and they argue strongly for their need for a medication to treat this anxiety. The risk is that the use of a benzodiazepine just adds another drug to the mix that the person is already abusing. If a person is still using alcohol or another drug, a benzodiazepine should generally be avoided. If a person relapses on alcohol or other drugs, benzodiazepines should generally be discontinued, even if the person protests about how much it is needed or how much worse the drinking or other drug use would be without it.

Many of the commonly used antidepressants can be helpful in the treatment of anxiety, including panic disorder, OCD, and PTSD. The medications can take a week or more to be effective and do not have the same feeling of rapid calm that comes from the benzodiazepines. On the other hand, they are safe, are not addictive, and do not add a new problem to the drug abuse the person already has.

Insomnia. Insomnia is probably the most common complaint from substance abusers. People often complain bitterly of their problems with sleep, and they explain that they drink or use other substances so that they can sleep better and that if they were to quit using, they would need something to help them sleep. Sleeping pills should be used very cautiously by people with active substance abuse patterns. It sounds tempting to use a pill, but often the same person is not engaged in good sleep habits and has not "learned" how to sleep without a chemical of one sort or another. Very often, the person cannot sleep even with a sleeping pill at a normal dose, and he may increase the dose or try one sleep medication after another with limited success. Over time the person is still abusing drugs and also now taking a sleeping pill on a regular basis. There can be a role for sleeping pills, on a temporary and monitored basis, for someone who is maintaining sobriety, but it is important not to allow the sleeping pill to become an additional problem. I do not prescribe sleeping pills for anyone who is continuing to actively drink or abuse other drugs. The person can always obtain over-the-counter sleep aids, but at least I can avoid being a participant in the pattern of abuse.

Medication in the treatment of withdrawal

Withdrawal from heroin, tobacco, cocaine, amphetamines, and marijuana can be very uncomfortable but is not medically dangerous. There are medications that may help allow the person to be a bit more comfortable, but there are no medications that can block the withdrawal or allow the person going through it to feel "good" or "normal." Sucking on a hard candy can help the person feel more comfortable during withdrawal. Clonidine (Catapres) or a related medication can help decrease some of the symptoms of opiate withdrawal, and these medications are themselves not addictive. These are medications typically used to treat high blood pressure, and they seem to block some of the increased reactivity of the body's system that can occur during opiate withdrawal. Nicotine patches, gum, or inhalers can ease some of the withdrawal from tobacco. Many medications have been tried, but there is no clear consensus on what medications help with the withdrawal from cocaine, other stimulants, or marijuana.

Withdrawal from alcohol, barbiturates, benzodiazepines, and other drugs classified as "sedative hypnotics" can be medically dangerous as well as uncomfortable. A person withdrawing from these drugs can have seizures as well as other medical complications. If someone has been using alcohol or a sedative hypnotic in significant doses for a significant period of time, especially if they have had any history of having had a seizure in the past, then medical monitoring of the withdrawal is required. Making sure that the person has been drinking water, and replacing needed vitamins and minerals, can be important.

People who have been seriously alcohol dependent and have become malnourished can develop thiamine deficiency, which can cause brain damage. Replacing thiamine either by pill or injection can be an important first step. People can also develop a magnesium deficiency, which increases the risk of seizures, and replacing that and other minerals may be necessary.

A number of medications can help decrease both the medical risk as well as much of the discomfort of the withdrawal. Traditionally, a benzodiazepine, either clonazepam (Klonopin) or lorazepam (Ativan) or a similar medication, has been used to treat withdrawal from either alcohol or other sedative hypnotics. These basically replace the alcohol or the drug, and they allow for a more controlled withdrawal that is less dangerous and less noxious. More recently, anticonvulsants, either sodium valproate (Depakote) or gabapentin (Neurontin), have become the primary medication of choice to control withdrawal. These have less risk of causing dependence and seem a safer way to help provide medication support during the withdrawal process.

MEDICATION IN THE TREATMENT OF ALCOHOL, OPIATES, AND TOBACCO ABUSE

The idea that a medication could help with the treatment of substance abuse is relatively new. It is also a very rapidly changing research area as we learn more about the underlying neuroscience of addiction and abuse. There are more different medications being developed with different pharmacological "targets," effective on more drugs of abuse. There are basically four approaches, or "targets," for a medication in the treatment of substance abuse. (1) A medication can discourage use by making the person sick if alcohol or the target drug is taken while the medication is in the person's system. Disulfiram (Antabuse) is the classic example of this. (2) A medication can replace the drug of abuse with a prescribed medication that can be better controlled, replacing one addiction with another that interferes less in the person's life. Methadone, which is used in the treatment of heroin and other opiate addiction, or nicotine patches used for smoking are examples. (3) A medication can decrease the pleasurable response to the drug, blocking the "high." Naltroxone, used in the treatment of alcohol dependence, is an example of this strategy. (4) A medication can decrease the withdrawal and the risk of being "triggered" to reuse. Acamprosate (Campral), used in the treatment of alcohol dependence, is an example.

Medication use in the treatment of alcohol abuse

Disulfiram (Antabuse): Disulfiram causes anyone taking it to become very sick if he or she drinks any alcohol. It interferes with the breakdown or metabolism of alcohol, so that one of the alcohol by-products called acetaldehyde builds up. A very small amount of this in a person's system causes all of the symptoms of a bad hangover. If a person drinks while taking disulfiram, a much higher concentration of acetaldehyde builds up, causing flushing, nausea, vomiting, sweating, a throbbing headache, breathing problems, chest pain, heart irregularities, rapid pulse, and dizziness. It is an extremely unpleasant experience. For someone with a bad heart or another medical condition, using disulfiram can be potentially dangerous. The decision to take a disulfiram tablet is a decision to not use alcohol for several days.

Disulfiram can be used in a number of ways. It can be given coercively, as part of conditions of parole or as part of an agreement to keep a job. In these situations, taking the medication is often supervised. A spouse can agree to stay in a marriage if the person agrees to take disulfiram as a way of guaranteeing sobriety. In other situations, a person who is committed to sobriety does not trust his own impulsivity to use alcohol, and he may take disulfiram as a way of guaranteeing that he cannot get triggered by an event or stress and start drinking without having enough control to think through all of the consequences. In yet another possible scenario, a person who has achieved a period of sobriety may know that she will be in a very high-risk situation. For example, she may want to join her family for a holiday, yet she knows that everyone in her family uses alcohol and there will be pressure for her to drink as well. Disulfiram can allow her to join her family and yet know that she will not give into the pressure to use alcohol. Disulfiram has some side effects and risks, but in the right situation it can be extremely helpful in helping the alcohol-dependent person maintain sobriety.

Naltrexone (ReVia): Naltrexone blocks opioid receptors in the brain. Initially, naltrexone was used to block the "high" from heroin and other opiates. Some of the reinforcing properties of alcohol work through these same receptors, and blocking them with naltrexone makes using alcohol less pleasurable and less reinforcing. When used by people who are alcohol dependent, naltrexone decreases the craving for alcohol, increases the number of days to a person's first drink, increases the time to return to heavy drinking, and decreases the number of days when heavy drinking occurs. Naltrexone does not "cure" alcoholism or prevent relapse, but it can help.

One of the problems with naltrexone is that people tend to stop taking it. It is available in a long-acting injection that can be given every 4 weeks. This is effective and well tolerated but is very expensive.

Acamprosate (Campral): Acamprosate seems to work by decreasing the overexcitement of nerve cells that continues for a long time after alcohol withdrawal. The theory is that while the most visible symptoms of alcohol withdrawal are over in a few days or a week or so, there are subtle elements of withdrawal, with an overexcited nervous system that can trigger relapse. Acamprosate decreases some of this overactivity. It works best when given to someone who has been sober for at least a few days or to someone who is motivated to stop drinking. It requires a lot of pills; someone would need to take two large pills three times a day, so taking the medication can be difficult for many people. Results have been mixed, but it appears to be helpful for some people with alcohol dependence.

Topirimate (Topamax): Topirimate is a medication commonly used to control seizures and treat headaches. Several studies have shown that it decreases heavy drinking and also increases the number of days of abstinence when given to alcohol-dependent men. It can cause thinking and memory problems in some people. These side effects are dose related and are decreased if the medication is started at a low dose and the dose is then increased slowly.

What you can expect from medications used in the treatment of alcohol abuse and dependence. If you have taken disulfiram (Antabuse) in the last few days and you drink, you will likely become very ill. Knowing this is enough to keep most people from drinking. It is common for a person to feel the need to "test" the effect and drink once just to see what it feels like. This can be dangerous and is definitely not recommended, but people do this anyway. Some people experiment with how much they can drink without becoming ill. For the vast majority of people, the answer is very, very little. Even very small amounts of alcohol will make most people taking disulfiram sick. The idea of disulfiram is to help keep someone from impulsively drinking. Disulfiram means that if you want to drink, you cannot do it today or tomorrow or even the next day. It means that you can still make a decision to drink, and the decision to stop taking disulfiram is in fact a decision not to drink. This cannot be an impulsive decision.

Naltrexone, acamprosate, and topiramate all decrease the urge to drink, the craving to drink, and the risk of getting into yet another out-of-control drinking period. None of these medications will keep you from drinking, none of them will increase your motivation toward sobriety, and none of them will fix the problem. All of them can give you a bit more control over your drinking, decrease some of the cravings that may make sobriety more difficult, and decrease the positive effects of alcohol that can keep a drinking bout going. As part of an AODA program and when used along with lifestyle changes that support sobriety, they can all help. They may not stop all drinking, but they can help decrease the frequency of relapses and can be very helpful in decreasing the risk that a relapse will turn into a major binge.

Medication use in the treatment of opiate addiction

Historically, opiate addiction meant addiction to opium, which was typically smoked. Later, opiate addiction in the United States meant an addiction primarily to heroin and other opiates taken by intravenous injection. More recently, the distribution of very pure, less expensive heroin has led to increasing numbers of new users—people who would never have used an IV needle but who smoke heroin, get hooked, and then at times move on to IV use. There has also been a growing problem with people abusing and becoming dependent on morphine, oxycodone (OxyContin), methadone, and other opiates that are either prescribed or obtained illegally.

Many people can "kick" opiate addiction with appropriate support and treatment. Some people who are opiate dependent will continue to relapse and be unable to maintain themselves drug–free. For this group, there are currently two medications in widespread use. Both are effective, but each has different advantages and disadvantages.

Methadone: Methadone is an opiate that works similarly to heroin or morphine or meperidine (Demerol). It has the advantage of having a half-life of around 22 hours, much longer than the other opiates. This means that after 22 hours, half of the methadone is still in the person's body, which means that if it is taken once a day the person will not go through significant withdrawal, even if he is physiologically dependent on it. This is a "mean" or average duration, and it can vary enormously from one person to another. A person can have a half-life as short as a few hours or as long as four days. The duration needed to prevent withdrawal is much longer than the time methadone is effective for pain control, which means that it must be taken more frequently when used for pain control. A person who is addicted to another opiate can be put on methadone and build up to a high-enough dose that the addition of another opiate will not add much additional effect. Essentially, the methadone can block the effect of other additional opiates. True methadone itself is addictive, but someone can effectively trade an addiction to street drugs that are short-acting and need to be taken multiple times a day at high cost to avoid withdrawal, to using a drug that can be taken once a day in a controlled amount and decreases the likelihood that the person will use other drugs.

Methadone is effective in helping someone with an opiate addiction lead a much more stable life. There are, however, a number of problems. For one, it replaces one addictive drug with another addictive drug, albeit one that allows for a more stable life. Methadone is itself a drug that can be abused, and methadone clinics must be tightly controlled to try and minimize diversion. Even with these tight controls, people sometimes sell their methadone in order to purchase other opiates that act faster and give a better "high." The nature of methadone clinics and the need for very tight monitoring tends to be expensive, and people on methadone must be very tightly connected to methadone clinics. While this can be helpful in supporting stability and decreasing other drug use, it can interfere with developing a life that is not focused on drug use or drug treatment. While a person on prescribed methadone can try to taper off it after a period of many months or years, the chance of relapse is much higher if the methadone is discontinued.

Buprenorphine (Subutex and Suboxone): Buprenorphine is a "partial agonist." This means that it both blocks the opiate receptor so that other opiates cannot further stimulate it, and it also weakly stimulates the receptor itself. This means that it blocks the "high" or the euphoric effects of other opiates while also being slightly addictive itself. Buprenorphine is much less likely to be abused than a drug that fully stimulates the receptor such as methadone. If taken in an overdose, methadone and other opiates can be very dangerous. Buprenorphine is much safer in an overdose, and because its effects are limited and it does not cause the same high as an opiate, people who use it are less likely to abuse it and are much less likely to try and increase the dose in an effort to get high. Because buprenorphine is both safer and less subject to being abused, clinics that dispense it are less tightly controlled, which allows people who are doing well on it to be less involved in a treatment clinic on a daily level. It still is much more effective in helping people overcome their opiate addiction if it is used as part of an integrated AODA treatment program.

Suboxone is a combination of buprenorphine and a small dose of naloxone. While buprenorphine is not likely to be abused when taken by mouth, if it is dissolved and injected it can cause a high and can be abused. If it is dissolved and injected, the naloxone in the Suboxone blocks opiate receptors, and this will prevent any opiate from being effective. This effectively prevents Suboxone from being dissolved and injected as a drug of abuse. When it is taken sublingually (under the tongue since it is not absorbed well if swallowed), the naloxone breaks apart before it becomes active and it has no effect. The addition of naloxone to the buprenorphine in the same pill decreases the risk that the drug could be injected and abused. Subutex is just buprenorphine without the naltrexone. This is prescribed for pregnant women, since there is some concern about possible birth defects from naltrexone. Otherwise, Suboxone, rather than Subutex, is prescribed.

What you can expect from medications used in the treatment of opiate dependence. Both methadone and Suboxone block the euphoric effects of opiates and stop the symptoms of withdrawal. They trade addiction to the opiate of abuse with addiction to a medication that is easier to take in controlled amounts. This can help someone lead a more stable and less drug-focused life. A person can still miss the euphoric "high" that comes from an illicit opiate, the excitement of the lifestyle, and the circle of friends that were part of that life. Even people who are stable on methadone or Suboxone may feel some desire to return to their old lifestyle and chase a "high." At the same time, these medications taken as part of a clinic with urine drug screens and counseling can help people reestablish stable lives. Just being drug-free or being on a replacement medication that allows a stable life is not enough. Often people have to learn new skills, make new friends, and begin new ways of living.

Medication use for treatment of tobacco addiction

When people talk about drugs, they commonly think of alcohol, cocaine, or heroin, but not tobacco. Tobacco kills more people than any other drug. It is as addictive as any other drug, and it is harder to stop than most other addictive drugs. The damage from smoking builds up over time, and it causes not only lung cancer and emphysema but also heart disease and other cancers. After years of abstinence, some but not all of the damage can be reversed. There has been a major public health campaign to try and decrease smoking in the U.S. population. The primary treatment to help people stop smoking is support groups that train people about the cues that promote smoking and the triggers that cause relapse. While medication can help, medication is not the primary focus of smoking cessation.

Alternative nicotine delivery systems: The problem with smoking is not with the use of nicotine; it is with the tobacco that serves as the delivery system for the nicotine. If someone uses nicotine without tobacco, it can cause blood pressure elevation, and a person can overdose on nicotine if he or she takes too much, but there are few serious medical problems from nicotine used in reasonable doses. Unfortunately, nothing is quite the same as smoking tobacco. Smoking tobacco is a bit like smoking freebase cocaine. Smoking gives a very fast pulse of nicotine to the brain receptors, which is different from the slow increase that comes from gum or bathing those same receptors in a low level of nicotine from a patch. Alternative nicotine delivery systems, such as patches, lozenges, gum, and inhalation systems, can decrease some of the symptoms of withdrawal but they will not substitute for the feel and the act of smoking. Some of the newer delivery systems such as the smokeless cigarettes and inhalers "feel" more like a cigarette and provide some of the same behavioral cues as smoking, but the brain will not be completely confused.

Bupropion (Wellbutrin, Zyban): Bupropion is an antidepressant that makes it easier for people to stop smoking. It seems to help both craving and withdrawal. This effect on smoking is not connected to its antidepressant activity, and it works even for people who are not depressed. Bupropion has a mechanism of action very different from other antidepressants, and it is the only antidepressant currently available that is effective for helping people to quit smoking.

Varenicline (Chantix): Varenicline works by blocking the effects of nicotine on the brain. It can be combined with bupropion and is much more effective if used as part of a comprehensive quit-smoking program. It can increase moodiness and depression in some people, and it can cause or increase suicidal thinking in some people. Hostility, irritation, and threats to others have also been reported. Despite these risks and concerns, it continues to be used because it is very effective. Warning a person about the potential risks is very important. The potential changes in mood and increase in suicidal thinking do not happen to everyone who takes the medication. When the medication does cause these side effects, they do not appear all at once but build up over days or weeks. If a person taking the medication is aware of the possible risks, he or she can stop the medication if any of the mood changes do appear, before they become a serious problem. Varenicline is usually used for 12 to 24 weeks, and it is not commonly needed as an ongoing medication.

What you can expect from medications used in the treatment of tobacco dependence. Varenicline and bupropion can help decrease some of the cravings for tobacco, and nicotine replacement patches, gum, or inhalers can decrease some of the withdrawal effects. None of these medications will replace the ability to focus and the alertness that comes from a cigarette. People continue to miss the effects of cigarettes even after years of not smoking. A person can enjoy being able to breathe better, be healthy, and save money, but he can still miss the cigarette.

What to expect from medication in the treatment of cocaine, amphetamine, marijuana, or hallucinogen abuse. There is no widespread consensus or convincing research on the use of medications to help treat abuse of cocaine, amphetamine, marijuana, or hallucinogens. Using a medication, especially medication that can have its own abuse potential such as some sleeping pills and some antianxiety medications, can add a second drug of abuse to the person's preexisting problems.

MEDICATIONS FOR ALCOHOL ABUSE

disulfiram	Antabuse	makes person very sick if alcohol is used
acamprosate	Campral	decreases long-term craving
naltrexone	ReVia	decreases "high" from drinking

MEDICATIONS FOR OPIATE ABUSE

methadone	Dolphine	blocks "high" from opiate
buprenorphine/ naltrexone	Suboxone	blocks "high" from opiate
buprenorphine	Subutex	blocks "high" from opiate

MEDICATIONS FOR CIGARETTE ABUSE

nicotine patch	Nicoderm CQ	nicotine replacement, once a day, less effective for some people
nicotine inhaler	Nicotrol Inhaler	nicotine replacement
nicotine gum	Nicoderm, Nicorette, Nicotinell	nicotine replacement, bite down on gum but do not chew

nicotine lozenge	Commit	nicotine replacement
bupropion	Wellbutrin, Budeprion, Zyban	stimulates dopamine receptors
varenicline	Chantix	stimulates nicotine receptors

6

Schizophrenia and other Psychotic Disorders

Think about what it would be like to hear the voice of God giving you special messages that no one else can hear, or hearing a panoply of unknown people talking to you loudly and incessantly with no way to shut the voices off. It can be terrifying to feel that you cannot determine what is real and what is not, and it is even worse to be absolutely sure that some belief or event or perception is real and then have no one else believe you. It is easy to be overwhelmed when you feel that you cannot trust anyone else or when you feel that you cannot trust your own brain.

The common description of psychosis is "going crazy," having a "nervous breakdown," or "going insane." These are imprecise terms and none of these have a medical definition, but they all reflect the terror of losing control of your own mind. Psychosis is the medical term that refers to a loss of touch with reality. Psychosis is a symptom, not a specific illness. Like other symptoms, psychotic symptoms can be intrusive and interfere with one's ability to function, or they can be mild and cause less of a problem. Some people hear voices or have other experiences that could be considered "psychotic" but seem to have little apparent distress or dysfunction and they would not think of seeing a psychiatrist or getting treatment. For most people, however, psychotic symptoms are profoundly disturbing and often cause major functional problems.

A number of different disorders can cause psychotic symptoms. A person can develop psychotic symptoms as part of a manic episode or as part of a psychotic depression. In these situations, the psychotic symptoms typically resolve as the underlying mood disorder improves. A person can develop a brief psychotic episode from extreme stress and sleep deprivation. This usually resolves once the stress is relieved and the person is able to sleep. Drug use can lead to psychotic symptoms. Depending on the drug and the use pattern, psychotic symptoms can continue for days, weeks, or even longer after the drug use is discontinued. A number of prescribed medications and medical illnesses can also cause psychotic symptoms. Delirium, a state of confusion caused by a medical problem affecting the brain, can be easily be confused with a psychotic disorder. There is also concern that some drug use, specifically heavy marijuana use, can precipitate schizophrenia in someone who is susceptible to such a disorder.

SCHIZOPHRENIA

Schizophrenia is only one possible cause of psychotic symptoms, but it is the most common cause of symptoms that continue over months and years without another obvious cause such as drug use, brain damage, or a medical condition. Schizophrenia typically develops when a person is in his or her late teens or twenties. It is a terrible disease that attacks people when they are just starting to develop dreams about what they want their lives to be. It often begins with a period of increased anxiety or decreased function before any psychotic symptoms are apparent. It is an illness with a high rate of mortality. Up to 5 percent of people with schizophrenia kill themselves, and on average people with schizophrenia die 25 years earlier than those in the general population (Hor & Taylor, 2010). While the psychotic symptoms of schizophrenia are most dramatic, there are other parts of the illness that can be even more disabling. Many people with schizophrenia develop "negative symptoms," which are the loss of motivation, spontaneity, initiative, and persistence. They also develop "cognitive symptoms," which are problems with thinking clearly and making decisions. These negative and cognitive symptoms can interfere with functioning more than hearing voices or having unusual beliefs (Diamond, 2004).

There are many misconceptions about schizophrenia. One false belief is that it always leads to disability. Although many people with schizophrenia are too disabled to work full-time, others can function quite well holding full-time jobs, having friends, and having lives that are fulfilling. There are a growing number of first-person autobiographies that recount both the difficulties and the possibilities of living with schizophrenia (McLean, 2005; Steele, 2002). Like most other illnesses, schizophrenia can be severe or mild; some people will have major functional impairment or relatively less impairment. Another false belief is that the lives of people with schizophrenia always take a downhill course and that people with schizophrenia get worse over time. Actually, a number of long-term studies demonstrate that, over decades, the course of schizophrenia is very heterogeneous, with some people doing very poorly and others doing very well. In one study that followed up on people for more than 20 years, a third of the people with schizophrenia diagnosed by research criteria were living fairly normal lives without currently receiving medication or other treatment. Another third of the group was doing well, although still requiring medication and other services. Only a third of the group was significantly impaired or unstable at the time of follow-up (Harding et al., 1987).

These long-term follow-up studies changed our ideas about schizophrenia and began an ongoing discussion about recovery. The term "recovery" has been used in two very different ways when applied to schizophrenia. One meaning is that there is a complete absence of symptoms or the disease is cured (Andreason et al., 2005). This can happen, but it is not something that everyone with the illness can achieve. The other meaning of "recovery" is the process of getting one's life back, despite ongoing illness, of striving to have the best life despite the possibility of ongoing disability. Recovery in this sense is an ongoing journey of discovery that focuses on the person's own life goals (Diamond, 2006). This could mean getting a friend or a job or going back to school. It often means learning to live and function despite ongoing symptoms. Too often, a person with schizophrenia is defined by his or her illness. The person becomes "a schizophrenic," and the other parts of personhood become lost. Someone may have been an artist or musician, a father or brother, someone who enjoyed playing sports or just watching sports. He may be very bright, very athletic, or very focused on helping other people, but all of that can get lost in the diagnosis. An important part of the process of recovery is learning to think of oneself and be thought of as more than just having an illness. The process of recovery is making as much out of one's life as possible, despite the illness. This is similar to the person who lives as full of a life as possible despite diabetes, rheumatoid arthritis, or becoming a paraplegic.

Psychotic symptoms

The most obvious and dramatic symptoms of schizophrenia are positive, or psychotic, symptoms. Psychotic symptoms include hallucinations, delusions, false beliefs, illusions, and misinterpretation of real stimuli.

Hallucinations: False perceptions. Any sense can be the source of false perceptions. A person can hear voices or music or sounds that no one else can hear, see objects or people that are apparently not real, experience smells or tastes without clear reason, or even feel tactile sensations on his skin, such as bugs crawling. While people with schizophrenia and other serious psychiatric disorders can have these kinds of psychotic symptoms, not everyone with schizophrenia experiences hallucinations, and not everyone with hallucinations has a serious mental illness. There are people who are functioning well, are working, and are living their lives without any need to see a psychiatrist but who regularly hear voices and do not see this as a major problem. Up to 15% of the population will at some point experience hypnogogic hallucinations: hallucinations when half asleep, either while waking up or going to sleep. People under enough stress will sometimes experience psychotic symptoms, usually for a brief period of time. Psychotic symptoms can also appear as part of a delirium, a medical condition that interferes with normal brain function. There is also a cultural component to hearing voices. Some cultures support the idea of hearing the voices of dead relatives, not as pathology but rather as a natural part of life.

Voices and other hallucinations can be quietly in the background or can be very intrusive and interfere with normal thinking. They can be constant or come and go with stress and with other activities. It is common for people with schizophrenia to report that voices are louder and most intrusive when there is nothing to do or nothing to focus on, and that the voices recede with activity or conversation. People with stress-related voices are likely to get improvement after sleep. The patterns of voices and what makes them better or worse are very different for each person.

Delusions: False beliefs. Some beliefs are so improbable that there would be widespread consensus that they do not reflect the reality of the world. This sounds as though it would be easy to know which beliefs are based in reality and which are not. If a person's beliefs are so outlandish that no one else could believe them, then they are probably psychotic. While the distinction between "reality based" and "psychotic" is usually clear, philosophically it is worth considering those cases that are more confusing.

There are groups of people who believe they have had personal contact with UFOs, experienced miracles that have no scientific explanation, or believe with certainty that the world will end on some specific date and plan their lives around this to the extent of giving away possessions and preparing for their next life. How many people have to share an unusual belief for it to no longer be psychotic? Many people have beliefs about various conspiracies, from the death of John F. Kennedy to the involvement of the U.S. government in 9/11. It is not always clear when a strongly held political belief becomes a paranoid delusion.

It is difficult for any of us to assess the veracity of our own beliefs. For example, I believe that I am a psychiatrist, and I have firmly held on to this belief for many years. I can point to many kinds of evidence to support this belief: my name on my office, my business cards, the reactions of my family and colleagues, the paperwork connected with my medical license and my university position. But if these pieces of evidence were to disappear, if I appeared at work and my name was not on my office door and my key no longer worked in the lock and my colleagues refused to recognize me and my official paperwork was all lost, I would still believe that I was a psychiatrist. And if people around me tried to convince me that my belief was in error or delusional, even if all of the supporting evidence was missing, I would continue in my belief. Beliefs are just that, beliefs, and we tend to hold on to them with or without evidence. Of course, some beliefs are held onto with more tenacity than others. It would be much easier to convince me that I had misremembered the date of my daughter's birthday, even though I am pretty certain of it, than that I did not really have a daughter.

Illusions: Misinterpretations of real stimuli. It is easy to develop beliefs about the interpretation of what is happening. Two men are talking in the corner of the room and occasionally look in my direction. I can believe with complete certainty that they are talking about me. I may hold onto this belief even when the men say they are not talking about me, when they do not know me and have no reason to talk about me. I can become absolutely certain of this belief and can even start behaving based on it. This kind of belief can be connected to other ideas of reference, beliefs that something is connected to me when there is little reason to support that belief. I may believe that a specific TV commercial was designed specifically for me, that the people who wrote it wanted to give me a specific message and perhaps even knew I would be watching it at this exact time.

Negative symptoms

You can think of positive symptoms as experiences that schizophrenia gives you that you do not want. Negative symptoms are parts of normal behavior that the illness takes away or makes more difficult. These include losses of spontaneity, motivation, and persistence. Spontaneity is being able to think of something to say as part of a casual conversation. When spontaneity is lost, conversation becomes difficult. Motivation is the ability to forcing yourself to study, go to work, or exercise. When this is lost, it becomes easy to sit and feel overwhelmingly passive. Our motivation is what allows us to push ourselves to overcome limits, and when this is the element that is damaged, all other behavior becomes difficult. Persistence is the ability to continue with a task until it is done, to not just give up and lose interest. Without persistence, work and school and even friendship become very difficult. As already mentioned, these negative symptoms of schizophrenia can cause more disability and dysfunction than do the more dramatic psychotic symptoms.

Cognitive symptoms

Cognitive symptoms include verbal memory deficits, or an inability to hear some piece of information and then use it later. For example, a person with a verbal memory deficit could be told to do something, but then have great difficulty using this memory to carry out a task, even if it is a task she would like to do. She could also have a problem with executive function, an inability or difficulty thinking about what will be needed later and making a decision about an abstract problem. Going grocery shopping requires thinking about how much money you have for the month, how much you can afford to spend today, what you can buy that will not go bad before you have time to cook it, and what you might want to eat the day after tomorrow. All of these decisions are abstract; they include thinking about facts and consequences that are not immediately present. Severe problems with executive function mean that you cannot successfully grocery shop, which means running out of money or out of food. Even the simple parts of living in our complex society require using memory and thinking through abstract problems. Cognitive symptoms also include disorganized thinking. Someone with disorganized thinking may jump from one idea to another without any logical connection, making his conversation jumbled and hard to follow. He may string words together so that they have no logical connections, and while it sounds like he is saying something, when you listen it makes no sense.

Not everyone with schizophrenia has problems in all of these areas, and even if present, the deficits can be mild or severe. In her autobiography, Elyn Saks (2008) describes graduating as valedictorian of her university while she had psychotic symptoms; despite her continuing problem, she went on to earn a master's degree in philosophy from Oxford and then Yale Law School degree. Her schizophrenia made her life much more difficult but made no part of it impossible.

THE ROLE OF MEDICATION IN THE TREATMENT OF PEOPLE WITH SCHIZOPHRENIA

Antipsychotic medication is central for the treatment of people with schizophrenia. This simple statement overlays a number of complexities. (1) Most people with schizophrenia will have more stable lives and have less chance of relapse and less risk of hospitalization if they consistently take antipsychotic medications. Despite this, the majority of people with schizophrenia will not take medications as prescribed. (2) Medications primarily help the positive, psychotic symptoms of the illness. Medications seem to have less effect on the negative and cognitive symptoms that often cause the most disability. (3) While most people with schizophrenia will benefit from medication, some will not. This means that at least some of the people with schizophrenia who say that medications do not help are being accurate. (4) Medication alone is almost never enough. Even with medications, there are a variety of psychosocial interventions and supports that will be required to help a person with schizophrenia achieve a reasonable quality of life.

1. Most people with schizophrenia will do better, have fewer re-hospitalizations, and more control over psychotic symptoms if they consistently take antipsychotic medications

Most people with schizophrenia will have less distress from their symptoms, less recurrence of symptoms, and more stability in their community if they consistently take antipsychotic medications. People with schizophrenia who discontinue their medication, or are switched to a placebo during research studies, are much more likely to relapse. People who stop taking antipsychotic medications may not relapse right away, but over weeks and months the risk of relapse increases. This is the reason why there is a focus on medication as a central part of treatment; for most people, medication helps because it decreases psychotic symptoms and can help people to avoid hospitalization. Unfortunately, there can be so much focus on medication that the person with the illness may feel that that is all that family and clinicians care about. Treatment can be completely focused on getting a person with schizophrenia to take medication, without considering why a person may want to avoid medication, or what the medication is not doing, or the possibility that medication is not helping in ways that are important to that person.

The reality is that many people with schizophrenia do not take antipsychotic medication consistently (Velligan et al., 2009). This should not be a surprise. Many people with chronic illnesses, from high blood pressure to diabetes, do not consistently take medication as prescribed. People with schizophrenia have the same trouble taking medication as do other people with a chronic disease. In addition, many people have troublesome side effects from the antipsychotic medications that are commonly recommended for schizophrenia. Common side effects range from weight gain to tremor to extreme motor restlessness to tiredness. People often stop medications as a way of avoiding these side effects. People with other medical illnesses have a choice to take prescribed medication. People with schizophrenia are often under considerable pressure to take their prescribed medication: either through informal pressure from family or clinicians or more formal pressure from the courts who order treatment. Some of the objection to taking medication is a reaction to this loss of control and choice and a reaction against everyone in the person's life focusing on medication compliance.

Because of this focus and concern on medication as being central to treatment, and the frequent resistance of people with schizophrenia to taking medication, it is difficult to have an objective discussion about what medication is or is not doing for any specific person. Many people with schizophrenia say that the medication does not help, when to family and friends it seems very obvious that the medication appears to be helping a lot. These experiences reinforce the assumption that people with schizophrenia have little insight into their need for medication. At times, however, a person will say that the medication is not helping, and he or she may be correct. Family and even clinicians may have such a strong belief in the effectiveness of antipsychotic medication that it can be difficult to objectively consider whether it is working for an individual person.

2. Antipsychotic medications primarily help the positive, psychotic symptoms of schizophrenia

Antipsychotic medications usually help decrease the intensity and intrusiveness of positive symptoms of schizophrenia. A person may still be hearing voices, but the voices are often easier to ignore or cause less distress. A person may still have a variety of beliefs that seem out of touch with reality, but they often recede into the background and become less of a constant focus. Most often, hallucinations and delusions do not completely disappear. The voices are still there, and the underlying beliefs have not changed. Someone may be able to hold a more normal conversation without the voices interfering, or he may be able to concentrate enough to read a book. A person may still have the belief that he is God, has special powers, or has a chip implanted in his brain, but he can have a conversation without needing to bring these issues up. A man I worked with for many years believed he was God, that he was able to control the weather, and that he and his friends would live forever. Despite these beliefs, he was able to hold a full-time competitive job, drive a car, and buy a house. These beliefs did not change when he was taking medication, but he was able to get his work done and not talk about his beliefs to others.

Unfortunately, medications that are available today have less impact on negative symptoms, such as loss of motivation or problems with spontaneity, and with cognitive symptoms, such as memory deficit and problems with abstract reasoning. Insofar as these negative symptoms are partly caused by distraction and distress from positive symptoms, the medications can help. Loud, intrusive voices or passionate beliefs that no one else believes can interfere with concentration and focus and make negative symptoms worse. Medication can help some people with schizophrenia with negative and cognitive symptoms, but their impact is usually less impressive. While medication can help someone be less bothered by psychotic symptoms, she may still have major problems living independently, getting a job, being successful in school, and developing friends. On the other hand, psychosocial supports, including case management, skill training, and cognitive behavioral therapy, can help many people live more effective lives despite their negative and cognitive symptoms, and can complement medications to increase treatment effectiveness.

3. Not everyone with schizophrenia responds to medication

The same research studies that demonstrate that antipsychotic medications are effective for most people with schizophrenia all include some subjects who do not seem to improve. It seems clear that antipsychotic medications are not effective for everyone with schizophrenia, yet it is very unusual for a person with schizophrenia to be taken off all medication because they have all been tried and found to be ineffective. It is difficult to even have a discussion about the idea that medication may not help everyone. Many, perhaps most, of the people with schizophrenia who say that medications do not help seem to have fewer symptoms and more life stability when they take medication. Many of the people who argue that medication does not help have family or friends who can point to very specific ways in which the medication does seem to make things better.

The person with the symptoms and her family, friends, and clinicians all have different points of view. There may be different ideas about what counts as "improvement" or different views about how much the medication has helped facilitate the change. Some of the disagreement may be from the lack of insight of the person with schizophrenia, or the blinders imposed by the hopes and expectations of family and friends who have a fervent belief in the efficacy of medication. While most people with schizophrenia will have a better quality of life if they use antipsychotic medication, the side effects and the effectiveness vary enormously from one person to another. To someone taking a medication, the improvement in symptoms may be outweighed by the side effects.

What is rarely discussed is the reality that some people do not get much help from medication, and some of the people who say that medication does not help may be reporting accurately. There is concern that giving too much credence to this possibility may reinforce those people who do seem to respond to medication but who maintain that they do not.

4. Medication alone is almost never enough

Different people with schizophrenia are very different. This should be obvious, but too often an assumption is made that all people with schizophrenia are equally impaired, have similar problems, and will need similar treatment. The reality is that some people with schizophrenia are very bright, some are academically very successful, some are great at budgeting money, some are extremely consistent about holding a job, and some are able to cook and care for an apartment without problem. Treatment needs to start with the person's own life goals, and then there needs to be targeted treatment to assist the person in meeting those goals. For example, a person with schizophrenia may have the goal of living independently. One person may be able to achieve this without any help. Another may be too shy or disorganized to find an apartment, fill out an application, and organize the move in. If someone is helped in these initial steps, the other parts of living independently may follow with little problem. Yet another person may only be successful in independent living if he or she has help budgeting money or paying bills, or keeping the apartment clean, or even help dealing with the inevitable problems that can come from interacting with neighbors or a landlord. One person who has the goal of going back to school may achieve this with little help, while another may need help with study skills and structuring time and even special tutoring. One person may be able to make friends easily, while another may need help learning how to have a conversation and feedback about appropriate ways of interacting with others.

Some people with schizophrenia will require intensive services with multiple contacts a week and regular outreach of staff into the person's home to maintain stability. Another person may need psychological support to handle the stress of trying to meet more ambitious goals. Yet another person may benefit from specific therapy that helps the person overcome psychotic symptoms by learning to question automatic thoughts and assumptions.

Start with the person's own goals. Too often, family and clinicians will have their own goals about what is good for the client, what counts as "getting better" and what kind of treatment is required. Most people with schizophrenia have life goals that turn out to be similar to everyone else's life goals: a nicer place to live, a way of feeling useful, a reason to wake up in the morning, a car, friends, a bit more money to spend any way you want. Treatment is much more likely to be effective if it is designed to help a person get what he or she wants. An important part of treatment is in giving both the person with schizophrenia and his or her family information about the illness, about different treatment options, and about recovery and hope (Mueser & Gingerich, 2006). The National Alliance for Mental Illness (NAMI) is a national organization that has local chapters that provide support and education to people with major mental illnesses and their families (www.nami.org).

Medication should never be a goal of treatment. Medication is a tool that can help someone achieve goals, but taking medication should never be a treatment goal. A treatment goal is the person's own life goals: getting a job, having more friends, getting back in touch with her family, staying out of the hospital. Medication is just a tool; it is like a hammer or a screwdriver that may be helpful for a person trying to achieve these goals. Medication is not "good" or "bad," but is instead "rather useful" or "not useful." A person will be much more likely to take medication if he believes that it is helping him to meet his own goals, and he will be much less likely to take a medication if he feels it is not helping him to meet his own goals. Medication and other parts of treatment must be integrated; one cannot be considered without the other.

A young man with a diagnosis of schizophrenia and a history of several hospitalizations and two arrests took medication consistently for a year, and then he abruptly stopped it. During the year while taking medication he looked much better to staff and to his family. He was able to stay out of the hospital, live independently, and get a volunteer job that he enjoyed. He interacted with others much more appropriately, and he seemed more relaxed and generally in less distress. When asked why he had stopped the medication, he said that it was not working.

He had gone on the medication in the hope that it would help him get a girlfriend, and after more than a year on the medication he felt no closer to this goal than before. The clinical chart confirmed that at regular visits he reiterated his desire for a girlfriend, but it was obvious that the staff spent little time or attention in really helping him pursue this goal. When the staff took his goal seriously and started teaching him how to talk to a girl and how to meet girls, even bringing in a female student so that he could practice his new conversation skills with her, he was willing to restart taking his medication.

ANTIPSYCHOTIC MEDICATIONS

The primary medications used in the treatment of schizophrenia are labeled "antipsychotic." These medications are not "antischizophrenic"; they do not reverse all of the symptoms of the disorder. They do help decrease the frequency and intensity of psychotic symptoms. They are all diagnostically "nonspecific." If someone has psychotic symptoms from a wide variety of causes, from drug use to other illnesses, then antipsychotic medications are likely to help. This means that a positive response to one of these medications does not mean that the person necessarily has schizophrenia.

While these medications are labeled "antipsychotic," they can be very effective in other conditions even when a person is not psychotic. For example, some people with depression who do not respond to antidepressant medication alone may respond better when a small amount of an antipsychotic medication is added, even if the person has no psychotic symptoms. Antipsychotic medications can be effective mood stabilizers for people who become manic or who have moods that fluctuate up and down. These medications can help some people with autism, and in rare situations they can be used by people who are very agitated. These medications can even be used for severe nausea and vomiting. Their ability to decrease psychosis is their main reason for use, but they can be very effective in a number of other conditions as well.

History of antipsychotic medications: Typical and atypical antipsychotic medications

The antipsychotic medications are often categorized as being either "first-generation" or "second-generation," or "typical" and "atypical." "Typical" refers to medications that are very likely to cause motor or extrapyramidal side effects. "Atypical" refers to medications that are much less likely to cause these motor side effects. These distinctions are beginning to blur. Some of the older "first-generation" or "typical" medications, such as loxapine, seem to have relatively less motor side effects. There are significant differences among the different, newer "atypical" medications, with some causing less motor side effects, and others causing more side effects as the dose of medication is increased. Despite these misgivings, I will use the classifications of "typical" and "atypical" in this book.

The first effective antipsychotic medication, chlorpromazine (Thorazine), was introduced into the United States in 1953. A number of different antipsychotics over the next 20 years, including trifluoperazine (Stelazine), thothixene (Navane), and haloperidol (Haldol), all had the same mechanism of action. These medications had slightly different side-effect profiles, but none of them were any more effective than another. The first antipsychotic that was really different was clozapine. Initially developed in 1961 and first used in research studies with people in 1962, clozapine was discovered to have a mechanism of action and a side-effect profile very different than any of the then-available medications. The major side-effect concerns before clozapine were related to motor- or muscle-related side effects, such as tremor, stiffness, motor restlessness, and tardive dyskinesia. Tardive dyskinesia was of particular concern because it is a potentially permanent movement disorder that often continues even after the medication is stopped. Clozapine has many fewer of these motor side effects and a much lower frequency of tardive dyskinesia. More importantly, it was the first antipsychotic medication that was markedly more effective than all of the others.

Clozapine worked for many patients who had not responded, or not responded well, to other antipsychotic medications. Clozapine had its own problems. It had many side effects, even if its risk of tardive dyskinesia was low. Approximately 1% of people who start taking clozapine will stop making white blood cells that are required to fight infection, and if this is not caught early these people will die of infections that would normally be fought off by a person's immune system. There was a rush to understand how clozapine worked and to develop other medications that were as effective as clozapine without this problem with white blood cells. A number of second-generation or atypical antipsychotic medications were developed that did not have this same problem with white blood cells. These medications were labeled "atypical" because they were much less likely to cause motor side effects than the typical antipsychotics. Unfortunately, none of these other atypical antipsychotic medications were as effective as clozapine, and some of them have the same risk of weight gain and diabetes as clozapine.

There is an ongoing controversy about whether the atypical antipsychotics, other than clozapine, are really more effective than the older, typical medications. There are clear differences in the side-effect profiles between the typical and atypical medications. Typical or first-generation medications are much more likely to cause tardive dyskinesia and other motor-related side effects than the second-generation, atypical medications. Many people feel much more comfortable taking the newer medications than the older ones. On the other hand, at least some of the atypical antipsychotics are more likely to cause weight gain and increase the risk of diabetes. Efficacy is more controversial. There are a large number of research studies that show that the atypical antipsychotics are more effective than older medications, but most of these were funded and designed by the pharmaceutical companies making the new medications. The three largest studies that were government–funded did not show much difference between the newer and older medications. These were all very complicated studies that can easily be criticized and are hard to interpret. At the same time, if there were large differences between the typical and atypical antipsychotic medications, one would expect them to show up, despite the methodological problems with the studies. On the other hand, the studies had flaws that may explain the lack of difference even if one does exist.

My own belief is that there are significant differences between the typical and atypical medications, at least for some people, but it may take many months or more for these differences to become apparent. I also believe that the atypical medications are permissive. That is, if a person is in a socially rich environment where personal growth and change is supported, the new medications will show benefit over the older typical medications. On the other hand, if the person is in an environment that does not support recovery, then the subtle but important advantage of the atypical medications may not become apparent.

Typical or first-generation antipsychotic medications

The first-generation medications vary from one another primarily by different patterns of side effects. These medications are more or less "potent." A more potent medication is not more effective than one with lower potency; it just takes fewer milligrams of medication to accomplish the same thing. Potency just refers to how many milligrams of medication are needed for the dose to be effective. High-potency medications that are effective at lower doses are more specific for dopamine receptors, and as a result they tend to have more motor side effects. Lower-potency medications that require a higher number of milligrams to be effective tend to have fewer motor side effects, but they may have more weight gain, sedation, dry mouth, or other side effects. The first-generation antipsychotic medications are primarily used to decrease psychotic symptoms. They can also be used in the treatment of agitation, psychotic depression, and acute mania.

TYPICAL ANTIPSYCHOTIC MEDICATIONS

	Motor Side Effects (EPS)	Sedation	Anti-cholinergic
Chlorpromazine/Thorazine	+ +	+ + +	+ + +
*Fluphenazine/Prolixin	+ + + +	+ +	+ +
*Haloperidol/Haldol	+ + + +	+	+
Loxapine/Loxitane	+ + +	+ +	+ +
Molindone/Moban	+ + +	+ +	+ +
Perphenazine/Trilifon	+ + +	+ +	+ +
Thiothixene/Navane	+ + +	+ +	+ +
Trifluperazine (Stelazine)	+ + +	+ +	+ +

+ = low; + + = moderate; + + + high; + + + + extremely high
Source: DeBattista & Schatzberg, 2006.
*Available as a long-acting injection.

Atypical or second-generation antipsychotic medications

Atypical antipsychotic medications vary from each other much more than do the typical medications. With the exception of clozapine, and despite many conflicting studies, my belief is that none of the atypical medications are any more effective than another for a group of people. On the other hand, one of these medications may work much better than another for a particular individual. One person may respond much better to risperidone than to quetiapine, while another person may respond better to quetiapine. This means that if one medication does not work, it is worth trying a second and then a third and then a fourth before deciding that no medication will work.

While it is difficult to predict who will respond best to which medication, it is easy to predict whether a medication is more or less likely to cause a particular side effect. For example, olanzapine is highly likely to cause substantial weight gain in people taking it. Risperidone is likely to cause some weight gain in most people, and ziprasidone is "weight neutral" for most people. There are individual differences that interact with these differences between medications; one person may gain a lot of weight from risperidone, while another person gains no weight. Despite these individual differences, different medications vary enormously in the potential to cause specific side effects and can be a reason to initially try one medication rather than another. For example, olanzapine tends to cause much more weight gain than other antipsychotic medications, and it may not be a good initial choice for someone worried about this or who has a family history of diabetes. Risperidone is more likely to cause amenorrhea than some of the other atypical antipsychotics and may not be a good choice for a woman who would be distressed by this. Considering likely side effects can help someone to choose a medication that will be better tolerated.

The atypical antipsychotic medications are effective in many conditions in addition to psychosis. They are effective mood sta-bilizers, and can be used to augment the effectiveness of antide-pressants for both severe depression and obsessive-compulsive disorders, and have some role in other severe anxiety disorders. There is concern about the increasing numbers of advertise-ments, directed at both physicians and potential patients, to use these medications for anxiety and depression. These medica-tions can work for these disorders, but they should be reserved for those people who have not responded to multiple trials of antidepressants and other treatments.

ATYPICAL ANTIPSYCHOTIC MEDICATIONS

	Motor Side Effects (EPS)	Sedation	Weight Gain <
Aripiprazole/Abilify	+ +	+	+
Asenapine/Saphris	+ +	+	0
Clozapine/Clozaril/FazaClo	0	+ + + +	+ + + +
Iloperidone/Fanapt	+	+ +	+ +
Quetiapine/Seroquel	0	+ + +	+ +

	Motor Side Effects (EPS)	Sedation	Weight Gain <
*Paliperidone/Invega	+ +	+	+ +
*Risperidone/Risperdal	+ +	+	+ +
Olanzapine/Zyprexa	0/ +	+ + +	+ + + +
Ziprasidone/Geodon	+ +	+	0

Source: DeBattista & Schatzberg, 2006.
*Available as a long-acting injection.

Clozapine. Clozapine is significantly more effective than any other antipsychotic medication. It is effective in some people who have had no response to other medications, and it can allow further improvement in someone who may have had a partial response to another medication. Anyone with severe problems from schizophrenia who has not responded to other medications should try clozapine before deciding that medications do not work. Clozapine is not used as the first medication tried because of the requirement for regular blood tests, and its many side effects. These include potentially dangerous side effects, such as the loss of white blood cells and the increased risk of seizures and increased risk of diabetes. Anyone taking clozapine is required to get a blood test, initially weekly and then less often, to monitor the white blood cell number so that the medication can be stopped if there is a problem. Some of the side effects are not dangerous but are hard to live with, such as increased drooling and sedation. Clozapine can require significant lifestyle changes to avoid serious problems. For example, clozapine interferes with temperature regulation and increases the risk of fatal heat stroke in someone who stays out in the heat, does not have air conditioning in a hot climate, or becomes dehydrated on a very hot day. The most common and concerning side effect from clozapine is weight gain. Not everyone on clozapine gains weight, but many people do and the mean weight gain on clozapine is around 22 pounds in the first year of use. Diet and exercise can help, but weight loss is difficult for most of us and is much more difficult for a person on clozapine.

Unfortunately, the list of potential side effects and risks has kept many people from trying clozapine, even when other medications have not worked. Not everyone experiences severe side effects, and the promise of something that can really work makes it worth considering. Clozapine is generally underused, and many people who may be able to achieve a much better quality of life do not even consider it.

Side Effects From Antipsychotic Medications

Side effects from antipsychotic medications can be put into four groups. (1) Motor or extrapyramidal side effects; (2) metabolic side effects; (3) NMS and other medically serious side effects; and (4) side effects that are not medically dangerous but are bothersome and interfere with quality of life.

Motor or extrapyramidal side effects (EPS). The biggest problem with the typical or first-generation antipsychotic medications is their tendency to cause motor side effects, often referred to as extrapyramidal side effects, or EPS. The voluntary control over muscles is carried through nerves that run through what look like pyramids in the spinal column. The involuntary coordination of muscles is controlled by nerves that are outside of these pyramids, or extrapyramidal. Dopamine is one of the two main neurotransmitters in the extrapyramidal system, and any medication that blocks it will cause EPS. EPS can have a number of different forms. *Dystonias* are relatively rare. They can consist of a muscle spasm, usually dramatic and sometimes painful. Dystonias are a risk within days of starting or increasing the dose of an antipsychotic medication. A person can develop a *tremor* that looks just like the tremor of Parkinson's disease. This is typically a coarse, three-per-second tremor called a "resting tremor" because it is apparent when the person is not using his hands. *Akinesia* is the loss of normal movements. A person with akinesia looks stiff and wooden, may have decreased facial movements, and loses the normal "bounce" that comes with a normal walking gait. The most uncomfortable, and the most common EPS, is *akathisia*, a motor restlessness that compels the person to keep moving. People will jiggle their legs while sitting in a chair, or they may feel the need to keep walking even when exhausted. At times there is a subjective sense of motor restlessness even when it is not apparent to others. Akathisia has been associated with an increased risk of suicide and can develop very rapidly or after weeks of being on the same medication.

All of these extrapyramidal side effects listed above will go away when the medication is discontinued. Tardive dyskinesia (TD) can be permanent. It is most commonly the slow movement of a person's tongue or lips or fingers, but it can appear in any part of the body. It is something that happens in the background of a person's thought. When someone pays attention, the movement can often be stopped, only to come back when attention is pulled away to something else. It can be a minor, barely noticeable movement of a finger or the corner of a mouth, but it can also be a large and very obvious movement that can increase social stigma. Forty percent or more of people using a typical antipsychotic medication will develop TD. The percentage is much lower for the atypical medication, although the frequency of risk is debated. Of people taking atypical antipsychotic medication, probably less than 5%, and perhaps substantially less than that, will develop TD. It does tend to get better if the medication is stopped, especially if it is stopped shortly after the TD symptoms appear. This does not guarantee that it will disappear even when medication is discontinued, and often it may not be possible to stop the medication without the person suffering a relapse of the underlying mental illness.

Metabolic side effects. Many medications cause weight gain, including many of the antidepressants, such as lithium and valproic acid. Some of the atypical antipsychotic medications can cause substantial weight gain, enough that it has become a major issue of concern. Olanzapine and clozapine cause an average weight gain of 22 to 30 pounds in the first one to two years of use (Alvarez-Jiménez et al., 2008). Not everyone gains weight, which means that some people gain much more than 25 pounds. Substantial weight gain increases the risk of developing diabetes and cardiovascular disease, and it is part of the reason why people with major mental illnesses die 25 years younger than the general population. Not all of the antipsychotic medications have the same risk of weight gain. Haloperidol and ziprasidone are "weight neutral." While some people may gain a bit, others may lose a bit and the overall weight for a group of people does not change. Risperidone and quetiapine cause some weight gain: 6 to 10 pounds on average in the first year. This is enough to be a concern and enough to increase the risk of diabetes at least a bit, and some people will gain substantially more. Overall, the issues of weight gain and risk of diabetes is a concern that should be considered in choosing a medication, and anyone taking any antipsychotic medication should have weight and other metabolic markers monitored.

NMS and other medically serious side effects. Neuroleptic malignant syndrome (NMS) is a very rare but potentially life-threatening syndrome associated with all of the antipsychotic medications. It is a risk in the first few days or weeks of starting a medication or increasing the dose. Symptoms include fever, severe muscle stiffness, and confusion. The person typically looks ill. If anyone develops a fever within a few weeks of starting a new antipsychotic medication, he should call his physician for advice or go to an emergency care center for evaluation.

Antipsychotic medications are also associated with a number of other rare but potentially dangerous side effects. For example, clozapine can increase the risk of fatal heat stroke, seizure, and some kinds of heart problems. All of the antipsychotic medications can increase the mortality rate in older people with dementia. There is a very rare incidence of people just dying for no clear cause and this has been associated with antipsychotic medication. For the most part, other than the weight gain and the EPS discussed above, these medications have side effects that are bothersome but not usually dangerous.

Side effects that are not medically dangerous but are bothersome. There are many side effects that vary depending on the specific medication. At least some sedation is common with most of them, and it is a significant problem with some. Some of the medications can cause dry mouth or constipation or dizzy spells. The biggest problem is feeling "drugged" or "medicated." Probably an even more frequent problem is the psychological one of needing to acknowledge that the medication is needed and that something is wrong with your brain. Family and friends and clinicians can get so focused on the medication that it can feel like that is all that anyone cares about. At times, someone will stop the medication just to feel in control of all of the pressure that is pushing him to take the medication. The psychological feeling of being told that an antipsychotic medication is needed may be the most difficult side effect of all.

Summary

Most people with schizophrenia, and people with ongoing psychotic symptoms, will have fewer problems with symptoms and more stable lives if they take antipsychotic medications. This can make it easier to accomplish life goals: getting a job, living in an apartment, having friends. Not everyone with schizophrenia will respond to medication, but the vast majority will. Medication alone is never enough. The medications will not cure the schizophrenia or equally help all of the problems caused by the illness, but medication can often make it possible for other kinds of help to be more effective. Most people with schizophrenia will have a better quality of life if they continue taking medication. Some may be able to eventually discontinue medication after some years, but little is really known about how to predict who will eventually be able to discontinue medication and still maintain their quality of life. The goal should not be to stop medication but to live the life you want to live. Medication is not "good" or "bad" but is a tool that is either effective or not effective. Taking medication should never be a treatment goal, but it is a tool that can help overcome life problems caused by illness and help a person get closer to his or her life goals.

7

Personality Disorders

There is something strange about the entire idea of a "personality disorder." Does it mean that a person's entire personality is disordered, or is just a part of it not okay? Does it mean that the person is just not very likable, or does it mean something more than this? Do all of us have some degree of a "disordered personality," or does the term really refer to something out of the ordinary? Finally, if there is such as a thing as a personality disorder, how could a medication possibly help? Can a medication change your personality?

PERSONALITY

Before thinking about personality disorders and how medications could potentially influence people's personalities, it is useful to think about the nature of personality. Our personality is our pattern of responses to the world—our characteristic ways of reacting to the world. Some of us tend to be more organized, while others are more spontaneous. Some of us are more emotional or more reactive, while others tend to react in a more logical, less emotional way. Some of us plan everything, and some of us pride ourselves on rarely planning anything. Some of us are open and trusting with total strangers, while others of us may instinctively be more guarded. The pattern of all of these reactions and responses is our personality. If we change some of these characteristic ways of responding, then to that extent we change part of our personality. If we become more or less tolerant of being frustrated, more or less likely to behave impulsively, more or less driven to the excitement of something entirely new as against enjoying the old, then our personality shifts. Typically, if this is a short-lived change we consider these kinds of changes as just changes in behavior, but if the pattern changes over time then it makes sense to talk about personality change.

Recent research strongly suggests that many aspects of personality are much more determined or at least strongly influenced by biology. Impulsivity, the ability to tolerate frustration, novelty seeking, emotional moodiness, and other parts of the personality seem to have strong genetic components. There is always interaction between a biological predisposition toward a certain kind of behavior or way of organizing the world and the behaviors that are reinforced as the person develops. The actual personality is always a complicated amalgam of biology, early development, and later life experience (Reichborn-Kjennerud, 2008).

An important part of our personality is its flexibility. If we are characteristically very organized and like to plan, can we be more creative and spontaneous when the situation calls for it? The rigidity or flexibility of our characteristic responses is an important part of how adaptable we are to different kinds of situations.

Our personality will work better in some situations than in others, no matter what personality style we have. Being very organized and very detail-oriented may work well for an accountant, but it may work less well in an intimate relationship. Being very emotionally available may get you lots of friends, but it can be a problem in a job that requires a professional detachment. We tend to like some of our own and our friends' ways of reacting to the world, and we also like less some of the other parts of our and our friends' personalities.

WHAT IS A "PERSONALITY DISORDER"?

People often talk about someone having a "bad personality" or a "personality disorder." This typically means that the person is not liked or that some of the ways that the person characteristically behaves are not liked.

A formal diagnosis of a personality disorder is something entirely different than a way of describing or labeling someone whom you do not like or who causes problems. A formal diagnosis means that the person's ongoing behavior fits a set of specific requirements that define the specific personality disorder. Among other things, it requires that someone's personality has caused major life problems in multiple life areas. It refers to a person whose characteristic pattern of responses to the world does not work very well, and this pattern is both fixed and inflexible. It also refers to a person whose way of being in the world is so problematic that it interferes with the normal ability to function, and as a result the person faces recurrent personal and social problems. We all have personality styles, but we do not all have personality disorders.

A formal diagnosis of a personality disorder should not be applied just because someone is a bit difficult or has some characteristics in common with one of the diagnoses listed below. Many of us have some characteristics of one or more personality disorders, and sometimes these characteristics get us into trouble. One can skirt the truth or even lie without being a sociopath; one can be concerned about what people are saying or concerned about privacy without having a paranoid personality disorder; and one can like being dramatic and the center of attention without having a histrionic personality disorder. The concept of disorder applies when the personality pattern causes overwhelming, enduring problems in multiple areas of someone's life.

Labels always give very incomplete information, and this is particularly true of the label of "personality disorder." A person with a very maladaptive style of living in the world—a person with a personality disorder—may be very bright or not very bright, may be a virtuoso musician or tone deaf, may be very successful in some parts of their professional lives or not at all successful. What it does mean is that there are major problems with how they fit into the world, not just at work or with intimate relationships, but in multiple areas of their lives.

What kinds of personality disorders are there?

The current diagnostic system used in psychiatric practice is called *DSM-IV-TR*, for the *Diagnostic and Statistical Manual, Fourth Edition, Text Revised*. A new system called *DSM-V* will be published in 2013, and it is expected to reorganize the diagnoses of personality disorders. The same people and problems will remain with the advent of *DSM-V*, but the categories and labels will change significantly. Many of the *DSM-IV* personality diagnoses will be revised to be reflected by a description of a core impairment in personality functioning rather than a specific diagnosis. The *DSM-IV-TR* separates personality disorders into three different groups.

Cluster A: Odd or Eccentric	Cluster B: Dramatic, Emotional, or Erratic	Cluster C: Anxious or Fearful
• Paranoid	• Antisocial	• Avoidant
• Schizoid	• Borderline	• Dependent
• Schizotypal	• Histrionic	• Obsessive-compulsive
	• Narcissistic	

DSM-IV-TR Table of Personality Disorders

Cluster A refers to people who are odd or eccentric, and this category includes paranoid personality disorder, schizoid personality disorder, and schizotypal personality disorder. People who are paranoid are just that; they are not psychotic but are extremely guarded and suspicious of everyone. People who are schizoid tend to be extreme loners who do not relate to others. And people who are schizotypal have odd beliefs and odd ways of thinking about the world; these ways are odd in some of the same ways as someone with schizophrenia but without any clear psychotic symptoms. Again, someone with a paranoid personality is not just a bit guarded or someone who prefers to lock their car and keep their blinds down at night. Rather it refers to someone whose persistent fear of what other people are doing or could be doing significantly interferes in his or her ability to live in the world normally.

For the most part, people with Cluster A personality disorders rarely see psychiatrists or seek treatment for their problems, and they often are perceived as "odd" but otherwise draw little attention to themselves. At times, external pressure or a complete inability to function will force someone into contact with a mental health clinician, but most often people with one of these concerns will try to avoid mental health treatment. People with paranoid disorders may experience considerable distress because of their constant fear and social isolation, but this is directed to fear of what are considered real outside threats or potential threats. People with schizoid personality disorders just want to be left alone, and it is only a problem when this is not possible. They typically have few friends and an extremely limited support system, and their disorder is of more concern to their family than to themselves, if in fact they have remained in contact with their family. Someone with schizotypal disorder may be in enough distress to seek treatment, especially if his odd way of thinking and behavior interferes with the accomplishment of personal goals.

Cluster B refers to people who are very dramatic or emotional, and this category includes borderline, antisocial, histrionic, and narcissistic disorders. People with these labels very often bring attention to themselves. Their behavior often forces a response from people around them, and most often this response is negative.

Borderline disorder is the personality disorder that most commonly brings a person into mental health treatment. It is also the personality disorder where medications are most commonly used. It causes tremendous distress both for the person with the disorder and for friends and family and other people trying to help the person. Borderline disorder will be the major focus of this chapter and will be discussed in more detail later.

Antisocial personality disorder refers to people who continuously and pervasively disregard the rights and feelings of other people. This pattern goes back to childhood, and anyone with this disorder as an adult would fulfill criteria for conduct disorder in childhood. While people with sociopathic disorder commonly engage in illegal activity, this is not a required part of the diagnosis. And while everyone who is a criminal or involved in gang behavior is commonly called a sociopath, there are crucial differences between those criminals who have a sense of connection and trust at least within their own peer group, and those who treat their own peers with the same disregard that they treat everyone else. The formal *DSM-IV* diagnosis includes impulsiveness, lying, aggressiveness, irresponsibility, and lack of remorse. Substance abuse is common but not required. People with sociopathic personality disorder more often end up in jail or prison than in a psychiatrist's office. Since for the most part the person does not feel much distress and is rarely interested in changing her own behavior, treatment is unlikely to be very effective. Hervey Cleckley (1950), who first described sociopathy, described it as the complete absence of any kind of conscience or of any guilt or shame or internal constraints on one's behavior.

People with histrionic personality disorder have patterns of excessive emotionality, attention seeking, and the need for approval. Often there is a seductive quality to the attention seeking, with seductive clothing and behavior. Someone's emotions often seem exaggerated, almost theatrical, but also shallow. Many people with this disorder are often able to function well but have trouble achieving stability in their lives. Medical complaints and concerns about physical appearance are common. They often come into mental health treatment with complaints of depression and frustration about how their lives are going.

Narcissistic personality disorder refers to a person with an extreme self-centeredness and grandiosity about his or her own importance; someone with this disorder would think that he is special and deserves admiration for his talents. This is not the temporary grandiosity of someone who is manic, pressured, and hyperactive, but rather the ongoing arrogance of someone who believes that he is better than other people. Most people with this disorder feel entitled to special treatment and become frustrated and angry that it is not forthcoming, but they rarely seek mental health treatment since they do not feel that the problem is within themselves.

Cluster C refers to people who are extremely anxious or fearful, and this category includes obsessive personality disorder (which is different from obsessive-compulsive disorder), avoidant disorder, and dependent disorder. Obsessive personality disorder refers to people who require a sense of order and exactness and who need rules and organization. People with obsessive personality disorders do not have the intrusive thoughts or repetitive behavior of someone with an obsessive-compulsive disorder. The most important characteristics are perfectionism, rigidity, and stubbornness. Avoidant disorder refers to people who are so afraid of real or perceived criticism that they stay away from other people. People who are schizoid (discussed above) do not want or need social interaction. People with avoidant disorder are so afraid of their own perceived social ineptness that they stay away from other people rather than face what they feel will be inevitable criticism. Dependent disorder refers to people who have a pervasive and excessive need to be taken care of by others, with the belief that they are unable to function without the help of other people to make all their decisions for them.

TREATMENT OF PEOPLE WHO
HAVE PERSONALITY DISORDERS

People with personality disorders are, by definition of having the diagnoses, causing major life problems both for themselves and for the people around them. Some of these ways of living are less amenable to change and less treatable than others. If a person feels significant distress and if she does not like the way she is and would like to change, change is more likely to happen. For the most part, while the world would like people with antisocial disorder to change, the person with this disorder rarely sees that there is anything wrong. Similarly, the person with schizoid personality disorder does not typically want to change: he just wants to be left alone.

Some of the personality disorders are associated with more personal pain and distress than others. Personal distress provides motivation to change and will lead to ongoing pain if change is not made. People cannot make a new personality for themselves, but they can modify, mute, or change elements of their personalities so that they and the world get along better. A person in more distress is typically more motivated to change, and while this does not guarantee that change will happen, a very real personal stake in change is a good beginning.

It would be nice to have a pill that would make everyone nicer, friendlier, more patient, and less angry. There is no medication that will "treat" a personality or a personality disorder. On the other hand, we do have medications that can be helpful in treating some of the symptoms connected to a personality disorder, and some medications can potentially decrease some distress and dysfunction. For example, many people with schizotypal disorder are quietly eccentric and do not feel the need for any treatment. Some people with this disorder find their thinking to be too disorganized or find themselves becoming a bit paranoid, and they welcome the stabilizing effect of a low dose of an antipsychotic medication. A person with a narcissistic personality disorder who becomes depressed may respond to an antidepressant medication. Medication will not change the underlying personality disorder, but it could help the person to feel and function somewhat better.

This attempt to use medication can lead to problems that make the situation worse rather than better. Someone may request and even demand medication, even if the problem has not responded to medication in the past and is unlikely to in the future. There may be overreliance on medication as a solution to a problem that medication will not fix. Dependency, especially with antianxiety medications and sleeping pills, can be a significant concern. As with other conditions, medications may be able to help, but they also come with risks and side effects, and at times they can make someone's overall life worse rather than better.

Borderline Personality Disorder

Of all of the personality disorders, people with borderline personality disorder (BPD) are most likely to come into contact with mental health clinicians. People with BPD live in a state of tremendous distress, and they cause tremendous distress for those around them. When a mental health clinician refers casually to a "personality disorder," the specific reference is most often to people with BPD. The behavior of people with BPD often evokes strong feelings from people around them, friends, family, and clinicians. People with this disorder are often "blamed" for their behavior, and it is hotly debated whether they are responsible for their own behaviors. It is important to remember that no one chooses to "be borderline," and if people could choose to live their lives in a different way, they would.

What is borderline personality disorder? What is it "borderline" to? "Borderline" is an unfortunate, outdated term that refers back to psychoanalytic theory and no longer makes much sense. The idea was that a person could get "stuck" in different stages of development. If a person got "stuck" very early, it would lead to a psychotic disorder like schizophrenia; if he got "stuck" later, it would lead to a neurotic disorder; and if he got stuck between these two developmental points, he would be on the borderline between psychosis and neurosis and would have some characteristics of each. This is not our current understanding of the problem of the people that end up with this label, and it is expected that a more descriptive diagnostic term will be used in DSM-V.

The current *DSM-IV-TR* diagnostic criteria for BPD describes people who become frantic when they feel that someone close to them might leave; people who have very intense but very unstable relationships with other people; people whose sense of self is overwhelmingly defined by the reflections of others rather than having an internal sense of who they are; people with self-damaging impulsiveness such as gambling, promiscuity, or recurrent suicidal or self-mutilating behavior, such as cutting oneself in an attempt to feel better; people who have moods that are constantly up or down and not stable, chronic feelings of emptiness or boredom, inappropriate anger, and dissociative symptoms; and people who "space out" in ways that they do not remember. Not everyone with a borderline personality disorder necessarily has all of these symptoms, and many people have some of these symptoms some of the time. It is the overall fixed pattern of these symptoms and how they interfere with the person's life that is central to the specific diagnosis.

It is important to always keep in mind that any label gives very incomplete information. A diagnosis, whether it be a diagnosis of BPD or anything else, does not say whether the person is very smart or not very smart, whether he or she is a musical virtuoso or not at all musical. Personality disorders by definition are present early in life and are relatively enduring. A diagnosis of a personality disorder should not be made because of how one behaves in reaction to stress or a temporary event.

A major problem with a BPD diagnosis is the stigma that is attached to it. We react negatively to the "borderline" diagnosis. "Having that diagnosis resulted in my getting treated exactly the way I was treated at home. The minute I got the diagnosis people stopped treating me as though what I was doing had a reason" (Herman, 1997).

Words that interfere with relationships. We commonly use words without thinking about their real meaning. The problem is that some of these words interfere with our ability to form relationships with people. By labeling somebody in particular ways, we no longer have to take them seriously, we no longer have to listen to them, and we do not need to think about our part in problems with the relationship. This is particularly a problem with people labeled as having BPD. We label people as "manipulative," "unmotivated," or "attention seeking." The problem with these words is that once a person is labeled as manipulative or attention seeking, other people no longer have to take her seriously. If she is "manipulative" or "just attention seeking," it gives other people permission to stop thinking about what she is really saying, what she says she needs, and what is happening in the relationship.

The behavior of people with BPD causes major distress both to themselves and to others around them. Even worse, there is a belief that the diagnosis and the attached behaviors are fixed and unchangeable and that change is impossible. Actually, people with BPD can change and grow just as other people can.

> I was diagnosed with BPD about 2 years ago. I'm not sure if I really agree with it, but I guess I do fit into the criteria, just not the stereotype. I think that almost everyone on earth could fit into the BPD criteria somehow though. I didn't feel bad about the diagnosis until I started reading about it. Then it seemed to be this horrid curse that labeled me a self-centered, attention-seeking jerk. I don't see myself this way. I hope I am not. (Source: consumer list-serv discussion on borderline disorder.)

Core deficits of people with borderline personality disorder. Another way to think about BPD is to think about the core deficits in people who have it. This is different from a diagnosis, and as with all such explanations not everyone with a borderline disorder has each element, or has each to the same degree.

Affective instability: People with BPD tend to have moods that change rapidly and unpredictably. Much of this is probably based on biology, and it has usually been present since childhood. You can imagine what it must be like as a child growing

up to find yourself happy at one moment, and then unpredictably sad or angry or upset the next.

Impulsivity and low frustration tolerance: People with BPD
tend to be impulsive and will have trouble tolerating frustration.
This too is probably more biological than most people think.
While there is some childhood learning connected to this, we
know there is also a large genetic component. Some of us are
better at tolerating not getting what we want now and knowing
that we will have to wait.

Sense of self as being damaged/defective/not good: Most
people with BPD believe that there is something fundamentally
wrong with them. They realize they do not react to the world
the way other people do, and they realize the fault is within
them. They often fear that if they allow you to know them too
well, you will also realize that there is something defective or
even rotten at their core.

**Difficulty maintaining their own sense of identity/poor
object constancy:** Very young children only have what is immediately in front of them. If someone's mother is present, then
she is there. If she is away, or even out of sight for a moment, it
is as though she were gone forever. There is no sense of being
able to consider that she is still around, just not there right
now. As we get older we learn to hold onto the idea of our
mother or a favorite toy or our pet, even if she or it is not with
us right now. This sense is missing in many people with BPD.
It is not that the person is psychotic. If you ask someone with
BPD where her mother or friend is, she knows perfectly well
that her mother is still around or that her friend will be back
to visit tomorrow. Intellectually and cognitively, her system is
intact, but emotionally there seems to be a missing connection.
She will often feel as though her friend is gone forever and will
never return, even if intellectually she knows this makes no
sense. This can be very confusing to both the person with the
disorder, and to those around that person.

Connected with this is inconsistency in how someone thinks
about herself. All of us vary to some extent in our self-image. If

we are with friends who think we are smart and interesting, we will usually feel smarter and more interesting. At the same time, most of us have a sense of self that is not just a reflection of who happens to be around us or how we happen to feel that day. We may change our self-image a bit, but we hold onto whether we think of ourselves as smart or dumb, friendly or aloof, attractive or unattractive. This is much more difficult for people with BPD.

Poor understanding of rules of normal interpersonal relationships: We negotiate relationships all of the time, with our friends and family, work colleagues, and casual acquaintances. If we do not have the skills or understand how to carry out these negotiations, our relationships with other people fall apart very rapidly.

For example, suppose that a work colleague were to call you at home to discuss something that he felt was important, but he happened to call right before some friends were about to arrive for dinner. There would be a very rapid negotiation that neither of you would even be fully aware of: how important is the call, could it be put off till some other time, could it be made very brief, how much time do you have before your guests arrive, and so on. He might end up calling back at some other time or talking for a much briefer period than he intended, and you would tolerate some brief intrusion into your evening. You would negotiate some arrangement so that both of your needs were met. Now think about what would happen if he were not able to carry out this kind of negotiation. He would start talking and you would try to indicate that this was not a good time or that it needed to be a brief conversation. If he just went on talking and ignoring you, you would again try to end the call or reschedule it. And if he kept talking and kept talking and kept talking, eventually you would hang up on him. By this time you would be angry at yourself for hanging up on a colleague and angry at him for making you into the kind of person who hung up on people. If he were to call back about something else the following week, you might well be angry even before he starts talking, just because you are still angry about the last interaction and you know what is to come. He would wonder why you were angry when he had not done anything. This is the result of not being able to negotiate normal human relationships, and it is the experience of people with BPD.

We all negotiate all kinds of arrangements. "Give me some extra time and I won't ask you for it again"; then when the person does ask again, we react to her having broken or cheated on the implicit contract. "Give me some time and I will be safe," "Give me the medications and I will not misuse them," "Don't discharge me from therapy and I will not miss sessions in the future": The list is endless, but the basic structure of the arrangement is that the client asks you to do something now, and the client promises to do something in the future. When the client does not follow through, a clinician can become angry.

We now know that there is a biological basis for some of these problems with negotiation. There are specific parts of the brain that seem to be connected with understanding and negotiating with other people, and there are specific differences in the brains of at least some people with borderline disorder and some people without. This does not make it impossible to learn how to negotiate better, but it does explain why things that seem so obvious and simple to others can be much more difficult for people with BPD to figure out (Silbersweig et al., 2007; King-Cassas et al., 2008).

Sexual abuse and borderline personality disorder. Many people with BPD report childhood sexual abuse. Not all people with BPD have been abused, and many people who have been abused do not develop borderline disorder. Most abuse survivors do not develop a mental illness. It is worth noting the presence of symptoms of chronic PTSD in many people who have borderline disorder. Sexual abuse from a trusted adult is a profoundly invalidating experience. It causes confusion about how people should take care of each other, and it creates confusion about the difference between caretaking and hurting.

Long-term follow-up of BPD.

> Today is my birthday. Thoughts about growing up.
> My birthday is today. I am 42 years old. I feel as
> though I am in my early 20s emotionally. It is like I
> am finally shedding that hurt, rebellious, licentious,
> abused teenager. She is healing, and blossoming into
> a woman of faith, courage and integrity. That is how
> I would like to be remembered by my friends and
> loved ones someday when they and I no longer cross
> paths.
>
> Paris, 1988
> —(Angel Panda, posted on consumer
> list-serv, November 1, 1999)

Over a short period of time, people who are living chaotic lives will tend to continue to live those same lives. This often leads to the sense that people with BPD are incapable of change. There are now four well-done, long-term studies, and these all show that over a period of years many people with BPD will improve substantially.

General treatment approaches: What works, what doesn't. The most effect treatment for people with BPD is psychotherapy. Cognitive behavioral therapy, especially a modified form that is called dialectical behavioral therapy, which was developed specifically for people with borderline personality disorder, can be very helpful. Supportive psychotherapy, crisis planning, and crisis intervention can also be extremely useful. Unfortunately these treatments are not always available or may not be useful for all people.

There are now a number of excellent self-help books that are written both for people who suffer from BPD and for their families. The message from all of these therapeutic approaches is that people with this disorder can learn to cope in new and more effective ways. The other message is that this change is difficult and usually takes time.

The significance of a "healing relationship." The beginning of all treatment is the establishment of a stable relationship. This is not an easy thing to do, when the basic problem the person with BPD has is in the establishment of a stable relationship.

One problem that makes maintaining this relationship difficult is that people who are labeled or diagnosed with BPD evoke strong reactions in those around them. It is hard for most people to stay balanced in the maelstrom of the intense relationship expectations that people with BPD often generate. The core problem with people with BPD is their difficulty maintaining stable relationships, and this includes relationships with their therapist, clinicians, and helpers.

There are a number of assumptions about the lives of people with BPD that are useful to keep in mind in the course of providing services.

1. People with a borderline personality disorder are doing the best they can. If they could do better, they would.
2. People with a borderline personality disorder want to improve. No one wants to be borderline, and no one wants to live their lives the way most people with borderline disorder are living theirs.
3. Despite the fact that they want to improve and are doing the best they can, people with borderline personality disorders need to do better, try harder, and be more motivated to change. Even if the problem is not their responsibility or their fault, they are the ones who will have to change it.
4. People with borderline personality disorders may have not caused their own problems, but they have to solve them anyway.
5. The lives of suicidal borderline individuals are invariable as they are being currently being lived.
6. People with borderline personality disorders must learn new behaviors in all relevant contexts (adapted from Lenihan, 1993).

Cutting and other self-injurious behavior. The need to hurt oneself is very different from the desire to kill oneself. Cutting often serves a purpose. Cutting is both a solution to a problem and is a problem in and of itself. Some people feel less anxious after they cut themselves. Cutting can help a person focus on something other than more impulsive, more dangerous behavior. Cutting decreases dissociation, or "out of body, not here" feelings. It can help a person to feel alive when she has lost touch with her own inner sense of self. It feels familiar and allows for some sense of self-control. The problem is that people can lose control of their cutting just like other behaviors. They can cut more and deeper. They can almost become addicted to it.

> I can remember the first time I cut. . . . It was to see how hard it would be to slice my wrist. . . . Finally I took the chance and tried to kill myself. . . . It was an odd sensation . . . I suddenly felt better . . . this rush actually saved me, I didn't finish the suicide. . . . I tried two more times within a month . . . each of these times getting deeper and more dangerous. Again I feel better almost immediately. . . . I found it was like a drug. (Source: consumer listserv discussion on borderline disorder).

Pharmacological treatment for people who have borderline personality disorder

There is no medication that is formally approved for BPD or any other personality disorder. At the same time, most people with BPD are taking multiple medications. The distress of people with BPD is so intense that there is pressure to "do something," and often this means prescribing medication. The good news is that medication can be very useful in helping people with BPD cope with some of the specific symptoms, even if there is no medication that is effective for the entire constellation of symptoms. The bad news is that there is relatively little research supporting this use of medication in people with any personality disorder. The way medication is often used by people with BPD is also a significant problem.

It is difficult to prescribe medication that must be taken consistently for somebody whose life is inherently unstable, inconsistent, and impulsive. While some medications can be used now and again, only as needed, most medication is unlikely to be effective unless it is used consistently. Medication must also be taken long enough to see if it will really work. Finally, medications will only be used consistently if at least some side effects can be tolerated. All of this requires a stable relationship between the patient and the prescriber of that medication. Many people with BPD report that they have been on many different medications, none of which were very effective. A typical patient may report that she has been on Prozac for 2 days, Zoloft for a week, and Depakote for 1 day; she also tried a single pill of Risperdal and got a prescription filled for Seroquel but never took it. The summary is that none of these medications worked. An alternative way of thinking about the problem suggests that none of these medications were taken long enough or consistently enough with clear-enough target symptoms to know if they would have been effective or not.

Medication is often something that is done "to" a patient; a patient is often "medicated" by the physician. For a person who already has problems with stable, trusting relationships and who rapidly gets into control struggles with other people, the medication is just one more area of interpersonal instability. When the medication does not work immediately, or does not work enough, or causes any side effects, all of the positive hope and expectation that had initially been connected to the medication flips into the negative, and the medication is stopped or pushed away before it has had a chance to work.

Medication can also be used as a tool by someone to try and establish more control over her own life. This requires that it is the patient's medication, not the doctor's medication, and that the patient is making an informed, thoughtful decision about it. This also requires that there be a stable, trusting relationship with the prescriber. One's view of a medication is always connected, more or less, to one's view of the prescriber. In the case of a person with BPD, a trusting and consistent relationship with the prescriber is required before she can develop any kind of trusting and consistent relationship with the medication. It may take some time to develop that kind of relationship, to develop specific target goals, and to decide on specific medication trials that allow the medication to have any chance of being effective.

Finally, medication has meaning for everyone, but especially for people with BPD. Does the prescription indicate that there is still hope or that the doctor has not given up, or that there is nothing to be done except take the medication? Does it indicate that the person can get better, or that the problem is hopeless? Does getting a prescription "mean" that the problem is real and "not just in the head," or does it feel like you are dependent in one more way? Does taking a medication feel like you are using a tool to take more control over your own life, or does it feel that you are so out of control that some other person or medication needs to step in to take control? An effective medication trial requires a collaborative relationship with the prescriber who shares treatment goals with the client. If there is not clear agreement between prescriber and client, it is unlikely that a medication will be found that works for either.

ELEMENTS OF AN EFFECTIVE MEDICATION TRIAL

The structure of an effective medication trial will be discussed in more depth in chapter 8. While it is always important to think carefully about how to set up a medication trial, it is particularly important when the person using the medication is in extraordinary distress, is impulsive, is suicidal, has difficulty with stable relationships and stable behavior, and has a disorder that may or may not respond to medication. All of these issues are often present in people with BPD, which is why planning and structuring the medication trial is so critical.

1. **Identification of the specific symptoms or problems you are hoping the medication will help**. How would you know if the medication was helping? How would you know if the medication were making things worse? What side effects would be most difficult for you to tolerate, even for a short period of time?

2. **Clarify how big the problem is that you want medication to address.** How much does this problem interfere with how you want to live your life? What risk or discomfort would you be willing to consider to solve this problem? What else, besides medication, have you tried or are trying?

3. **Organize your medication history and share this with your prescriber.** What medication have you tried in the past? How long was each taken and at what dose? How well did the medication work? What problems did the medication cause? What side effects were bothersome?

4. **Could your symptoms be caused by some problem that would interfere with any medication working?** Could you have a treatable medical illness that could be causing some of your symptoms? Do you have a co-existing mental illness that could be part of your problem? Is your use of drugs or alcohol making your life more difficult?

5. **What commitment are you willing and able to make to taking medication?** Do you know how long it will take to see if the medication is working? How long will a reasonable medication trial take? What expected side effects could you tolerate or not tolerate?

6. **Make one medication change at a time.**

7. **Stop the medication if it is not clearly helping.** All medications have risks and side effects. It can be difficult to stop a medication if you are feeling a lot of distress, even if the medication is not really helping. Piling one medication on top of others increases risk, and it increases uncertainty of what medication is doing what. Medication can often help but rarely does enough by itself. There are many skills that people with BPD need to learn or relearn to improve their

lives. There are many techniques that have been developed to help people learn these skills. Just taking medication without working on life-changing skill development is rarely going to be effective.

Specifics of medication in the treatment of people who have borderline personality disorders

There is no medication specifically indicated for treatment of BPD. Despite this, most people with this diagnosis are either taking psychiatric medication or have tried it in the past. People are searching for a solution to their life dilemmas, and medication is often seen as something worth trying to see if it might help. There are symptoms that are common to people with that diagnosis that may respond to medication. The major categories of symptom-related problems each lead to a specific psychopharmacology trial.

Potential pharmacological "targets" for medication.

1. Mood instability
2. Depression
3. Anxiety
4. Disorganized thinking, paranoia, and/or temporary psychotic symptoms, related to stress
5. Hypersensitivity to the environment
6. Impulsivity/self-harm
7. Insomnia
8. Intrusive nightmares, flashbacks, and startle reflex from PTSD
9. Substance use/abuse

These are all symptoms or problems, but are not "borderline personality." There is very little research supporting the use of any medication for people with a personality disorder. This limited amount of research increases the importance of a careful assessment of the severity of the problem, as well as a careful evaluation of how well the medication is actually working.

This is not a book about psychopharmacology. I have not listed side effects or the risks associated with each of these medications, and I have not tried to list every medication that is potentially useful to a person with BPD. I have listed those targets and those medications that are most commonly used in the treatment of people with BPD. Where there are a number of different medications in a list, I have not tried to list them all but have provided representative examples. For more details on medications, please refer to my book *Instant Psychopharmacology* or to another reference book.

Mood instability. "Classic" mood stabilizers can decrease the intensity and frequency of mood swings in some people. Often they do not eliminate the mood swings but can make them easier to manage. Most of the classic mood stabilizers are more effective for the "up" side of the mood swings than for the "down" side of the mood swings.

> sodium valproate, valproic acid (Depakote)
> lithium carbonate (Eskalith, Lithobid)
> carbamazepine (Tegretal)

Atypical or second-generation antipsychotic medications have many different targets, completely apart from their anti-psychotic effects, which is what they are commonly named for. All of them have significant mood-stabilizing properties. For some people, they may be more effective or have more tolerable side effects than the classic mood stabilizers.

> risperidone (Risperdal)
> ziprasidone (Geodon)
> quetiapine (Seroquel)
> aripiprazole (Abilify)

Depression. Antidepressants can be very useful, but not everyone who is depressed will benefit from medication. Antidepressants can also increase mood instability. When used by someone who already has a problem with mood swings, it is important to monitor him to make sure that the antidepressant does not make this worse. There is no "right" antidepressant. SSRIs (selective serotonin reuptake blockers) are most commonly used, often useful, and are relatively safe when taken in an overdose.

>   fluoxetine (Prozac)
>   citalopram (Celexa)

SNRIs (selective serotonin and norepinephrine reuptake blockers) are similar to SSRIs, although they may be useful in some cases where SSRIs do not work and may be more effective for people in pain or with fibromyalgia. They may also cause more high blood pressure and may be slightly more dangerous in an overdose.

>   venlafaxine (Effexor)
>   duloxetine (Cymbalta)

Presynaptic acting antidepressants work by impacting the amount of serotonin and norepinephrine released by the nerve cell.

>   mirtazapine (Remeron): very sedating, which can be useful, or a problem

Dopaminergic antidepressants.

>   bupropion (Wellbutrin): not sedating and not helpful for anxiety or panic

MAOIs (monoamine oxidase inhibitors) work by inhibiting the enzyme that deactivates serotonin, norepinephrine, and dopamine. They are effective, but they have many drug-drug and food interactions and have more risks and side effects than other antidepressants.

> phenelzine (Nardil)
> tranylcypromine (Parnate)

Mood stabilizers with predominant action on the depressed side of mood instability.

> lamotrigine (Lamictal): complicated to use because of the need to start with a very low dose and decrease the dose very slowly

Tricyclic antidepressants are older medications that are now rarely used. They are effective but with more risks and side effects, and they are much more dangerous if taken as an overdose.

> amitriptyline (Elavil)
> nortriptyline (Pamelor)

Anxiety. Benzodiazepines are commonly prescribed in response to complaints of anxiety, but the risk of dependency is significant. Most people with BPD feel in tremendous distress and are often desperate. There is a very real risk of taking more and more medication in response to this sense of desperation. This is in addition to the abuse of drugs and alcohol common to people who have this disorder. Benzodiazepines should be used infrequently and only with careful monitoring. In general, their use by those with BPD is to be discouraged.

> diazepam (Valium)
> lorazepam (Ativan)
> alprazolam (Xanax)

Most of the antidepressants listed above also have significant antianxiety, as well as antipanic and anti-OCD properties. They are not addictive, generally safe, and are first-line medications for the treatment of anxiety in people who have BPD.

Buspirone (Buspar) is an antianxiety medication that has little to no abuse potential and is safe. It takes a week or more to work, must be taken continuously, and may not be all that effective for many people.

In extreme cases when anxiety is overwhelming, to the extent that the person's thinking starts becoming a bit disorganized and the person's ability to function is impaired, a low dose of an antipsychotic medication may be useful. These medications are effective, but they also have significant risks and side effects. The atypical antipsychotic medications listed above or any of the older typical antipsychotic medications can be used effectively, but the dose must be kept low to avoid significant side effects.

> quetiapine (Seroquel)
> risperidone (Risperdal)
> aripiprazole (Abilify)
> ziprasidone (Geodon)

Disorganized thinking, paranoia, and/or temporary psychotic symptoms, related to stress. Antipsychotic medications, listed above, are often useful in low doses to help with some of the disorganized thinking, paranoia, and very brief experiences of psychotic symptoms. Some people with BPD will do better if they stay on an antipsychotic medication, although these medications can often be used in fairly low doses. Other people with this disorder find that they can use these medications effectively as a "prn," taking them only when symptoms become a problem.

Hypersensitivity to the environment. Many people with BPD are exquisitely sensitive to whatever is going on around them. Too much noise, too many people, and any sense of possible criticism can all lead to overreaction. Antipsychotic medications can help to "filter out" some of this overwhelming "noise." Cognitive behavioral skill training to handle these issues is preferred, from the point of view of effectiveness and safety, but there may be a role for antipsychotic medications in some situations.

Impulsivity/self-harm. Mood stabilizers can sometimes be useful in helping decrease impulsiveness, especially "hair-trigger" explosive anger.

Topirimate (Topamax) is an anticonvulsant that works through a mechanism similar to the mood stabilizer valproic acid. Topirimate is not an effective mood stabilizer, but it is effective in decreasing some kinds of impulsive behavior, such as cutting.

Insomnia. A good night of sleep is extremely useful for helping people maintain stability. Insomnia is a very nonspecific problem caused by a wide range of problems, from sleep apnea and restless legs, to chronic pain, substance abuse, depression, or anxiety. Naps, lack of exercise, and even boredom can interfere with sleep. A careful assessment of the causes of the insomnia is important before medications are prescribed.

Sedating antidepressants have not been formally studied as sleeping agents, but they are not addictive and are very commonly used to promote sleep, even in people who are not depressed.

trazodone

Selective GABA agonists are similar to the benzodiazepines (Valium-type medications) but they are more selective to the sleep system and are less useful in the treatment of anxiety. They are supposed to be less likely to be abused than the benzodiazepines.

zolpidem (Ambien)

Intrusive nightmares, flashbacks, and startle reflex from PTSD. A history of childhood sexual abuse is common for people who have BPD, and symptoms of chronic PTSD are also common. Some of the nighttime terror can be reduced by using medications that commonly treat high blood pressure.

> guanfacine (Tenex)
> prazosin (Minipress)

Substance use/abuse. Substance abuse is a common problem for people who have BPD. There are medications that can be useful as part of a comprehensive treatment approach to helping people recover from substance abuse and dependence. There are medications that can be very useful in the treatment of alcohol and opiate abuse. Medications are less clearly effective in the treatment of cocaine and marijuana abuse.

FINAL THOUGHTS

Medications can sometimes help some of the symptoms of a personality disorder. Medications alone will not change the underlying personality, but medications may allow someone to live with a bit less distress for himself and his family and friends.

A person with a serious personality disorder is often in considerable distress. There is often pressure to "do something," and to do it now as though it were an emergency. Effective medication trials cannot be treated as an emergency. They need to be planned ahead of time, with careful attention to specific goals and target symptoms, attention to possible risks and side effects, and a shared understanding of how they can help or hurt. Medications are never the primary part of treatment for a person with a personality disorder. They are one tool that may help, and they are more likely to help if the goals are realistic and clear. Most important, a medication trial must be part of a collaboration between the client and the prescriber. Finally, medications do not work for everyone. If they help, then that is great. If they do not help, it is important to jointly decide with a prescriber whether it is worth pursuing a better response from yet another medication or whether medication is not likely to be a useful solution at this particular time.

8

Understanding the Problem

The general belief is that medications are used to treat an illness. It would seem that the decision about when to use a medication is pretty obvious; if you have an illness that is likely to respond to a medication, especially if the medication is effective and has few side effects, you take the medication. Actually, the decision about whether or not to use medication for a particular problem is much more complicated than this.

Most of us have some "physiological dysfunctions" that we do not even know we have, ignore, or decide not to get treatment for, or we use a variety of treatments other than medication. We have rashes or skin discoloration; we have allergies and colds; we have joint pain and headaches: we treat some of these conditions, and some we do not treat. Medications have now been developed to treat physiological dysfunction that we used to just live with in the past. For example, obesity, or at least some obesity, is now a recognized disease, treated not only with diet and exercise, but also with medication and surgery. Additionally, a wide variety of herbal medications and food supplements are available to "treat" various conditions. Whatever the problem, there is almost certain to be a medication or herbal supplement advertised to treat it, regardless of whether it is actually connected to a disease.

There is an important difference between a "disease" and an "illness." A disease is a physiological dysfunction, whether you know about it or not and whether you take action because of it or not. An illness is the recognition or the belief that something is wrong with your body, especially if this leads to some kind of activity related to this illness. A reaction to having an illness could include telling your friends that you are sick, getting to bed early, taking a medication, or requesting a day off from work. A person can have a disease that he or she takes no notice of, and he or she does not feel or act ill. On the other hand, someone can be ill and can act and believe as though he has a disease, when in fact no actual disease is present. While disease and illness are connected, they are not the same thing—one can occur without the other. When someone says that he is sick, or when he takes a medication, he is responding to a set of beliefs that he has a specific type of problem called an illness. Once he decides that he has an illness, then taking a medication is usually considered to be a reasonable solution to the problem. If he does not consider himself to be ill, then taking a medication is likely to be considered inappropriate. The issue is not actual physiological dysfunction but rather the set of beliefs and expectations that lead us to agree that someone has a particular type of problem called illness.

A common complication is that it is not always clear what problems are associated with a physiological dysfunction or a disease, and which problems are not. If we believe, and if those around us believe, that a problem is connected to some kind of physiological dysfunction, it is easy for all of us to agree to label the problem as an "illness." An elevated body temperature or a swollen and painful knee are examples where most would agree that the problem is an illness.

However, there can be considerable disagreement about what type of problem would be defined as an "illness." Homosexuality, for example, was at one point a theological or moral "problem," then it became a legal problem, then it was defined as an illness, and more recently it has come to be considered as a part of the normal biological spectrum and not a problem at all. Addiction to alcohol was once considered a moral failing, and it has been redefined as an illness.

Many of the disagreements about whether a medication is

indicated have more to do with the disagreement about whether a problem is an illness or something else. It is clear that a stimulant used by a hyperactive child will help that child attend better in school and fit into the classroom more effectively. There is little disagreement about the effects of the medication. However, those who believe that ADHD medications are overused believe that the problem is more in the structure of the classroom or in the child's home environment, and that these should be changed rather than giving the child a medication. Alternatively, those who believe that the hyperactivity is associated with a biological problem within the child's brain may agree that changes in the schools and the home environment might help, but they feel that the use of medication is also justified because the child has a problem caused by a disease.

Someone who is bothered by hearing voices that no one else can hear may feel strongly that she has telepathy, but people around her may label the same problem as symptoms of a disease. For one person, extreme sadness that continues for month or years may be part of a normal grieving process, while for another it is an indication of illness. The reality is that most interesting and complicated human problems have a biological component and also a social/environmental/moral component. In most cases, the issue is not whether it is one or the other, but how much of the problem has a biological component, and how much of the problem is caused or exacerbated by nonbiological issues.

However, if the question is whether or not to use a medication, the cause of the problem is only very loosely connected to the solution. For example, anxiety that is caused by job related stress may be helped by diazepam (Valium), even though the cause of the anxiety has little to do with any disease process and is certainly not related to a diazepam deficiency.

WHAT IS THE NATURE OF THE PROBLEM?

What is the problem that you feel that you would like help with? While the cause of the problem may be interesting, when considering possible solutions, it is often more productive to begin with a very clear description of the problem and a description of how it interferes with your life. People too often start by considering whether or not they want to take a psychiatric medication, or they think about what medication they want to take. Medication is a tool that can help fix, or at least improve, some problems. However, before deciding on what tool you want to use, it is useful to understand the problem as much as possible.

What are the symptoms or pieces of the problem
that you would like to solve? How long has it
been going on, and how did it start?

Example: My problem is that I am feeling depressed. My depression includes low energy, easy fatigue, poor concentration, inability to enjoy normal activities, and increased need to sleep. I have not been tearful, but I feel tearful inside. I am not suicidal, and I still hope that things can get better, but I am not sure what you can do to make this happen.

It started a couple of months ago. Initially I thought it was just a reaction to a round of layoffs that affected some friends, although I was not personally affected. I started worrying more and more about what if I had been laid off, and whether I would be laid off next, and then it just snowballed downhill. Initially, I could shrug it off but it seems to be getting more difficult to do this.

How does this problem interfere with your life?
What can you no longer do because of this problem,
do less of, or do only with difficulty?

Example: I am still able to go to work, but I feel that my impaired concentration and energy decreases my effectiveness. I feel that I have not been doing a very good job, but so far my supervisor has not said anything. My wife, on the other hand, has commented that I seem sad and somber and that I am less willing to do things with her, and I feel that my depression has put a strain on my marriage. I have resisted the urge to increase my use of alcohol, but it has been much harder to keep to my normal exercise pattern, something that I used to enjoy. I have stopped playing poker with my friends, and it is no longer enjoyable to go to movies because it is too hard to concentrate on the story, although I continue to go primarily to please my wife.

How big is the problem; how much does it interfere with your life?

Example: So far, I have not lost my job or my marriage, but things are clearly going downhill and if things do not get better it is not clear how bad things could go. On the other hand, my life has stopped being enjoyable and it is hard to just force myself to keep going. Right now my depression is a big problem, but if it does not start to get better it could become huge and overwhelming.

What appears to make it better?

Example: Nothing really makes it better. It is a bit less painful when I can just lie down by myself, pretending to watch TV that I am not really watching. I can keep up an okay front while I am at work, and perhaps I feel a bit better when I am forced to keep busy, but as soon as I get home I collapse.

What appears to make it worse? When is it worse?

Example: It is worse when my wife tries to talk with me and I do not know what to say. I start feeling even more guilty, like I am letting her and the kids down. I feel worse when anyone at work is critical. I have gotten so sensitive that I have been interpreting any suggestion as a criticism, and then I get angry with myself for being so sensitive.

What have you already tried in order to overcome this problem?

Example: I have tried to force myself to exercise and to spend time with friends, but it is harder and harder to do this and for the most part I have dropped out of most activities. I have tried to force myself to "snap out of it" but this just makes me feel worse. I have thought about going to church, but I have never been religious and going to church now does not make much sense. I have tried to talk to my wife about how I feel, but I do not know what to say and when I try to talk about it, it seems to scare her more than it helps.

Have you ever had a similar problem in the past,
and if so, how did you overcome it back then?

Example: I have had several other bouts of depression, once in my early twenties when I was in college and later in my early thirties shortly after I got married and shortly after my father died. During my first depression, in my twenties, I started drinking heavily, which seemed like the thing to do when you were in college. Between the depression and the drinking, I ended up dropping out of school for a year. It seemed that by the end of the year I was able to get on top of the depression, get control of my drinking, and pull my life together. When I got depressed in my thirties I was given some Prozac from my primary care doctor. I was also able to keep to my regular exercise pattern, which seemed to help.

What other life issues may be making
this problem better, or worse?

Example: I am sure that the layoffs at work got me to initially worry, and they seem to be connected to how this began. Now I am not sure. It seems as though my biggest stressor is dealing with the impact of the depression itself. So far I have avoided any use of alcohol. In fact, since becoming depressed I went from drinking an occasional beer to not using any alcohol at all, because I did not want to slide into using alcohol the way I was when I was younger. I do not have any particular medical problems, but I was recently started on a medication for high blood pressure.

What medications have you tried
to deal with this problem in the past?

Example: The last time I got depressed, some years ago, I was on Prozac for around a year. I am not sure if it helped or not, but I had been pretty stuck in my depression and after I started the Prozac it seemed as though I could fight the depression off more effectively. I did not like the sexual side effects of the Prozac, which was one of the reasons I stopped it after a year. Initially, when I started it, my sex drive was so low that no medication could have made it any worse, but after I started feeling better and my libido continued to be shot I thought it could be connected to the medication.

Is there any other personal or family history
that may influence your decision about how
you want to deal with this problem?

Example: My sister was on medication for a depression around 10 years ago, and when she mentioned it to my father, he kidded her about it and was clear that he thought psychiatric medication was all worthless. I know that she felt it had helped her, and she stopped talking about it. I assume she stayed on it but I am not sure. When I took some Prozac for my depression a few years ago, I did not let my parents or siblings know.

Answer: Your problem is that you are depressed: it is getting in the way of many things you would like to do, and it is not getting better. You have tried to put it out of mind and just get on with your life, but this has not worked. You have the feeling that if this does not get better, then your job and perhaps your marriage could be in trouble. On the other hand, you have been able to avoid using alcohol, which seemed to make things worse when you were depressed in your twenties.

What have you already tried to deal with this problem?
What will happen if it does not get better?

Example: I have a sense that eventually this depression will just go away on its own. The problem is that in the meantime I am miserable, and I am worried about the long-term impact on my job and marriage. Just waiting does not seem like a good option.

I have tried to force myself to exercise and do activities that I used to enjoy, but this has been very difficult and for the most part I have spent more time exhausted in bed and less time up and about. I have also tried to just push the depression away, telling myself that it is "all in my mind," but so far this does not seem to have helped.

How might medication help? What problems might medication cause?

Example: When I took medication in the past, I did not feel great but it did seem more possible for me to push myself into being active, and over time I was able to "pull myself up by my bootstraps" in a way that did not seem possible before taking the medication. It was not an instant cure, but it did seem to help.

I would expect that the medication would allow me to push myself, and that if it was working I would be able to start exercising, spend more time with friends, and spend less time in bed. I would also hope that I would be able to concentrate better at work, and start enjoying things more.

One big problem with taking medication is that I either have to keep it secret from my family, at least from my siblings, or face their attitude that I should be able to get better without medication. I guess I have some of this same attitude myself, which makes it feel like a weakness to use a medication. At the same time, I know this is irrational and that it has worked in the past.

I am concerned about the sexual side effects, but right now I do not have any sex drive anyway, so I can worry about this down the road when I feel better.

What else could **you** do that might help?

Example: I know that staying active and avoiding alcohol will help. I also know that exercise and staying active helps, and I

will make a schedule in order to commit myself to a more regular exercise program, even if I start by just taking a walk every
day.

I know that I fall into thinking really terrible, negative
thoughts that I expect just make it all worse. I start thinking
about it never getting better, about losing my job, and so on.
Every time someone looks at me or makes a suggestion I start
feeling that they dislike me or are being critical. I have heard
there are some self-help books that can help me redirect my
mind when this kind of thing happens. I will go to the library
and try and see if there is some book that can give me some better ideas about how to deal with all of these negative thoughts.

THINKING OF THE SOLUTION

It is important to have a very clear understanding of the problem before one tries to solve it. Often, human problems are
complicated, making it hard to clearly define the problem or
recognize all of its pieces. Human problems often have multiple
influences and causes. There are almost always multiple ways
to try and cope with or solve the problem. Starting a discussion with the question of whether or not to use a psychiatric
medication runs the very real risk of trying to come up with a
solution without fully understanding the nature of the problem.
Asking the question of whether one should use "medication or
therapy" assumes that the solution is one or the other. Actually,
for a complicated problem that is interfering with a person's
life, it is worth considering all of the possible solutions, and
then deciding which solutions to try first, in what order, and in
what combination.

The bigger the problem and the more it interferes with your
life, the more you may be willing to make life changes, or tolerate risks or side effects to get it fixed. If the problem is relatively
minor and not really interfering with your life, you will be less
likely to tolerate big risks or uncomfortable side effects to fix it.

While it may be tempting to speculate about the cause of a

problem, and to wonder if it is "biological" or "psychological," "genetic" or "related to current stress," the reality is that almost all real human problems have some mixture of factors from all of these areas. Therefore, the best approach is to understand the problem, figure out how big the problem is, consider how much risk or inconvenience the person is willing to tolerate to improve the problem, and decide what solution or package of solutions makes the most sense. The focus is not on the cause of the problem but on its solution. The cause and the solution may, or may not, be connected.

9

Setting Up an Effective Medication Trial: Increasing the Chance That Medications Will Help

You may have tried a psychiatric medication, but you are not sure if it really helped or not. You may now be taking a medication and you are not sure if you should continue it. You may have tried many psychiatric medications, none of which have worked, but on more careful assessment it turns out that you have never taken any of the medications for a long enough time, or at a high enough dose, so that they had much chance of working. You may have been told that you should take a medication, but you did not agree on the need for the medication or the reason why you were supposed to take it, and you stopped it as soon as possible. Medication is a tool, and it is important to ensure that the right tool is used, in the right amount, for the right problem (Deegan & Drake, 2006).

Before starting a medication, think about what you would like the medication to do. Most people will take medication for some period of time and then will want to know if it is worth continuing. Is it helping or not? To answer this all-important question, think about how you can best set up your medication trial to ensure that the medication has the best chance of being helpful. There are a number of steps to setting up a medication trial, which can increase the chance that the medication will work and can increase the chance that you will know if it works.

Setting up an effective medication trial requires collaboration between you, if you are the person who will be taking the medication, and your prescriber. This collaboration may also need to include your therapist, your spouse, a family member, or a friend. Who do you want involved in the decision making about your medications? Most of us do not decide on whether to take or stay on a medication completely by ourselves. Rather, we are influenced by friends, family, physicians, maybe even teachers or employers. Carefully consider whom you want to talk to about medication, and who can give you helpful feedback about whether it is working.

Now, before you take your first pill, consider the following points:

1. Develop clear "target symptoms" that make the goals for each medication concrete and measurable.
2. Decide on the "time frame" for the medication trial.
3. After you have been on the medication, make a clear decision about whether the medication is working or not.
4. Make one medication change at a time.
5. Combine medication with other ways to improve the problem.
6. Avoid alcohol and other substances that can interfere with the medication working.

1. COME UP WITH CLEAR "TARGET SYMPTOMS"

We take a medication if we believe that it will help us come closer to a goal that is important to us. If you are told to take a medication to achieve a goal or target that is not important, it is unlikely that you will take the medication. The target for you and for your prescriber may not always be in complete agreement. Sometimes the goals are not in agreement at all. A medication trial is likely to be much more effective if there are goals that are clear, specific, and shared.

Target symptoms are symptoms that can be measured as a way of assessing whether things are getting better or worse. Target goals are specific goals for the treatment. The more specific and measurable the target symptoms and goals are, the more they are behaviors that can be observed. As observable behaviors, they are more likely to be useful ways of measuring progress. It is great to "feel better," but this is a very vague description and it is hard to know what it means. The number of panic attacks, or the number of times leaving the house, or being able to concentrate enough to be able to read, or even a daily self-rating of mood all can allow a way of tracking changes over time.

> Example 1: John is a 45-year-old man with a history of having been seriously depressed three times in the past. During his last depression 3 years ago he stopped going to work and just stayed in the house for 6 weeks before forcing himself to go through the motions of going to work. The last time he was depressed he tried an antidepressant medication for a week or so during his last depression, but it just made him feel worse so he discontinued it. John is feeling so bad that he agreed to try an antidepressant again, although he did not feel that medication was very helpful the last time he was depressed.

John just wants to feel less depressed. However, wanting "to feel less depressed" is too vague to be a useful target symptom. Some parts of John's depression may respond more rapidly or more completely than other symptoms.

John's symptoms of his depression would include the following:

- Feelings of sadness, that life is over, that nothing matters;
- Decreased concentration;
- Decreased sleep;
- Decreased motivation;
- Inability to feel good about anything or enjoy anything;

- Not doing normal activities, exercising, going out with friends, or reading (all of which used to be favorite activities);
- A sense of hopelessness, that this will go on forever no matter what he does;
- Feeling like crying, although he has not; or
- Feeling vaguely like he wished he were dead, although he is not actively suicidal.

John and his physician decided on three initial target symptoms that he could track to determine whether his medications were helping:

- He would be able to start forcing himself to exercise regularly and to play cards with friends:
  - He will keep track of how many days a week he is now exercising.
  - He will track how many times in the last month he has gone out to play cards with his friends.
  - He will record on a calendar every time he exercises, and every time he goes out with friends.
- He would be able to concentrate enough to read:
  - He will track whether he is able to read, and what kind of material. Right now, he is not reading anything. He will see if he can concentrate enough to read, starting with short articles in his favorite magazines, and hopefully down the road, he will be reading books.
- He would feel less tearful and less depressed:
  - On the same calendar, he will also record a number reflecting his mood for the day. The scale runs from 1 = worst sadness he has had in this entire process, up to 10 = feeling really good.

Sometimes it becomes impossible to set up a medication trial with specific targets. This can occur when the person's expectations are so unrealistic that no medication is likely to work. At other times this can occur when the person is unable or unwilling to make other life changes that are necessary before target symptoms can realistically be achieved. In still other cases, past trials have indicated that medication is unlikely to work for this person in the way that one might hope.

Example 2: Susan is a 32-year-old woman with lifelong anxiety. For years, she has been afraid to leave her home without a family member being present. She has many specific fears. She is afraid of spiders that could be out in the yard, of dogs, and of being poisoned by eating the wrong food. She has tried many medications, none of which have freed her from her anxieties and allowed her to "feel normal." She would like a medication that would allow her to live a normal life. She feels so overwhelmed by her various fears and anxiety that she cannot imagine changing her life unless a medication takes her fears away. She cannot imagine leaving her house alone, and until she feels better she does not feel that she can even work on this goal.

It is unclear whether Susan and her physician can come up with any specific symptoms that would be appropriate targets for a medication. Possible medication targets would be to decrease her anxiety enough that she could work on leaving her home, even for very short visits outside. However, Susan is not willing to consider this goal unless and until the medication cures her anxiety. Another possible goal would be for Susan to learn to live a more complete life despite her various fears through a behavioral desensitization program of slowly being exposed to the causes of her fears until the fear is experienced as less intense. For example, Susan could first just think about eating in a restaurant, then go to a restaurant not to eat but only to sit, then perhaps get a glass of water at the restaurant, and then slowly proceed to eating something. The idea is to set up a hierarchy of behaviors that are less frightening to those that are more frightening, getting used to the anxiety at each level before proceeding to the next. Susan was not at all interested in this plan, and she was again looking for a medication.

Susan has some very real problems that are significantly interfering with her life, and she could probably be helped by treatment. At the same time, her hopes about what a medication could accomplish are so unrealistic that no medication is likely to meet any of her expectations. Her many past negative trials of medication support this point of view. The issue is not that medication could not help but that it would not likely help in ways that Susan would recognize. If she had never tried medication it might still be worth seeing if one would help enough for her to recognize improvement and be more flexible about the role of medication, but given multiple past medication trials, the focus needs to be on what Susan would need to do in addition to medication to live the more normal life that she desires. Supporting one more medication trial that is very unlikely to be helpful would only serve to reinforce Susan's belief that medication does not help, while at the same time distracting her from coming up with a plan that could more realistically help her change her life.

Example 3: Ralph is a man with ongoing complaints of severe insomnia and ongoing general anxiety. He is able to go to work and do many normal activities, but he is perpetually anxious. The only way that he can sleep is by having three or four drinks, and the only way that he can decrease his anxiety to a manageable level is to use alcohol throughout the day, starting when he wakes up. He has had one ticket for driving while intoxicated, but he does not see himself as an alcoholic and does not see alcohol as a problem. He would like a medication to help with his sleep and anxiety problems, and he feels that his drinking is likely to decrease once his anxiety is in better control.

Ralph wants a medication to replace the alcohol and do what the alcohol does— only better. There may be nonaddictive medications that will do what he wants and help him with his sleep and his anxiety, but without some focus on the role of alcohol in his life these medications are unlikely to be very useful. If he is given a prescription for one of the antianxiety medications with an abuse potential, for example, one of the Valium-type benzodiazepines, there is a significant likelihood that he will continue to abuse alcohol but will also become dependent to the prescribed antianxiety medication as well, leaving him with two addictions instead of just one. Treatment might help his anxiety and insomnia, and there might be a role for medication as part of this treatment, but effective treatment would have to include attention to his alcohol use.

> Example 4: José is a 55-year-old man who has had panic attacks since he was in his early twenties. He has had periods where these become more frequent and more bothersome, and there are other periods where he can go for weeks without having one. During the bad periods, he has always been able to force himself to go to work and stay involved with normal activities. A few weeks ago he began having multiple panic attacks every day. His activities had already been curtailed because of a back injury at work that was getting better but still causing significant pain, which had left him on temporary disability for the next few weeks. He was unable to play softball or run, which were his normal ways of "letting off steam." He now finds it more and more difficult to get out of the house, to go shopping, or even to go to watch his friends play softball because of his fear that he will have a panic attack while out.

José has panic disorder with agoraphobia. The panic attacks have left him afraid to go outside. All of this is complicated by his back pain, and also by his loss of his normal activities including work, softball, and running.

José's symptoms now include the following:

- Panic attacks several times a day;
- Not going out of the house, even to shop; and

- Decreased involvement in normal activities: some caused by his back pain but some connected to the fear generated by his panic attacks.

There are a number of strategies that could help José decrease his panic attacks. Cognitive behavioral therapy (CBT) would start with learning to recognize the very early cues indicating that a panic attack is just beginning before it builds up so much that it is impossible to do anything about it. Once José could recognize the early signs of an impending panic attack, he could learn techniques to actively distract himself as a way to stop or at least decrease the intensity of the attack. José was interested in this method, but he preferred a medication that might work faster with less effort. At the same time, José was well aware that he had become "gun-shy" of leaving the house, and that even after he had better control over his panic attacks, he would have to force himself out of the house and become more involved in normal things. He had struggled with this issue for years, and he felt confident that if the frequency and intensity of the panic attacks could be decreased, he could overcome the fear of going out.

These are the target goals developed by José and his physician:

- Work to decrease panic frequency and intensity of attacks:
  - He will measure the frequency of his panic attacks.
  - He will measure the intensity of his panic attacks.
- Increase the frequency and ease with which José can leave his home for normal activities:
  - José will measure how often he forces himself to leave his home, with a minimal goal of finding some excuse to leave the house to go shopping or visit a friend or go to some activity at least once a day.
  - José has a number of doctor appointments that are necessary but are not part of his normal life. He and his physician agreed that going to a doctor's appointment

would not count in his goal of going out at least once a day, unless he did something in addition to going to the doctor appointment.

2. Decide on an Appropriate Time Frame for the Medication Trial

Most medications take days or weeks to work. Taking a medication for a few days and then deciding it is not helping is not an effective way to decide whether this medication is useful. Before even starting a medication, you and your physician should discuss how long it will take to see if the medication is working and what a fair trial would be. For some medications, this can be one or two doses. If you are taking propranolol for performance anxiety, it will either work within a couple of hours of the first pill or it will not. It may be worth taking it for a second or third day and increasing the dose just to check, but if it is going to work, it will work rapidly. A trial of venlafaxine (Effexor) may take multiple weeks. This is a medication that must be started at a fairly low dose and increased over time, so it may take weeks before it can be increased to an effective dose. Once you are on a full dose, it may take several more weeks to see if it is going to do any good. A trial of venlafaxine could easily take 6 to 8 weeks or even longer before you know that this medication is likely to help.

Before starting a trial of a new medication, decide with your physician how long an appropriate trial would take. Commit yourself to a reasonable length of time for the medication trial. If you are only willing to tolerate a medication for a week, and if that medication often takes several weeks to work, it is probably not worth even starting it. You will have the risk and possible side effects of starting the trial, and you are unlikely to have any of the benefits that might come from the medication. Too often someone will start a new medication without thinking this through, and he will then stop the medication before it has any real chance of working.

If you have uncomfortable side effects, a medication trial can always be stopped early. On the other hand, if you are trying to find a solution to a really bad problem, and other solutions have not worked, then it might be worth tolerating some side effects, even if they are uncomfortable. Many side effects are temporary. Some people starting SSRI antidepressants can feel mild nausea, jitteriness, or a headache. These symptoms usually pass after a few days. However, other side effects are so frightening or uncomfortable that the medication must be stopped right away. Some people can become manic from an antidepressant medication. If you started an antidepressant and your thoughts began to race a mile a minute, your energy level increased 100%, you stopped needing very much sleep and started spending money wildly and behaved in other impulsive ways, you would want to stop the medication without going through a full trial period.

Often, you can decrease some of the side effects that might be associated with starting a new medication trial by simply starting at a lower dose and increasing the medication slowly. For example, many people have problems with diarrhea and nausea if they start lithium at a full dose. However, if the dose is then decreased and increased slowly over time, the discomfort can usually be avoided or minimized. If the medication is likely to provide important help, it is very important to work with your physician to jointly decide how to manage early side effects rather than to prematurely stop the medication.

3. MAKE A CLEAR DECISION ABOUT WHETHER MEDICATION IS WORKING

Often someone starts a new medication, and the problem is a "bit better" but not much. The depression is a bit better, but she may still be depressed and tearful and unable to go to work, or the anxiety is a bit better but she is still unable to leave her home and do routine things. At times it makes sense to use combinations of medications, and at times rational combinations are more likely to work than any single medication. Too often, the combinations of medications are not rational. The first medication might work a bit, so she may add a second, which also may be working, although it is not clear, and then a third is added. A person with a complicated set of problems can end up on a pile of different medications, and at times it may not be clear which is working and which is just adding more risk and side effects. If combining two medications is rational and thoughtful, then by all means do not get stuck with the idea that one should never be on combinations. On the other hand, if it is not clear that a medication is working, then it is probably not working well enough to be worth continuing.

At times, the person taking a medication may not be aware of how much she has changed. She may not feel that it is doing much good, but her family and friends may feel that it is helping a lot. There is not much subjective change and she may not feel much better, but her behavior or expression may have changed in ways that are very obvious to other people around her. For example, if she were recovering from a severe depression she could start engaging in more normal activities and start looking much better to family and friends, but feel just as depressed as before.

Alternatively, someone taking a medication may feel better with the medication, but family and friends may feel that his behavior has not changed at all. For example, a person paralyzed with anxiety may feel much better when taking antianxiety medication, but family and friends may observe no change in how he spends time, what he is doing during the day, or whether he has been able to recapture his normal life. A psychiatric medication can improve behaviors and a subjective sense of well-being. It is easy to judge effect if both change at the same time, but if one changes and the other does not, it can be confusing to determine if the medication is really doing very much good. Feedback from a support system can be very useful in trying to decide whether a medication is really helping, as can developing and following the change through clear target symptoms throughout the medication trial.

If a medication is really helping, you probably want to keep taking it. If the medication is not helping, you want to at least consider stopping it. Unfortunately, this is not always clear. If you are in a lot of distress, or if you are very anxious or very depressed even on the medication, it may be scary to stop it even if it is not doing much good. If you feel this bad while taking the medication, how bad would you feel without it? If you are not clear about whether a medication is helping or not, it sometimes feels safer to continue taking a medication even if it is not clearly helping. It is easy to start adding one medication to another in an attempt to get some relief, and you may end up on a complicated mixture of medication. Rational polypharmacy can be very useful; this means using medications in combination when it is fairly clear what each medication is doing or when there is a clear strategy about how they might work together to increase the effectiveness of each. At times, it can be very effective to use medications in combination. However, irrational polypharmacy means that you end up on a pile of medications without any clear idea of what is working and what is not, not as a plan but as the result of adding one medication to another to another without being clear at each point how to plan for the next step.

4. MAKE ONE MEDICATION CHANGE AT A TIME

If you are in distress and hurting, it can be very frustrating to make a medication change, wait, then make another change, then wait. We are all in a hurry, and there is a natural desire to make whatever medication change is needed to start feeling better. If you are very depressed and are on a low dose of an antidepressant, it is understandable to raise the dose of the medication and add a second medication at the same time, instead of waiting for weeks to see if the dose adjustment is enough. If you are having panic attacks and nightmares from PTSD, it makes sense to start some medication that might help the panic attacks and another medication that might help the nightmares. What happens, however, is that if you start feeling better and if the medication seems to be working, you have no idea whether the improvement came from the combination of the two medications, or only from one, and if from one, which one. If you have a really bad side effect, you have no idea which of the two medications was responsible, and you may be reluctant to try either one, even though one might be useful and one might not be. If you make multiple changes at the same time, you will almost always end up on complicated medication combinations with little sense of what each medication is doing.

Example: Jay came in for consultation to try and figure out what medications he really needed. He was complaining of being continually tired and did not have the energy to do much. He requested a prescription for a stimulant for his persistent tiredness and concentration problem. He had used Adderall in the past and felt that it had helped.

He had a history of a number of psychiatric hospitalizations and a history of psychotic symptoms, mania and depression, as well as a formal diagnosis of schizoaffective disorder. At the time of the consultation, he still heard some voices in the background but they were not really bothersome. His mood was a bit depressed but not too bad. He was on two different antipsychotic medications, two different mood stabilizers, two different antidepressants, a sleeping pill, and an antianxiety medication. Yet he had no clear sense of what was working, what was needed, and what was making him so tired.

He had stopped taking all medication when he was hospitalized for a manic episode 18 months earlier. He had a history of having been on many different medications, none of which had been very effective, although this was complicated because of his history of not taking medication very consistently. Because he was so agitated at the time that he entered the hospital, he was initially started on sodium valproate (Depakote) and risperidone (Risperdal). He continued to be agitated and manic, and after 2 days, quetiapine (Seroquel) was added in increasing doses. The mania continued and 5 days later, lithium carbonate was added. He was discharged after an 8-day admission; by that point, he was on two mood stabilizers, two antipsychotic medications, and a sleeping pill. At that point he became depressed, and an SSRI and bupropion (Wellbutrin) were both started. (Lamotrigine was considered but he did not take medication consistently enough for this to be considered a safe medication to try.) His primary care physician added diazepam (Valium) because he complained of ongoing anxiety.

There are times when starting a combination or making two changes at the same time does make sense. If you are very depressed and not able to sleep, sometimes taking a sleeping pill for a few days at the same time that you start an antidepressant may allow your sleep to regularize before the antidepressant has time to work, and the improvement in sleep may provide major help. There can be some confusion about whether the improvement is from better sleep or from the antidepressant, but if the sleeping pill is discontinued after a few days or so, the benefit from a short-term use of the sleeping pill may be worth it. A person who has psychotic symptoms associated with a severe depression will respond better to a combination of an antipsychotic medication and an antidepressant. It may be that the antipsychotic medication can be discontinued after the psychotic symptoms clear up, but there is good research support for using the combination from the beginning.

As a general rule, except for those specific combinations that have research support for combined use from the beginning, you are more likely to end up on an effective medication or combination of medications if you make one medication change at a time, give that change time to work, and then work with your physician to decide on the next step.

5. COMBINE MEDICATION WITH OTHER WAYS TO IMPROVE THE PROBLEM

Psychiatric medication can help, but medication alone is almost never enough. People who come in depressed or anxious, are not sleeping, or are obsessing, are almost always disappointed when they plan to take a medication and then wait for it to work. They find that the medication does not work at all, or does not work enough, or does not work nearly as much as they had hoped. They often try one medication after another, looking for a medication that will work well enough for them to get their lives back. While some people do have dramatic results from medication, for the most part medication can only help a person work on changing the parts of their lives that had been too hard to change without medication.

What do you want to be different in your life? What could you do to make these differences happen? How can medication help you to begin these changes?

> Example: Lucinda is so depressed that it is impossible for her to think about meeting friends, exercising, or even going over to her parents' home for dinner. The target symptoms that she developed for the medication included the following:
> - Crying less;
> - Getting out of the house to do some exercise at least once a day, even if this is initially just a walk around the block; and
> - Having contact with either a friend or family member at least every other day.

Note that while the first target, crying less, is not something that Lucinda has active control over, the other two targets—forcing herself to exercise every day and to have contact with family or friends—requires that she force herself to do these things. The medication, if it is really helping, may make this possible but she also has to be willing to exert effort to make this happen. There is a fine line between expecting too much of someone who is depressed or expecting too much of yourself and increasing your own sense of guilt, and not pushing yourself to try. If Lucinda cannot push herself to meet these targets, it may be that the medication is not working, that the targets were too difficult, or any number of other reasons. It is not her fault if she cannot accomplish these goals. At the same time, if she is going to recover from her depression she is going to have to push herself to behave in different ways, not because she feels like doing it or finds it easy, but because it is what will help her overcome her depression. It is not the medication that is overcoming her depression; instead, the medication, if it is working, can help her overcome her depression.

This "dialectic," the tension of it not being your fault if you cannot do it and your responsibility to do it anyway, has been best developed in a treatment approach called dialectical behavioral therapy (DBT). People who recover from depression, anxiety, schizophrenia, or just about anything else need to take active roles in their own recoveries.

6. AVOID ALCOHOL AND OTHER SUBSTANCES

I have already addressed the frequent overlap between mental health disorders and substance abuse. The overlap is common and understandable. It also makes treatment much more difficult. A person who is depressed is unlikely to get much benefit from antidepressants if he continues to drink heavily. The impact of the alcohol will outweigh any possible benefit from the medication. Similarly, a person is unlikely to stabilize his sleep problem, no matter what medication he takes, as long as he continues to abuse drugs. A person may feel that his medication did not work, but the reality is that the ongoing substance abuse will make it impossible to figure out whether the medication would have worked. Avoiding the use of drugs and alcohol, at least during the period of the medication trial, can give you important information about how well the medication might help.

10

Working With Your Doctor

You and your physician need to come up with a common understanding of your problem before you can decide on the best solutions. If one part of the solution is to take a medication, you need to jointly determine what medication makes the most sense. Without a common understanding of the problem, you and your physician are likely to go off in different directions, and it will be much more difficult to get a medication or any other treatment that will work for you. An important part of coming up with the right medication for the right problem is having the right communication with your doctor. You need to explain your problem accurately in the very limited time that is available during your medical appointment. Your physician needs to understand the problem that you are describing, when he or she may think about problems in a very different way than you do. This includes both you and your physician agreeing on the most important target symptoms for the medication and what side effects would be most difficult for you to tolerate. The decision must also include consideration of what you have heard about the various medications and the experience that your physician has had with various medications. After all of this, a medication is chosen and the prescription is written.

This entire process happens in a very limited period of time, between two people who do not know each other very well, and who often have very different concerns. If the process goes well, you come away with a medication that might help and that you are willing to take. If the process does not go well, you are given a medication that you are not willing to take or that is not likely to help the problem you are most concerned about, or it may be a medication that has more risk or side effects than you are willing to tolerate. The physician has the power to decide what medication is prescribed. You have the power to decide whether the prescribed medication is actually taken.

Just as there are ways that your physician can make this process more difficult or more effective, so, too, there are things that you can do to make it more likely that you and your physician will jointly come up with an effective solution to your problem, whether the solution is a medication or something else. Before your appointment with your physician, you should do (and prepare for) the following:

1. Develop a list of your priorities: What are your most important concerns, and what is most important about each of these concerns?
2. Write down your priority list, and note what you most want to tell your physician about each concern.
3. Practice being brief and to the point: The time with your physician is likely to be very limited.
4. Decide on a friend or support person to bring to your appointment with your doctor.
5. Ask your doctor to write down instructions.
6. Find accurate sources of information.
7. Ask questions.
8. Look for areas of agreement during the appointment: Think about where the communication is going well, and be aware of areas where you and your physician are not hearing each other.

1. Develop a List of Priorities

Every problem cannot be the most important problem to address first. It can be difficult to figure out what problem in a long list of problems is most important to focus on first, and what is a bit less important. Actually, you may have a number of problems that are all very important and that need to be addressed. Real people do not develop one problem at a time. Someone may be trying to cope with a depression, financial problems, the need to get a new apartment, gaining weight, getting older, wanting a girlfriend, wanting a new job, his mother's recent hospitalization, a fight with his sister, worries about his son who is abusing drugs, a car that seems to be needing a new transmission that he cannot afford, and peeling paint in his apartment. All of these are real issues, and all of them are important. They are all connected in the sense that all of them are likely to be contributing to his depression.

How could he focus on one thing and not be equally worried about all of the others? At the same time, it is easy to get so overwhelmed by the number of different concerns that none of them get enough attention to lead to a real understanding and an effective plan for what to do. It is easy for peeling paint and a fight with a sister to get on the list along with a clinical depression and concerns about a son's drug abuse. It can be difficult to know how to prioritize problems.

Different people will have differing priorities. For one person, a fight with a sister is a problem that must be addressed, because this sister is a very important part of his already precarious support system. For someone else, a fight with a sister is upsetting but may not be the most important issue to focus on at the time. For a person with diabetes and other health-related problems, weight gain may be on the high-priority end of the list. For another person, paying attention to eating right and exercise may be an important part of feeling in more control of other parts of her life. Each person will make a different priority list. What is important is that such a list should be made. You cannot concentrate on everything all at once.

Start with what is most important, and work down to the issues that are important but lower on the priority list. A clear list of priorities—what you really need to focus on now—can be the beginning of a more effective change process. Establish a focus so that you can come up with a change plan. Not everything is equally important. Other issues that are not currently the highest priority may need to be dealt with at some point, but they cannot all be focused on at the same time.

Consider what problems seem to be connected with each other and need to be responded to as an integrated whole, and what problems can be put off until later. Is getting a new job something that is required now, as something that would be required in any serious attempt to deal with your depression, or is this something that is a less pressing priority?

A clear listing of priorities can help determine whether medication is likely to play an important role in the change process. Once your priorities are clear, ask how or if a medication can help with the highest priority problem on your list.

2. WRITE DOWN YOUR PRIORITY LIST

Once you have decided on your list of priorities, write the list down, starting with the most important concern. It is one thing to prioritize one's issues and decide to focus on what is most important. It is another thing to actually be able to keep to this list during a doctor visit. This is true even for those of us who are doctors ourselves. We know that the time is very short, and there is a lot of information to cover and questions to ask in a few minutes. It is very easy to become flustered and anxious. All of a sudden, that question that was most important gets forgotten, and a question that is much less important is blurted out. Without a written list, it becomes very easy to walk out of the visit feeling that you ran out of time before you said what was most important.

Writing down a list of questions and concerns accomplishes a number of things. First, it requires that you have actually made your own priority list. You can feel that you know what is more important and what is less essential, but until you try and write it down you may be less clear about this than you think. Second, it helps to make sure that you start with the highest items on your priority list. Third, it will help you to keep moving through the appointment. If you have six items on your list, you will have a sense that you cannot spend all of your time on the first two items unless they are so important that the other items can be left out. Finally, having a list will help your physician also keep somewhat structured and move through the concerns based on your list, rather than his own list of questions.

Without the structure of a list, it is easy for an appointment to become structured more by the physician's concerns than by yours. He or she has his or her list of things to go over, and it is easy for the patient to become passive and just go along. The physician has the clinical chart to refer to, to jog memory. This is not to say that the physician's list is not important or can be disregarded, but your list is also important and having it written down increases the chances that your concerns will be addressed. Some of my patients bring in copies of their lists and hand them to me, so that I know right from the beginning of the appointment what they want addressed.

3. Practice Being Brief and to the Point

We can complain about how rushed our doctors are, we can wish it were different, and we can even get annoyed at physicians for their too-busy schedules. The reality is that a primary care physician may have 10 to 12 minutes for your appointment. Some of this must be spent reviewing your chart, reviewing labs, doing a physical exam, writing orders and a prescription, writing a clinical note, and so on, so the time available to understand your problem is very limited. A psychiatrist may have 15–25 minutes, including reviewing the chart, writing a note, and writing out a prescription. This is a luxury of time compared to the primary care physician's allotment but even so it is very brief. All of your concerns are important, but it is very unlikely that all of them will be covered during your appointment.

It is important to be as concise and focused as possible when you describe your problems; how you have coped with those problems, stressors, or responses to medication; and other parts of your life that directly bear on your problem. What information is most important for your doctor to know to work with you on a joint decision, and what is extraneous? Get to the point, stay on the point, think about what you most need to communicate, and practice staying focused just on that information.

This is much different than how we normally communicate. In a casual conversation, we wander around in our thinking, and even when we are focused we allow one idea to prompt an association to another idea. This can be useful and can provide very important information about both the primary problem and some possible solutions. It can also take up time that may not always be available. We often feel it is important to include all of the details about a potential problem. While this would be ideal, in reality this often means that time is spent on less important details, and more important details are omitted because time runs out. Physicians are trained to succinctly communicate just the facts that are needed for a specific decision. Time is always short and there is a premium on saying what needs to be said and nothing more. If you were to overhear two physicians talking with each other, or a nurse talking with a physician, you would overhear a very focused, almost abbreviated style of communication that is centered almost entirely on the problem at hand, and very little on the person with the problem. In our regular lives, our communication style is quite different.

Casual communication. *Example*: I have been depressed for quite a while, maybe a year or more. I have been depressed before but not like this. I am only coming in to see you now because my wife was getting frustrated with my moping around all of the time, and I guess I am getting tired of myself as well. I used to enjoy going out and horsing around with the kids, kicking a soccer ball around, playing touch football or whatever. We have always been a pretty active group, and with the boys now 12 and 14 it is a good age for me to do with them what my father never had time to do with me. Besides which, I kind of realize that my oldest is heading off to being a teenager and I expect this will change things. He is a really good kid, but I know how kids are and I get worried about the drugs and the girls and the booze that kids get into now. He spends a bunch of time up with his computer and just kind of "grunts" when I ask him what he is doing—I assume he is doing something for school or playing games but quite honestly I don't have a clue. I mean he could be going onto sex sites or learning how to blow up the world and I would not know anything about it. It's not like when I was a kid and my father knew everything I was doing. Anyway, I just find myself not doing much anymore. I don't play with the boys, don't want to take walks with my wife, and don't do anything. Work is a mess and I hate it, but I am not about to try and find a new job at my age in this kind of economy. I got a new supervisor about a year ago, some young "hot-shot" who does not need to listen to anything. I just keep my head down and do my job but it is not much fun. I can't concentrate and I just go through the motions waiting for the day to end. My boss keeps wanting to make points with his boss, so he keeps coming up with new ways to do things that we have either already tried and don't work, or just don't make any sense, or that he steals from someone else. I had an idea about how we could automate some of our stock ordering, and this guy takes the idea and passes it upstairs like it is his. So I sit and stew but it has all changed. I don't want you to think that it is just work. I could take this; I mean I have had ups and downs in my job before without getting knocked for this kind of loop. I would never kill myself, but I have even had thoughts of jumping off a bridge or something, crazy stuff that I would never do but it is scary to start thinking in that kind of direction. You probably remember, or maybe you don't, but actually I had this bad depression when I was in college and got really cruddy grades for a semester before pulling myself out of it. I almost had to drop out of school and once my folks found out about it all they got worried, and called our local doc, and I got put on this Prozac stuff but I was never convinced it did much good. I don't know if I need some drug or not. I can sleep OK but need a drink to drop off. Even my sex drive is shot—my fault. It is not like she pushes me away; just I don't have any urge to do anything with my wife. This has always been an up and down thing with us, but it had been getting better until I fell off this cliff . . . I don't know, maybe I need to go back onto Prozac but I feel like I should be able to do this without a drug.

Physician-to-physician communication. *Example*: John is a 43 y.o. man with a history of depression developing over the past year. He relates job stress and some concerns over his now 14 y.o. son, but he does not feel either of these is the cause of his depression. He was previously depressed when he was 20 and he seemed to respond well to Prozac, although he is not sure that the medication was the cause of his improvement. Currently he is anhedonic, with decreased concentration and libido, some suicidal ideation, and a vague plan of jumping off a bridge, but denies current suicidal intent. He has been using more alcohol than usual. He is willing to restart the fluoxetine that he had been on 20 years before during his last depressive period.

A casual conversational style includes the richness of a person's thinking and feeling and experience. Unfortunately, in the telling of this richness it is easy to get lost in the story and run out of time before the issue of suicide or alcohol use comes up, or before ambivalence about whether or not to take a medication can be discussed or whether the person can do something to help overcome his depression either along with or without medication. The richness of the details of one's life is important, but in the press of time, excess of detail and disorganization can keep other parts of the discussion from occurring.

The physician's abbreviated style can gloss over critically important issues and focus too much just on the medication decision or on other single elements of what is always a complicated human story. What did the person do to get over his

depression years ago, in addition to taking medication? Has he
had other periods of depression that does not get this severe?
What was going on at these times? What is going on with his
kids and his wife, and how does this fit into other parts of his
life or his family growing up? What has he typically done to stay
healthy, physically and psychologically, and is he doing these
things now? The issue is not to ignore all of the details but to
include those details that are most important in the time that is
realistically available.

4. BRING A FRIEND OR SUPPORT
PERSON TO YOUR APPOINTMENT

It can be very difficult to remember everything that has been
said during an appointment with your physician. There are
explanations of how the medication works, side effects, risks,
what to watch for, what to avoid or worry about, and more. A
support person is probably less anxious than you are, and this
can help. A support person is also a second pair of ears who you
can compare notes with after the appointment to help refresh
both of your memories. A support person can also help remind
you of what you wanted to say; you can also have a back-up
person to describe the benefits or side effects from a slightly different point of view. Finally, just having a support person present can help you feel less anxious. In a variety of ways, having
a support person present can help the "med check" be more
useful and less stressful.

If you are going to ask someone to join you for your medication appointment, it is important to choose the right person. You
want to think about who would support your point of view and
not just represent his or her own point of view. Having a support
person get into a fight with your physician, or go off on a tangent
that is not your concern, can get in the way rather than be a help.
If you are feeling that a medication might be useful, having a support person who is stridently against the use of medication might
make things more difficult. Similarly, you need to decide if you

want a support person who will support what you have to say or who will tend to "take over" and speak for you. You need to make sure that you are comfortable with this person hearing very confidential information about you. Questions about substance use, suicide, sexual behavior, and medical concerns are all legitimate parts of a medication appointment, and you want to make sure you are comfortable talking about these and other issues in front of your support person.

Inviting a support person into an appointment with a physician is the norm in many parts of the world, but it is somewhat unusual in mainstream American culture, especially if the visit is with a psychiatrist. For an appointment with other physicians, especially if the appointment is about a serious illness, the presence of a spouse or support person is increasingly common. It is now common for a spouse or close friend or sibling to come in with a patient to discuss surgery or options for cancer treatment, and diabetes educators commonly ask the patient to bring in a support person. The presence of a support person is still uncommon when seeing a psychiatrist. There is a feeling that psychiatric issues require more confidentiality than other serious medical problems. Perhaps most important, there is a long tradition of psychiatric treatment, at least in the United States, as a treatment where an individual is seen alone. Inviting a support person into a session that is not family therapy or couples therapy does not fit into the concept of normal psychiatric practice.

It is possible that a psychiatrist could become uncomfortable with the idea of a support person being present, and there may be times when a physician will ask a parent or sibling or spouse to leave, so that the issues of the patient and the support person can be clearly distinguished. A person can be so overwhelmed by the support person that his or her own needs become muffled. It is also possible that a physician could become defensive with a second person in the room. One of my patients asked to bring in his attorney, which left me feeling discomforted. However, it was still his session, and within limits he could use the time as he felt best.

5. ASK YOUR DOCTOR TO WRITE DOWN INSTRUCTIONS

Emergency rooms now commonly give patients written instructions about what medications they should take, what side effects they should look for, and where and when they should go for a follow-up. Often, instructions that seem clear during the appointment can be very hard to remember the next day or even the next hour. Pharmacies regularly provide written information about medications. There is information on the Internet about all medications, including their uses and side effects, although it can be difficult to determine what Internet information is accurate and what is not. At the same time, it can be difficult to remember how to take medications and what else you should do in addition to taking the medication. Are you supposed to take the medication in the morning or in the evening? Do you need to take it with food, or without? When are you supposed to get your next blood test? What was that rash or side effect that your doctor said to watch out for? These and other questions are commonly confused and misremembered.

Writing down instructions is always good practice, but it is not commonly done. It takes time when time is at a premium. Physicians are not used to writing instructions down. They write out a prescription, and there is a sense that this is enough. It can be hard for the physician to figure out what needs to be written down. Not everything can be written, and what one patient wants or needs is very different from what another person needs. At the same time, asking for written instructions about those things that are most important can be very useful, and it is something that you can ask for.

6. FIND ACCURATE SOURCES OF INFORMATION

There is a lot of information now available, on the Internet, from the pharmacy, from friends, from your doctor, from books, or from popular magazines. It can be very hard to know what to believe or how to weigh potentially competing sources of information. The personal story from a friend, about either how well a medication helped or some horrific side effect, tends to be remembered and given more weight. The direct experience of one person, whether good or bad, is more influential. Ads, on TV or in magazines, can be very convincing, but by providing simplistic and one-sided information they can actually confuse complicated decisions. Books can be useful but can also be out-dated, and each book, even my book on psychopharmacology, is written by someone with his or her own point of view. Pharmacists commonly provide information that is accurate and up-to-date, but it can be overwhelming; the pharmacists' printouts tend to discuss the medication itself, rather than how the medication fits into the context of your life and your problem.

One of the most common sources of information is the Internet. The problem is that accurate sites and inaccurate sites can look the same. There is no such thing as value-free information. All information is influenced by the bias and values of its authors, and few Internet sites clearly discuss the biases of the authors. It can be difficult to figure out if a site is hosted by a Scientologist (who tends to view medication as unnecessary) or by someone who is a fervent believer in the advantage of medication. A site hosted by the "APA" can be connected to the American Psychiatric Association or the American Psychological Association: these are two very dissimilar organizations with differing views on the value of medication. Even Internet sites that are generally considered an accurate source of information, such as www.nami.org, the website for the National Alliance for Mental Illness, tend to be somewhat "pro-medication." The fact that this orientation agrees with my personal views does not obviate the fact that values and biases are present in any source of information.

If there are no neutral or "value-free" sources of medication, what can you do? First, be aware that all sources of information have their own biases. This is not a reason not to listen to this information, but you should ask what the biases are. Second, be aware that some information is better than others. A single case, even the case of a friend, provides less information than a study done of many people. A statement about "this medication does" or "this medication does not" is less convincing than a research study that systematically examines the impact on many patients. A study where patients are randomly assigned to different treatments is much more convincing because it looks back at the experience of patients who happened to be treated in various ways, although the different outcomes may be related to the differences between patients rather than their varying treatments. This does not mean that every patient must be an expert in the methodology of research studies, but it would help to have some knowledge. Short of this, ask about the source of information and be willing to be just a bit skeptical. Information is a good thing and it is a critical part of making a good decision, but not all information is created equally.

7. ASK QUESTIONS

Ask questions. Listen for the answers, and ask the same questions again if you do not remember the answers or are confused by some part of the answers. It can be hard to ask questions. We have already discussed the very limited time that is available for an appointment with a physician. The structure of the appointment tends to leave the patient in a "passive mode," with the physician structuring the agenda and doing most of the talking. It is common for a patient to go into an appointment full of things that he or she wants to ask about, and then leave the appointment having not asked any questions at all, wondering "what happened"? Physicians also behave in ways that make asking questions more difficult. Most of the time, this is unconsciously done by physicians, but it can happen even with those doctors who try to be open and inviting of questions. Sometimes physicians can get so busy or so distracted that they may either ignore or just not hear questions that a patient may ask. Often, the appointment goes along at a fast clip until it is abruptly terminated, with the doctor writing a prescription and indicating that time is up. If the patient is waiting for a good time to ask questions, there may never be a good time and the questions may never be asked. Patients are often worried that their questions are stupid, that they should already know the answers, or that the question was asked during the last visit and not completely understood or remembered. At times, the questions are about something embarrassing, be it sexual function or weight gain or leaking urine.

8. BE AWARE OF COMMUNICATION

All relationships have good parts and more difficult parts. There are some topics that are easier to talk about, and there are other topics that are much more difficult to discuss. On some days a conversation with a friend goes well, and on other days, because one of you is tired or distracted, the conversation does not go as easily. Conversations with your doctor are likely to also have good and bad elements. It may be easy to discuss your difficulty with sleep, but it is more difficult when you try to discuss your diagnoses. It may be easy to talk about wanting to get a job, but you could feel annoyed by your physician's focus on your alcohol use, or your physician may become annoyed about your belief that acupuncture has been useful.

Even with a physician whom you feel listens well and respects your views, there will likely be some conversations that leave you feeling that you have not been heard. The important issue is to not give up. If you have generally had a good relationship with your doctor, it is important that an area of disagreement not get in the way of working together.

Example: Susan had been working with the same physician and the same treatment team for 6 years. Her mood was frequently up and down. She was often suicidal, and at times became so upset that she would cut herself in an effort to calm down. There were times when a brief hospitalization was a useful "time-out" that would allow her to center herself and get back in control. There were other occasions, however, where she would get more and more upset in the hospital, ending up in seclusion or restraints. Both Susan and her treatment team agreed that at times a hospitalization was useful, and at other times it seemed to make things worse. There was some disagreement about how to decide when to use the hospital, and when not to. Susan came in for an emergency appointment and then demanded hospitalization. She had recently had two respite admissions that had not been helpful. When the treatment team refused to support another hospitalization, Susan fired her physician, fired her treatment team, and maintained that no one was listening to her.

Even with a physician with whom you communicate well, there will inevitably be areas of disagreement. It is important to be able to talk about both disagreements and areas of agreements.

Example: Ralph was generally doing well in most areas of his life. His psychotic symptoms were under good control. He enjoyed his part-time job and was generally stable in his life. His physician kept bringing up both his smoking and his weight every visit. He realized that his physician meant well, but it made him feel bad about himself and just got him upset. It got to the point where he did not want to even see his doctor because he knew how the discussion would go. With the help of his case manager, Ralph was able to describe to his doctor how upset he was at being lectured about his weight and his smoking. In return, his doctor was able to talk with Ralph about how well he felt Ralph was doing, and how concerned he was about what he was doing to his health. In addition, his doctor talked about how he believed that Ralph could do things to become healthier, that he could start by taking walks with a friend and go from drinking regular soda to diet soda. The physician was better able to understand how sensitive Ralph was about his weight, and Ralph was able to get some sense that maybe he could do things to feel healthier.

11

What Else Can You Do In Addition To Taking Medication?

Medications can be very helpful in the treatment of many psychiatric disorders, but this does not mean they are the only thing that can be helpful. If you are hurting or anxious or depressed, you want some way to feel better rapidly. It may feel as though medication is the only solution, or at least the only fast solution, to feeling better. It is important to ask what else you can do, either along with medication or instead of medication, to stay well, to handle the current crisis, and to feel better.

One problem is that it is hard for any of us to be at our most creative about solving a problem when we are anxious or depressed or in pain. Often, there are strategies that have worked for us in the past or that we have heard about but that we do not consider because we get so focused on one solution, be it medication or something else. There are a number of questions that can help you to rethink a wider array of potential strategies to cope with your current problem.

1. What has helped you stay well in the past?
2. When you have felt bad in the past, what has helped you to feel better?
3. What do you think is adding to your current bad feeling?
4. What do you think you could do to help yourself feel a little bit better, or at least feel a little less bad?

5. What keeps you from doing these things that you know might help?
6. How can you change your own thinking patterns in ways that might help?
7. What risks are worth taking?

One of the problems is that you already know all of this. You know, or with a few minutes of thought can rapidly remember, what has helped you stay well in the past, what has helped you feel better when you feel bad, what may be making the problem more difficult, and all of the rest. The real problem is deciding how to remember and to use problem-solving strategies that you know but are not using. For the most part, the solution does not necessarily mean learning new behaviors but using those behaviors you already know.

Write your ideas down. Make written lists of what you already know, what you need to do, and what you need to change. When we are calm and rational and when we are feeling pretty good, it is easy to be smart and organized and to remember what we need to do. When we are upset, depressed, anxious, scared, angry, or are otherwise in distress, all of this logical thinking becomes much more difficult. Parts of your own history, decisions that you have made, and what you know about yourself are completely forgotten when you are upset. At difficult times, you will not remember the commitments of what you have promised yourself about how you will behave in specific situations. Even simple coping strategies that you know will work are forgotten or avoided when you are upset. So write them down. Make lists. Put simple statements that you want to remember onto 3 x 5 cards that you can stick in your pocket, or hang a list on your refrigerator so that you will see it in the course of your day. You need a way to jog your memory, to keep conscious of what you know and what you have decided.

When we are feeling calm and organized, we think with our cortex, the smart part of our brain. When we are upset, angry, depressed, or scared, we think with the more primitive parts of our brain that operate on instincts and emotions. We need to find ways to keep our cortex turned on, and written lists or other memory prompts can help. One person I worked with put a number of simple statements onto small, laminated cards and every morning she would select one to attach to her keychain. This process of selecting her thought for the day, and then having it on her keychain as a constant reminder, was her way to stay in control of her own thinking, her own memories, and her own behavior.

1. WHAT HAS HELPED YOU STAY WELL IN THE PAST?

Most of us have a variety of activities that help us to stay healthy. Some of these activities are conscious; we do them specifically because we know they are good for us. This might include healthy eating, exercise, limiting our alcohol use, or trying to keep to a regular sleep cycle. Some of these activities are closely connected to staying healthy, but we do not consciously do these activities for this reason. We stay connected to our friends, find reasons to get out of our homes, listen to music, and engage in activities that we enjoy and that make us laugh. Often, these activities allow us to feel productive and creative. We draw, or paint, or journal, or write poetry, or work in a scrapbook. These are activities that we enjoy and that keep us connected to the world. Besides being activities that we enjoy, these are activities that can keep us healthy.

It can be difficult to continue these activities just when we need them the most. When we are feeling depressed or anxious or overwhelmed, we too often stop those activities that have helped us to stay healthy in the past. Most of us have gone through better periods, and also more difficult periods. When we start feeling bad, we often stop doing just those things that help us to feel better. We do not have the energy or motivation, or we just want to stay away from other people, or we feel too anxious and overwhelmed to continue activities that were fun in the past but now are just too much to consider.

It can be very helpful to ask yourself what you were doing differently when you were feeling better. Were you spending more time exercising, spending more time with friends, or doing more activities that were enjoyable? Were you working at a different job, living with your family, or living alone? Going back to the way that you were living when you were feeling better, or going back to activities that you used to enjoy, will not necessarily cause you to feel better. On the other hand, it may be worth trying. Often a person who is depressed or anxious or otherwise hurting stops doing the things that she used to. If you used to enjoy being part of a softball team, going to movies, playing cards, or spending time with friends, what has caused you to stop these activities?

A person in distress often feels that he does not "want" to spend time with friends or does not feel like reading or painting or exercising. An alternative approach is to ask what the "healthy" thing is to do, rather than what you "feel" like doing. Doing the healthy thing may be very different from doing what you feel like doing.

2. When You Have Felt Bad in the Past, What Has Helped You Feel Better?

Most of us have gone through periods of feeling overwhelmed or depressed or anxious. It would be unusual for this to be the first time you were feeling bad. So how did you overcome your bad feelings? Most of us have a variety of things that we do to calm ourselves or feel better. We listen to music, take a walk, call a friend, or write in a journal. Each of us has a mental list of how we can feel better when we are feeling bad. The problem occurs when the things on the list, the "normal" things we do to feel better, do not work. Then we give up on them entirely.

Actually there are at least two different ways that our common ways of coping "do not work." It may be that we try our normal coping activities and we still feel bad. Often, while we are doing the activity—while we are listening to music or talking to our friends—we do feel a bit better, but the good feeling is not enough or it does not last. As soon as we stop, we go back to feeling as badly as we did before. This does not mean that these ways of coping are not working. Often we feel even worse when we give up trying to do them. Even if a coping behavior is not enough, if it is helping some it is probably worth continuing it. If listening to music or talking to a friend helps even for a short period of time, this is still better than not feeling better at all. If drawing or taking a walk still leaves you feeling depressed or scared, this may still be better than not even having a brief break from the bad feeling.

A somewhat different problem occurs when you do not have the energy or motivation to even try those behaviors that have been fun or relaxing in the past. It does not feel like you want to do those activities, or you cannot imagine being able to force yourself to even try. This inability to motivate yourself can be a huge problem. After all, if the basic problem is lack of motivation, it is hard to motivate yourself to change this. It can be useful to change the question from "what do I feel like doing?" to "what would be healthy or helpful for me to do?" People are often aware of what the healthy choice is, even if it is not the choice that they feel like making. We take medication that does not taste good because we want to get better from an illness. We must act in the same way in that you should force yourself to take a walk or call a friend or start a painting, not because you want to or feel like it but because you know that it will help you in your self-treatment.

There are tricks that might help. Involve another person whom you trust, who can remind you of your decision and your commitment. Hang a calendar in some public place in your home, and mark it every day that you do some coping behavior that you have decided might help. This is a visual motivator and a reminder to engage in coping behavior. It is a way to remind the smart part of your brain, the part that is turned off when you are most upset, to turn back on and start taking more control.

3. What Do You Think Is Adding to Your Feeling Bad?

At times, it is obvious why we are feeling bad. We are out of money, or have no friends, or hate our jobs, or are in physical pain. Even when the cause of our distress is obvious, it is rarely the complete story. If we are honest with ourselves, we can see that we start feeling sorry for ourselves because we are out of money and this feeling adds to the distress, or we start obsessing about how much we hate our jobs so that we carry it around with us even when we are not at work. We may not know exactly why we are depressed, but if we are honest we acknowledge that staying alone in a dark room is probably not helping. We may not know why we are having panic attacks, but giving into the fear of having another attack to the extent that we are afraid to leave the house is also not helping us improve our quality of life.

Often, our own behavior is part of the current problem, even if it was not what initially caused the problem. For example:

> "I was feeling so bad that I started drinking alcohol every night, and now I cannot stop drinking."
>
> "I was so depressed for so long that it became scary to even hope that I could feel good again, because I did not want to be disappointed."
>
> "I could not get myself to do any of the things that I wanted and needed to, like applying for a new job, so I just smoked dope every night."

Make a list (a written list is often much more effective) of all of the things that you are doing that could be making the current problem worse. This may include what caused the problem, but it may include behaviors that are making the problem worse even if the problem was initially caused by something else entirely. It may include some behaviors that you are willing to change, and others that you do not want to change. It may include some behaviors that you would like to change but have no idea how to do so.

For example, you may have become depressed because you lost your job and have been left with little money and even less self-esteem. The more you tried to look for work, the worse you felt so at some point you just gave up looking. On reflection, you decide that none of your behaviors caused your feelings of depression—the depression started when you were laid off. On the other hand, you have been very irritable with your friends and your parents, which has caused them to stay away, leaving you feeling isolated. You may be staying up all night watching TV, which leaves you tired and out of sync with the world. You have gotten into the "habit" of thinking that your current predicament will never change, that even things you used to think of as "good" are actually bad, and you are thinking very negative thoughts about yourself. You find that you are constantly criticizing yourself, calling yourself stupid or lazy or ugly. You may not be ready to change all of these behaviors, but at least you can be clear that what you are doing is making the situation worse.

This is not to blame you or anyone else for your depression or your anxiety or your fears. It is only to point out that even when you are dealing with a clearly biological illness, or reacting to a very real problem imposed on you from the real world, you are also a participant in how you are feeling. You can be part of the solution to overcoming these bad feelings. Even if you decide to take medication to help, that is your decision to make, and there are almost always other decisions in addition to the one about medication that you can make as well.

It may be easier to think about what to change once you figure out what things are making your situation worse. Write it down; make a list. It is important to be as honest as possible about such a list. Putting a behavior on the list does not commit you to changing it. It does allow you to look at it. At times, you can ask your friends or family what they think is making the current situation worse. It is always easy to point to those things outside of yourself that you cannot change. This exercise is to be clear about those things that you are doing and to consider how the ways that you are reacting are making things even harder.

4. What Do You Think You Could Do to Help Yourself Feel Better?

Once you have created the list of what is making things worse or helping to keep things bad, then you can decide what you are able to change and what you want to change. Some things may be more difficult than others. It may be almost impossible to go out with friends, but it may be possible to start taking walks. It may be too hard to start writing again, but it may be possible to sit on the corner of your bed and at least listen to music. Some things cannot change in isolation. For example, most people cannot just stop using alcohol without making other changes in their lives. If you drink with friends who will continue to drink, not drinking means changing who you spend time with. If drinking is how you use up time because you have nothing else to do, then not drinking requires that you find some other more productive and less damaging way to fill your time.

Put together a plan. Write it down with a timeline and dates. Start with things that you can really change. Get help from your family and friends to make the changes that you want to make. People often feel that they have to do it all alone. In reality, most change is much easier and much more likely to happen if you involve other people. Sometimes identifying who is on your personal support team is the first step toward change.

The idea is not to change everything: The idea is to change something (Minkoff & Cline, 2004). It is not to decide that you will wake up tomorrow and will yourself to feel great. Decide tomorrow that you will do one small thing that will help yourself to feel a bit better than you do now.

Some changes are more obvious than others. If you are staying alone in a dark room, then you may decide that you need to force yourself to get out. If you are drinking too much, you need to stop drinking. If you are avoiding all of your friends because you are too embarrassed to face them, you may need to get reconnected. How to actually do these things can be much more difficult than just writing the item down on a list. It is often very helpful to be very specific and very detailed about what step you want to take first. You may decide to talk a walk around the block, or you might e-mail a very short note to a friend or call your brother. The idea is to start with some kind of change. One change might be going to an AA meeting, even if you are just going for curiosity and have no real intention to stop drinking. You may want to pick up a self-help book about anxiety disorders or sleep disorders or depression in order to educate yourself and see what ideas other people have come up with. If a big change is too much to consider, find some small change that seems less overwhelming.

5. WHAT KEEPS YOU FROM DOING THESE THINGS THAT YOU KNOW MIGHT HELP?

We all have a long list of things we could do to improve the quality of our own lives, and most of the time we do very few of the things on that list. We "should" . . . eat healthier, exercise more, stay in touch with old friends, drink less alcohol, learn to be less scared, and the list goes on. If it were easy to change our own behaviors, we would have made all of these changes a long time ago. The reality is that change is hard. There are many reasons for this. We get in the habit of doing things a particular way. We do not have the energy to change. If we try to do something differently, it could go even worse. If we really try and it does not work, we could end up feeling worse than if we had not even tried. We do not know how to change or even how to think about beginning a change. We are too angry to change, and we want to hang on to our anger. We want to make sure that if we do change, someone else does not get "credit" for our change. We are feeling so hopeless that we are already convinced that change is impossible or will not help even if we try.

Change can make things better, but it can also make things worse. If we stop drinking alcohol, we may be unable to sleep, or we may feel even more anxious or lose our drinking buddies. If we try to go out of the house we may become even more anxious. If we try to exercise, even walking around the block, it may take the little amount of energy we have, and if we try and it does not help we will likely feel even more tired for no good reason.

There is almost always some very good reason to not change, to keep things just the same. Often, we try to push ourselves into a change, and our friends and family try to push us into a change, and the more there is a push from ourselves or from others the more stuck we become. Instead of getting pushed and pushing ourselves when this has not helped in the past, try making a list.

Start with a list of how you want your life to be. What would you like to be different? How would you like to spend time? How would you like to feel? If thinking about your ideal life is too hard, think about some part of your life that you would like to be better. Write it down.

Write down all of the reasons why change could make things worse. Write down how change would be difficult, or scary, or could end up leaving you in an even worse predicament. There are some very good reasons that keep you from making the changes that you have already identified as possibly being helpful. Instead of ignoring these reasons or trying to pretend they do not exist, be clear about all of them. Be specific. If your concern is that trying to reconnect with your brother could lead you to feeling even more rejected, try to figure out how realistic this is. What is your brother likely to say? If you are concerned that you will become even more anxious if you attempt to drive, try and be specific about what you would be anxious about and realize the nature of your biggest fear.

Think about the list of how you would like your life to be, and think about why change is so difficult, and try to balance these ideas out. It may be that the risk of change is so great that it is better to just give up and agree to stay the way you are. It may be that some of the risk of changing is less than we thought, or it may be that the way you are living your current life means that some risk is worth it. It may be that there could be ways to make a change easier. For example, you can invite a friend to do something with you rather than trying to do it alone, or you can try something for some set amount of time rather than feeling that any change has to be permanent and forever. Whatever you decide, it is your decision to make.

6. How Can You Change Your Own Thinking Patterns in Ways That Might Help?

We all get into the habit of thinking in particular ways. There are many ways to describe this, but one common experience is to think about the background thoughts that most people have most of the time. It is almost as though we have tapes playing in the backs of our minds. Sometimes we pay attention to these tapes, and sometimes they recede into the background so that we barely notice them. These "automatic thoughts" are part of our normal experience. Even when we do not pay much attention to these automatic thoughts, they can influence how we feel and how we react to the world. Sometimes these background thoughts can be helpful, supportive, or reflective. At other times they can be critical and can amplify our own anxiety and fear.

Think of a psychology experiment where you are asked to wear headphones for 30 minutes, and then rate your mood. If the voice in the headphones was critical and repeated your own worst fears, that you were stupid or that no one liked you or that you were going to get fired from your job, your mood at the end of the 30 minutes is very likely to be upset. On the other hand, if the voice in the headphones reinforced that you were smart, that your boss liked you, that your friends liked you, that you were a great person, then your mood is likely to lighten. There is no need for any part of this to be hidden. The voice in the headphones will influence your own mood even if you are completely aware that this is a psychology experiment and that the voices have nothing to do with you. Think how much more powerful the impact would be if it were your own voice and the voice expressed not the random thoughts of a stranger but your own worst fears or your own best hopes. In the same way, your automatic thoughts influence how you feel and how you react to the world.

It is very difficult to decide to feel happier, to feel less frightened, or to feel less anxious. We do not have much direct control over our own feelings. We do have control over what we choose to pay attention to. While you cannot decide to feel happier, you can decide to think about some wonderful afternoon you had, smelling the air of the afternoon and listening to the sounds that were present. You can decide to listen in your mind to your favorite piece of music, or you can remember the best meal you have eaten in the past month. If you focus on these pleasurable activities your mood will go up. In the same way, if you focus on your worst fears or some very negative event, your mood will go down. While you cannot directly control your mood, you can learn to control what you pay attention to.

Of course, controlling what you choose to think about is much more difficult than just deciding to change your thinking. For example, you cannot decide not to think about something. If you try to avoid thinking about pink elephants, you will think about them even more. Even if pink elephants were not in your thoughts before, the attempt to avoid thinking about them puts them into your thoughts. What you can do is to learn to focus your thoughts and your attention on positive experiences, on things you like and situations where you were able to do well. This, too, is much more difficult than just deciding to do it. The technical term for learning to take control of one's automatic thoughts is called cognitive behavioral therapy, and there are a number of self-help books that can be useful for learning how to do this on your own. Mindfulness is another technique that might help. Mindfulness refers to trying to stay very much in the immediate present rather than allowing yourself to dwell on fears, past failures, and future expectations. Other ways to achieve a similar effect include meditation or relaxation therapy.

It is, of course, difficult to change one's characteristic way of thinking about the world. If you are afraid that something bad might happen, it is natural to mull over the risk, to prepare yourself for it, to think about every possibility. At some point, this does not help but just reinforces the fear and the depression. If you have gone several nights without sleeping, the fear of not sleeping is what will be most likely to keep you from sleeping tonight. Yet as you prepare to get to bed it is difficult to not become anxious about whether you will or will not sleep, and then you become more and more anxious when this fear cycles into another night of insomnia. If you are so afraid of having another panic attack that you cannot leave your home or drive a car, the real possibility of another panic attack is always present so it can be difficult to determine when thinking about a fear is being realistic and when it is part of the problem. For many people, the focus on the fear and the negative has become the problem.

The bottom line is to become aware of your own automatic thoughts. Be aware of how these background thoughts influence your own mood and attitudes, and then learn to control your own attention. It is possible to learn how to control what one chooses to pay attention to. Pay less attention to your fears, anxieties, and thoughts of failure, and pay more attention to your hopes, accomplishments, and memories that feel good.

7. What Risks Are Worth Taking?

This is a book about the role of psychiatric medication in the treatment of human problems. As part of this discussion, it is important to understand how we hope a medication might help and to know what risks and side effects a medication can cause. All medications, without exception, come with some risk and with the potential for some side effects. We must also consider the risks of nonpharmacological attempts at change. What is the risk of trying something new, or working to behave in some different way, or changing one's characteristic way of thinking and reacting to the world? Finally, it is important to consider the risk of not changing, of not taking the risk of trying to make things better.

If the problem, if the fear or anxiety or insomnia or bad feeling, is not intruding into your life, then it may be reasonable to decide to avoid the risk of other changes. If, however, your problem and your symptoms are interfering with how you want to live your life, then the risk of trying something new may be less than the risk of continuing to live with the way things are now.

Medication is only one of the ways that you can try to change your life to be closer to what you would like it to be. At times, medication can be very effective, and it will allow other changes to occur that would be virtually impossible otherwise. At other times, medication can help other changes to occur, but it is only part, and perhaps a relatively small part, of what is needed. And with other problems and in other situations, we might desperately hope for some kind of pill that will solve the problem, when in reality medication may have little to offer.

Medication is not "good" or "bad." Medication has no intrinsic moral value. Medication is a tool that is either useful or not useful. It either allows us to change in ways that are helpful, or it does not. Medication either facilitates those other life changes that we very much want to make, or it can interfere by causing side effects or by causing us to focus so much on the medication that we do not pay attention to other ways that we can make our own lives better.

Medication List by Brand Name

Brand Name	Generic Name	Medication Type
Abilify	aripiprazole	antipsychotic: atypical
Abilify disc-melt	aripiprazole fast dissolve	antipsychotic: atypical
Adderall	amphetamine/ dextroamphetamine	ADHD/stimulant
Adderall XR	amphetamine/ dextroamphetamine	ADHD/stimulant
Akineton	biperiden	anti-Parkinson medication
Ambien	zolpidem	$gaba_A$ agonist/sleeping pill
Anafranil	clomipramine	tricyclic antidepressant used for OCD
Antabuse	disulfiram	treatment of alcohol dependence
Aricept	donepezil	Alzheimer's medication
Artane	trihexphenidyl	anti-Parkinson medication
Ascendin	amoxapine	tricyclic antidepressant
Ativan	lorazepam	benzodiazepine/antianxiety
Benadryl	diphenhydramine	anti-Parkinson medication

Brand Name	Generic Name	Medication Type
Buspar	buspirone	antianxiety
Campral	acamprosate	treatment of alcohol dependence
Carbatrol	carbamazepine	mood stabilizer
Catapres	clonidine	PTSD treatment
Celexa	citalopram	SSRI/SNRI antidepressant
Chantix	varenicline	smoking cessation
Clozaril	clozapine	antipsychotic: atypical
Cogentin	benztropine	anti-Parkinson medication
Concerta	methylphenidate	ADHD/stimulant
Cymbalta	duloxetine	SSRI/SNRI antidepressant
Cytomel	liothyronine	thyroid hormone: T3
	D-cycloserine	augments behavioral therapy
Dalmane	flurazepam	benzodiazepine/sleeping pill
Daytrana	methylphenidate patch	ADHD/stimulant
Depakote	divalproex sodium	mood stabilizer
Deplin	L-methylfolate	active metabolite of folic acid
Desoxyn	methamphetamine	stimulant
Desyrel	trazodone	sedating antidepressant used for sleep

Brand Name	Generic Name	Medication Type
Dolphine	methadone	treatment of opiate dependence
Effexor	venlafaxine	SSRI/SNRI antidepressant
Elavil	amitriptyline	tricyclic antidepressant
Emsam	selegiline patch	MAOI antidepressant
Eskalith	lithium	mood stabilizer
Exelon	rivastigmine	Alzheimer's medication
Fanapt	iloperidone	antipsychotic: atypical
FazaClo	clozapine	antipsychotic: atypical
Focalin	dexmethylphenidate	ADHD/stimulant
Geodon	ziprasidone	antipsychotic: atypical
Halcion	triazolam	benzodiazepine/sleeping pill
Haldol	haloperidol	antipsychotic: typical
Haldol decanoate	haloperidol long-acting injection	antipsychotic: typical
Invega	paliperidone	antipsychotic: atypical
Invega Sustenna	paliperidone long-acting injectin	antipsychotic: atypical, long-acting injection
Klonopin	clonazepam	benzodiazepine/antianxiety
Lamictal	lamotrigine	antidepressant/mood stabilizer
Latuda	lurasidone	antipsychotic: atypical

Brand Name	Generic Name	Medication Type
Lexapro	escitalopram	SSRI/SNRI antidepressant
Librium	chlordiazepoxide	benzodiazepine/antianxiety
Loxapine	loxitane	antipsychotic: unusual typical
Ludiomil	maprotiline	antidepressant
Lunesta	eszopiclone	$gaba_A$ agonist/sleeping pill
Luvox	fluvoxamine	SSRI/SNRI antidepressant
Lyrica	pregabalin	neurogenic pain/fibromyalgia
Marplan	isocarboxazid	MAOI antidepressant
Mellaril	thioridazine	antipsychotic: typical
Metadate	methylphenidate	ADHD/stimulant
Minipress	prazosin	PTSD treatment
Mirapex	pramipexole	restless legs syndrome
Moban	molindone	antipsychotic: unusual typical
Namenda	memantine	Alzheimer's medication
Nardil	phenelzine	MAOI antidepressant
Navane	thiothixene	antipsychotic: typical
Neurontin	gabapentin	neurogenic pain/fibromyalgia
Norpramin	desipramine	tricyclic antidepressant

Brand Name	Generic Name	Medication Type
Nuvigil	armodafinil	stimulant
Orap	pimozide	antipsychotic: typical
Pamelor	nortriptyline	tricyclic antidepressant
Parnate	tranylcypromine	MAOI antidepressant
Paxil	paroxetine	SSRI/SNRI antidepressant
Pristiq	desvenlafaxine	SSRI/SNRI antidepressant
Prolixin	fluphenazine	antipsychotic: typical
Prolixin Decanoate	fluphenazine long-acting injection	antipsychotic: typical
Prosom	estazolam	benzodiazepine/sleeping pill
Provigil	modafanil	stimulant
Prozac	fluoxetine	SSRI/SNRI antidepressant
Razadyne	galantamine	Alzheimer's medication
Remeron	mirtazapine	antidepressant; sedating
Requip	ropinirole	restless legs syndrome
Restoril	temazepam	benzodiazepine/sleeping pill
ReVia	naltrexone	treatment of alcohol dependence
Risperdal	risperidone	antipsychotic: atypical
Risperdal Consta	risperidone long-acting injection	antipsychotic: atypical

Brand Name	Generic Name	Medication Type
Risperdal M-tabs	risperidone fast dissolve tablets	antipsychotic: atypical
Ritalin	methylphenidate	ADHD/stimulant
Rozerem	ramelteon	sleeping pill
Saphris	asenapine	antipsychotic: atypical
Savella	milnacipran	fibromyalgia
Serax	oxazepam	benzodiazepine/hypnotic
Seroquel	quetiapine	antipsychotic: atypical
Seroquel XR	quetiapine long-acting	antipsychotic: atypical
Serzone	nefazodone	antidepressant
Sinequan	doxepin	tricyclic antidepressant
Sonata	zaleplon	$gaba_A$ agonist/sleeping pill
Stelazine	trifluoperazine	antipsychotic: typical
Strattera	atomoxetine	ADHD: not a stimulant
Suboxone	buprenorphine/naloxone	treatment of opiate dependence
Subutex	buprenorphine	treatment of opiate dependence
Surmontil	trimipramine	tricyclic antidepressant
Synthroid	levothyroxine	thyroid hormone: T4
Tegretol	carbamazepine	mood stabilizer
Tenex	guanfacine	PTSD treatment

Brand Name	Generic Name	Medication Type
Thorazine	chlorpromazine	antipsychotic: typical
Tofranil	imipramine	tricyclic antidepressant
Topamax	topiramate	treatment of alcohol dependence
Tranxene	clorazepate	benzodiazepine/antianxiety
Trileptal	oxcarbazepine	mood stabilizer
Trilifon	perphenazine	antipsychotic: typical
Valium	diazepam	benzodiazepine/antianxiety
Vistaril	hydroxyzine	sedating antihistamine
Vivactil	protriptyline	tricyclic antidepressant
Vivitrol	naltrexone long-acting injection	treatment of alcohol dependence
Vyvanse	lisdexamfetamine	ADHD/stimulant
Wellbutrin	bupropion/Bude-prion	antidepressant
Xanax	alprazolam	benzodiazepine/antianxiety
Xyrem	sodium oxybate	fibromyalgia
Zoloft	sertraline	SSRI/SNRI antidepressant
Zyprexa	olanzapine	antipsychotic: atypical
Zyprexa Relprev	olanzapine long-acting injection	antipsychotic: atypical long-acting injection
Zyprexa Zydis	olanzapine fast dissolve tablets	antipsychotic: atypical

Medication List by Generic Name

Generic Name	Brand Name	Medication Type
D-cycloserine		augments behavioral therapy
methamphet-amine	Desoxyn	stimulant
acamprosate	Campral	treatment of alcohol dependence
alprazolam	Xanax	benzodiazepine/antianxiety
amitriptyline	Elavil	tricyclic antidepressant
amoxapine	Ascendin	tricyclic antidepressant
amphetamine/ dextroamphet-amine	Adderall	ADHD/stimulant
amphetamine/ dextroamphet-amine	Adderall XR	ADHD/stimulant
aripiprazole	Abilify	antipsychotic: atypical
aripiprazole fast dissolve	Abilify Discmelt	antipsychotic: atypical
armodafinil	Nuvigil	stimulant
asenapine	Saphris	antipsychotic: atypical
atomoxetine	Strattera	ADHD: not a stimulant

Generic Name	Brand Name	Medication Type
benztropine	Cogentin	anti-Parkinson medication
biperiden	Akineton	anti-Parkinson medication
buprenorphine	Subutex	treatment of opiate dependence
buprenorphine/naloxone	Suboxone	treatment of opiate dependence
bupropion/budeprion	Wellbutrin	antidepressant
buspirone	Buspar	antianxiety
carbamazepine	Carbatrol	mood stabilizer
carbamazepine	Tegretol	mood stabilizer
chlordiazepoxide	Librium	benzodiazepine/antianxiety
chlorpromazine	Thorazine	antipsychotic: typical
citalopram	Celexa	SSRI/SNRI antidepressant
clomipramine	Anafranil	tricyclic antidepressant used for OCD
clonazepam	Klonopin	benzodiazepine/antianxiety
clonidine	Catapres	PTSD treatment
clorazepate	Tranxene	benzodiazepine/antianxiety
clozapine	Clozaril	antipsychotic: atypical
clozapine	FazaClo	antipsychotic: atypical
D-cycloserine		augments behavioral therapy
desipramine	Norpramin	tricyclic antidepressant

Generic Name	Brand Name	Medication Type
desvenlafaxine	Pristiq	SSRI/SNRI antidepressant
dexmethylphe-nidate	Focalin	ADHD/stimulant
diazepam	Valium	benzodiazepine/antianxiety
diphenhydramine	Benadryl	anti-Parkinson medication
disulfiram	Antabuse	treatment of alcohol dependence
divalproex sodium	Depakote	mood stabilizer
donepezil	Aricept	Alzheimer's medication
doxepin	Sinequan	tricyclic antidepressant
duloxetine	Cymbalta	SSRI/SNRI antidepressant
escitalopram	Lexapro	SSRI/SNRI antidepressant
estazolam	Prosom	benzodiazepine/sleeping pill
eszopiclone	Lunesta	$gaba_A$ agonist/sleeping pill
fluoxetine	Prozac	SSRI/SNRI antidepressant
fluphenazine	Prolixin	antipsychotic: typical
fluphenazine long-acting injection	Prolixin Decanoate	antipsychotic: typical
flurazepam	Dalmane	benzodiazepine/sleeping pill
fluvoxamine	Luvox	SSRI/SNRI antidepressant
gabapentin	Neurontin	neurogenic pain/fibromyalgia
galantamine	Razadyne	Alzheimer's medication

Generic Name	Brand Name	Medication Type
guanfacine	Tenex	PTSD treatment
haloperidol	Haldol	antipsychotic: typical
haloperidol long-acting injection	Haldol Decanoate	antipsychotic: typical
hydroxyzine	Vistaril	sedating antihistamine
iloperidone	Fanapt	antipsychotic: atypical
imipramine	Tofranil	tricyclic antidepressant
isocarboxazid	Marplan	MAOI antidepressant
L-methylfolate	Deplin	active metabolite of folic acid
lamotrigine	Lamictal	antidepressant/mood stabilizer
levothyroxine	Synthroid	thyroid hormone: T4
liothyronine	Cytomel	thyroid hormone: T3
lisdexamfetamine	Vyvanse	ADHD/stimulant
lithium	Eskalith	mood stabilizer
lorazepam	Ativan	benzodiazepine/antianxiety
loxitane	Loxapine	antipsychotic: unusual typical
lurasidone	Latuda	antipsychotic: atypical
maprotiline	Ludiomil	antidepressant
memantine	Namenda	Alzheimer's medication
methadone	Dolphine	treatment of opiate dependence

Generic Name	Brand Name	Medication Type
methamphet-amine	Desoxyn	stimulant
methylphenidate	Concerta	ADHD/stimulant
methylphenidate	Metadate	ADHD/stimulant
methylphenidate	Ritalin	ADHD/stimulant
methylphenidate patch	Daytrana	ADHD/stimulant
milnacipran	Savella	fibromyalgia
mirtazapine	Remeron	antidepressant; sedating
modafanil	Provigil	stimulant
molindone	Moban	antipsychotic: unusual typical
naltrexone	ReVia	treatment of alcohol dependence
naltrexone long-acting injection	Vivitrol	treatment of alcohol dependence
nefazodone	Serzone	antidepressant
nortriptyline	Pamelor	tricyclic antidepressant
olanzapine	Zyprexa	antipsychotic: atypical
olanzapine fast-dissolve tablets	Zyprexa Zydis	antipsychotic: atypical
olanzapine long-acting injection	Zyprexa Relprev	antipsychotic: atypical long-acting injection
oxazepam	Serax	benzodiazepine/sleeping pill
oxcarbazepine	Trileptal	mood stabilizer
paliperidone	Invega	antipsychotic: atypical

Generic Name	Brand Name	Medication Type
paliperidone long-acting injectin	Invega Sustenna	antipsychotic: atypical, long-acting injection
paroxetine	Paxil	SSRI/SNRI antidepressant
perphenazine	Trilifon	antipsychotic: typical
phenelzine	Nardil	MAOI antidepressant
pimozide	Orap	antipsychotic: typical
pramipexole	Mirapex	restless legs syndrome
prazosin	Minipress	PTSD treatment
pregabalin	Lyrica	neurogenic pain/fibromyalgia
protriptyline	Vivactil	tricyclic antidepressant
quetiapine	Seroquel	antipsychotic: atypical
quetiapine long-acting	Seroquel XR	antipsychotic: atypical
ramelteon	Rozerem	$gaba_A$ agonist/sleeping pill
risperidone	Risperdal	antipsychotic: atypical
risperidone fast-dissolve tablets	Risperdal M-tabs	antipsychotic: atypical
risperidone long-acting injection	Risperdal Consta	antipsychotic: atypical
rivastigmine	Exelon	Alzheimer's medication
ropinirole	Requip	restless legs syndrome
selegiline patch	Emsam	MAOI antidepressant

Generic Name	Brand Name	Medication Type
sertraline	Zoloft	SSRI/SNRI antidepressant
sodium oxybate	Xyrem	fibromyalgia
temazepam	Restoril	benzodiazepine/sleeping pill
thioridazine	Mellaril	antipsychotic: typical
thiothixene	Navane	antipsychotic: typical
topiramate	Topamax	treatment of alcohol dependence
tranylcypromine	Parnate	MAOI antidepressant
trazodone	Desyrel	sedating antidepressant used for sleep
triazolam	Halcion	benzodiazepine/sleeping pill
trifluoperazine	Stelazine	antipsychotic: typical
trihexphenidyl	Artane	anti-Parkinson medication
trimipramine	Surmontil	tricyclic antidepressant
varenicline	Chantix	smoking cessation
venlafaxine	Effexor	SSRI/SNRI antidepressant
zaleplon	Sonata	$gaba_A$ agonist/sleeping pill
ziprasidone	Geodon	antipsychotic: atypical
zolpidem	Ambien	$gaba_A$ agonist/sleeping pill

Resource List

BOOKS

Adult ADHD

Kelly, Kate, and Peggy Ramundo. *You Mean I'm Not Lazy, Stupid or Crazy?* New York: Scribner, 2006.

Safren, Steven, Susan Sprich, Carol Perlmand, and Michael Otto. *Mastering Your Adult ADHD: A Cognitive Behavioral Treatment Program Client Workbook.* New York: Oxford University Press, 2005.

Binge eating/anorexia

Fairburn, Christopher. *Overcoming Binge Eating.* New York, NY: Guilford, 1995.

Bipolar disorder

Basco, Monica Ramirez. *The Bipolar Workbook.* New York, NY: Guilford, 2005.

Copeland, Mary Ellen. *Living without Depression and Manic Depression.* Oakland, CA: New Harbinger, 1994.

Miklowitz, David. *The Bipolar Disorder Survival Guide.* New York, NY: Guilford, 2010.

Borderline disorder

McKay, Matthew, Jeffrey Wood, and Jeffrey Brantley. *The Dialectical Behavior Therapy Skills Workbook: Practical DBT Exercises for Learning Mindfulness, Interpersonal Effectiveness, Emotional Regulation, and Distress Tolerance.* Oakland, CA: New Harbinger, 2007.

Linehan, Marsha. *Skills Training Manual for Treating Borderline Personality Disorder*. New York, NY: Guilford, 1993.

Mason, Paul T., and Randi Kreger. *Stop Walking on Eggshells: Taking Your Life Back When Someone You Care About Has Borderline Personality Disorder*. (2nd ed.). Oakland, CA: New Harbinger, 2010.

Couples and family counseling

Christensen, Andrew, and Neil Jacobson. *Reconcilable Differences*. New York, NY: Guilford, 2002.

Glass, Shirley. *Not "Just Friends": Protect Your Relationship from Infidelity and Heal The Trauma of Betrayal*. New York, NY: Free Press, 2004.

Gottman, John, and Nan Silver. *The Seven Principles for Making Marriage Work*. New York, NY: Crown, 1999.

Johnson, Sue. *Hold Me Tight: Seven Conversations for a Lifetime of Love*. New York, NY: Little, Brown, 2008.

Snyder, Douglas, Donald Baucom, and Kristina Coop Gordon. *Getting Past the Affair: A Program to Help You Cope, Heal, and Move On—Together or Apart*. New York, NY: Guilford, 2007.

Dementia

Rabins, Peter, and Nancy Mace. *The 36-Hour Day: A Family Guide to Caring for People with Alzheimer Disease, Other Dementias, and Memory Loss in Later Life*. (4th ed.). Baltimore, MD: Johns Hopkins University Press.

Depression

Addis, Michael E., and Christopher R. Martell. *Overcoming Depression One Step at a Time*. Oakland, CA: New Harbinger, 2004.

Burns, David D. *The Feeling Good Handbook*. New York, NY: Plume, 1999.

Copeland, Mary Ellen. *The Depression Workbook*. Oakland, CA: New Harbinger, 2002.

Greenberger, Dennis, and Christine Padesky. *Mind over Mood*. New York, NY: Guilford, 1995.

Martell, Christopher R., Michael E. Addis, and Neil S. Jacobson. *Depression in Context: Strategies for Guided Action*. New York, NY: W. W. Norton, 2001.

General anxiety

Bourne, Edmund. *The Anxiety and Phobia Workbook.* Oakland, CA: New Harbinger, 2005.

Craske, Michelle G., and David H. Barlow. *Mastery of Your Anxiety and Worry: Workbooks.* New York: Oxford University Press, 2006.

Lejeune, Chad. *The Worry Trap: How to Free Yourself from Worry and Anxiety Using Acceptance and Commitment Therapy.* Oakland, CA: New Harbinger, 2007.

Hoarding

Neziroglu, Fugen, Jerome Bubrick, and Jose Yaryura Tobas. *Overcoming Compulsive Hoarding: Why You Save and How You Can Stop.* Oakland, CA: New Harbinger, 2004.

Insomnia

Epstein, Lawrence, with Steven Mardon. *A Good Night's Sleep.* New York, NY: McGraw-Hill, 2006.

Glovinsky, Paul, and Art Spielman. *The Insomnia Answer.* New York, NY: Perigee, 2006.

Kradow, Barry. *Turning Nightmares into Dreams.* Available at http://sleeptreatment.com/.

Mindfulness-based stress reduction (coping with depression, anxiety, pain, etc.)

Brach, Tara. *Radical Acceptance: Embracing Your Life With The Heart of a Buddha.* New York, NY: Bantam, 2004.

Forsyth, John P., and Georg H. Eifert. *The Mindfulness and Acceptance Workbook for Anxiety: A Guide for Breaking Free from Anxiety, Phobias, and Worry Using Acceptance and Commitment Therapy.* Oakland, CA: New Harbinger, 2008.

Hayes, Steven C. *Get Out of Your Mind and Into Your Life: The New Acceptance and Commitment Therapy.* Oakland, CA: New Harbinger, 2005.

Kabat-Zinn, Jon. *Full Catastrophe Living.* New York, NY: Delta, 1990.

McKay, Matthre, Jeffrey Wood, and Jeffrey Brantley. *The Dialectical Behavior Therapy Skills Workbook: Practical DBT Exercises for Learning Mindfulness, Interpersonal Effectiveness, Emotional Regulation and Distress Tolerance.* Oakland, CA: New Harbinger, 2007.

Stahl, Bob, and Elisha Goldstein. *A Mindfulness-Based Stress Reduction Workbook*. Oakland, CA: New Harbinger, 2010.

Williams, Mark, John Teasdale, Zindel Segal, and Jon Kabat-Zinn. *The Mindful Way Through Depression: Freeing Yourself from Chronic Unhappiness*. New York, NY: Guilford, 2007.

OCD: Obsessive Compulsive Disorder

Foa, Edna, and Reid Wilson. *Stop Obsessing*. New York, NY: Bantam, 2001.

Hyman, Bruce M., and Cherry Pedrick. *The OCD Workbook: Your Guide to Breaking Free from Obsessive-Compulsive Disorder*. (2nd ed.). Oakland, CA: New Harbinger, 2005.

Purdon, Christine, and David Clark. *Overcoming Obsessive Thoughts*. Oakland, CA: New Harbinger, 2005.

Panic disorder

Beckfield, Denise Fisher. *Master Your Panic and Take Back Your Life: Twelve Treatment Sessions to Conquer Panic, Anxiety, and Agoraphobia*. (3rd ed.). Atascadero, CA: Impact, 2004.

Psychopharmacology

Diamond, Ron. *Instant Psychopharmacology*. (3rd ed.). New York, NY: W. W. Norton, 2008.

PTSD

Herman, Judith. *Trauma and Recovery*. (Rev. ed.). New York, NY: Basic Books, 1997.

Rothbaum, Barbara Olasov, Edna Foa, and Elizabeth A. Hembree. *Reclaiming Your Life from a Traumatic Experience: Workbook*. New York, NY: Oxford University Press, 2007.

Schizophrenia

Copeland, Mary Ellen. *Wellness Recovery Action Plans (WRAP)*. Available at http://www.mentalhealthrecovery.com/.

Mueser, Kim, and Susan Gingerich. *The Complete Family Guide to Schizophrenia*. New York, NY: Guilford, 2006.

Social anxiety

Antony, Marin M., and Richard P. Swinson. *The Shyness and Social Anxiety Workbook: Proven Techniques for Overcoming Your Fears*. Oakland, CA: New Harbinger, 2008.

Stress reduction

Davis, Martha, Elizabeth Robbins Eshelman, and Matthew McKay. *The Relaxation and Stress Reduction Workbook*. (6th ed.). Oakland, CA: New Harbinger, 2008.

Trichotillomania

Keuthen, Nancy, Dan Stein, and Gary Christenson. *Trichotillomania: Help for Hair Pullers*. Oakland, CA: New Harbinger, 2001.

WEBSITES

Death and dying

Growth House, Inc.: provides specialized resources for bereaved families; links provide additional resources for grief and terminal illnesses. http://www.growthhouse.org/death.html.

General information about mental illness and treatment

Mayo Clinic: a website designed to provide the public with information about a variety of different diseases, including mental illness. http://www.mayoclinic.com/.

National Alliance on Mental Illness (NAMI) website: an excellent source for reliable information about mental illness, with specific information about the medications commonly used in treatment of mental illness. It has a wide variety of different kinds of information for clients, families, and professionals. http://nami.org/.

National Institute of Mental Health (NIMH) website: http://nimh.nih.gov/health/topics/.

Substance Abuse and Mental Health Services Administration (SAMHSA): National Mental Health Information Center. http://mental-health.samhsa.gov/.

Mindfulness/relaxation

Mindfulness meditation practice tapes and CDs, available through http://www.mindfulnesstapes.com/.

Relaxation exercises and sounds: free MP3, available through http://forms.uhs.wisc.edu/relaxation.php.

Personality disorders

Treatment and Research Advancements National Association for Personality Disorders (TARA): self-help organization run by and for people with personality disorders. http://www.tara4bpd.org/dyn/index.php.

Trauma and PTSD

VA website on trauma and PTSD: www.ncptsd.va.gov.

Women's mental health

Information regarding women's mental health issues: www.womensmentalhealth.org.

References

Alvarez-Jiménez, M., González-Blanch, C., Crespo-Facorro, B., Hetrick, S., Rodríguez-Sánchez, J. M, Pérez-Iglesias, R., & Vázquez-Barquero, J. L. (2008). Antipsychotic-induced weight gain in chronic and first-episode psychotic disorders: A systematic critical reappraisal. *CNS Drugs, 22*(7), 547–62.

Amsterdam J.D. & Shults J. (2010). Efficacy and safety of long-term fluoxetine versus lithium monotherapy of bipolar II disorder: a randomized, double-blind, placebo-substitution study. *American Journal of Psychiatry, 167*(7) 792–800

Andreasen, N. C., Carpenter, W. T., Kane, J. M., Lasser R.A., Marder, S.R. & Weinberger, D.R. (2005) Remission in schizophrenia: Proposed criteria and rationale for consensus. *American Journal of Psychiatry, 162*(3), 441–49.

Baghai, T.C. $ Moller, H.J. (2008) Electroconvulsive therapy and its different indications *Dialogues Clin Neurosci* 10(1) 105-17

Barone, M. T., & Menna-Barreto, L. (2010, August 30). Diabetes and sleep: A complex cause-and-effect relationship. Diabetes Research and Clinical Practice.

Bouton, M. E., Kenney, F. A., & Rosengard, C. (1990). State-dependent fear extinction with two benzodiazepine tranquilizers. *Behavioral Neurosciences, 104*(1), 44–55.

Brown, T. E. (2005). *Attention deficit disorder: The unfocused mind in children and adults.* New Haven, CT: Yale University Press.

Budhiraja, R., Budhiraja, P., & Quan, S. F. (2010). Sleep-disordered breathing and cardiovascular disorders. *Respiratory Care, 55*(10), 1322–32.

Caspi, A., Sugden, K., Moffitt, T. E., Taylor, A., Craig, I. W., Harrington, H. L., McClay, J., Mill, J., Martin, J., Braithwaite, A., & Poulton, R.

(2003). Influence of life stress on depression: Moderation by a poly-morphism in the 5-HTT gene. *Science, 301,* 386–89.

Cerdá, M., Sagdeo, A., Johnson, J., & Galea, S. (2010). Genetic and environmental influences on psychiatric comorbidity: A systematic review. *Journal of Affective Disorders, 126*(1–2), 14–38.

Christakis, D. A., Zimmerman F. J., DiGiuseppe, D. L., & McCarty, C. A. (2004). Early television exposure and subsequent attentional prob-lems in children. Pediatrics, *113*(4), 708–13.

Churchill, W. N., & Furukawa, T. A. (2009). Combined psychotherapy plus benzodiazepines for panic disorder (review). Cochrane Library, Issue 1.

Cleckley, H. (1950). *The mask of sanity.* St Louis, MO: Mosby Medica Library.

Cloos, J-M. (2010). Benzodiazepines and Addiction: Long-Term Use and Withdrawal (part 2) *Psychiatric Times, 37*(8), 34–36.

DeBattista, C., & Schatzberg, A. F. (2006). *The Black Book of Psycho-tropic Dosing and Monitoring.* 10th ed.: Supplement] *Primary Psy-chiatry*

Deegan, P. E. & Drake, R. E.. (2006). Shared Decision making and med-ication Management in the recovery process. *Psychiatric Services, 57*(11), 1636–39.

Diamond R. J. (2004). What primary care physicians need to know about people with schizophrenia. *Wisconsin Medical Journal, 103*(6).

Diamond, R. J. (2006, August). *Recovery from mental illness: A psychia-trist's point of view.* Post Graduate Medicine Special Report: New Directions in Schizophrenia, 54–62.

Fehm, L., & Schmidt, K. (2006). Performance anxiety in gifted adoles-cent musicians *Journal of Anxiety Disorders, 20*(1), 98–109.

Fournier, J. C., DeRubeis, R. J., Hollon, S. D., Dimidjian, S., Amster-dam, J. D., Shelton R. C., & Fawcett, J. (2010). Antidepressant drug effects and depression severity: A patient-level meta-analysis. *Jour-nal of the American Medical Association, 303*(1), 47–53.

Frances A., et al. (2000). *Diagnostic and statistical manual of mental disorders.* 4th ed. Washington, DC: American Psychiatric Associa-tion.

Freeman, M. P, Fava, M., Lake, J., Trivedi, M. H., Wisner, K. L., & Mischoulon D. (2010). Complementary and alternative medicine in major depressive disorder: The American Psychiatric Association Task Force report. *Journal of Clinical Psychiatry, 71*(6) 667–68.

Harding, C. M., Brooks, G. W., & Ashikaga, T., Strauss, J. S. & Breier, A.. (1987). The Vermont longitudinal study of persons with severe mental illness II: Long-term outcome of subjects who retrospectively met DSM III criteria for schizophrenia. *American Journal of Psychiatry, 144*(6), 727–35.

Herman, J. (1997). *Trauma and recovery: The aftermath of violence— from domestic abuse to political terror.* New York, NY: Basic Books.

Hor, K., & Taylor, M. (2010). Suicide and schizophrenia: A systematic review of rates and risk factors. *Journal of Psychopharmacology, 24*(4 Suppl.), 81–90.

Johns, M. W. (1994). Sleepiness in different situations measured by the Epworth Sleepiness Scale. *Sleep; 17,* 703–10.

Katusic, S. K., Barbaresi, W. J., Colligan, R. C., Weaver, A. L., Leibson, C. L., & Jacobsen, S. J. (2005). Psychostimulant treatment and risk for substance abuse among young adults with a history of attention-deficit/hyperactivity disorder: A population-based, birth cohort study. *Journal of Child and Adolescent Psychopharmacology, 15*(5), 764–76.

Kessler, R. C., Adler, L., Ames, M., Demler, O., Faraone, S., Hiripi, E., Howes, M. J., Jin, R., Secnik, K., Spencer, T., Ustun, T. B., & Walters, E. E. (2005). The World Health Organization Adult ADHD self-report scale (ASRS): A short screening scale for use in the general population. *Psychological Medicine, 35*(2), 245–56.

Kimberly, S. J. (2005). Behavioral genetics and child temperament. *Journal of Developmental and Behavioral Pediatrics, 26*(3), 214–23.

King-Cassas, B., Sharp, C., Lomax-Bream, L., Lohrenz, T., Fonagy, P., & Montague, P.R. (2008) The Rupture and repair of cooperation in borderline personality disorder. Science, 321(5890), 806-10

Lader, M., Cardinali, D. P., & Pandi-Perumal, S. R. (Eds.). (2006). *Sleep and sleep disorders: A neuropsychopharmacological approach.* New York, NY: Springer Science.

Lenihan, M. (1993). *Cognitive behavioral treatment of borderline personality.* New York, NY: Guilford.

Manigilio, R. (2009). The impact of child sexual abuse on health: A systematic review of reviews. *Clinical Psychology Review, 29*(7), 647–57.

McLean, R. (2005). *Recovered, not cured: A journey through schizophrenia.* Crows Nest, Australia: Allen & Unwin.

Miller, W. R., & Rollnick, S. *Motivational interviewing: Preparing people for change.* 2nd ed. New York, NY: Guilford.

Minkoff, K. & Cline, C. (2004). Changing the world: The design and implementation of comprehensive continuous integrated systems of care for individuals with co-occurring disorders. *Psychiatric Clinics of North America, 27,* 727–43.

Mueser, K. T., and Gingerich, S. (2006). *The complete family guide to schizophrenia.* New York, NY: Guilford.

Owen R.T. (2009). Selective histamine H(1) antagonism: a novel approach to insomnia using low-dose doxepin. *Drugs Today, 45*(4), 261–67.

Patrick, C. H. (1970). *Alcohol, culture, and society.* New York, NY: AMS Press.

Philip, P., Sagaspe, P., Lagarde, E., Leger, D., Ohayon, M. M., Bioulac, B., Boussuge, J., & Taillard, J. (2010, October 18). Sleep disorders and accidental risk in a large group of regular registered highway drivers. *Sleep Medicine.*

Ramtekkar, U. P., Reiersen, A. M., Todorov, A. A., & Todd, R. D. (2010). Sex and age differences in attention-deficit/hyperactivity disorder symptoms and diagnoses: Implications for DSM-V and ICD-11. *Journal of American Academic Child and Adolescent Psychiatry, 49*(3), 217–28.

Reichborn-Kjennerud, T. (2008). Genetics of personality disorders. *Psychiatric Clinics of North America, 31*(3).

Reiss D., & Leve, L. D. (2007). Genetic expression outside the skin: Clues to mechanisms of genotype x environment interaction. *Developmental Psychopathology, 19*(4), 1005–27.

Rush, A. J. & Siefert S. E. (2009). Clinical issues in considering vagus nerve stimulation for treatment-resistant depression. *Experimental Neurology, 219*(1), 36–43.

Saks, E. (2008). *The center cannot hold: My journey through madness.* New York, NY: Hyperion.

Schonfeldt-Lecuona, C., Cardenas-Morales, L., Freudenmann, R.W., Kammer, T., & Herwig, U. (2010). Transcranial magnetic stimulation in depression—lessons from the multicentre trials. *Restorative Neurology and Neuroscience, 28*(4), 569–76.

Silbersweig, D., et al. (2007). Problems learning rules of cooperation in a multi-round economic exchange game. Failure of frontolimbic inhibitory function in the context of negative emotion in borderline personality disorder. *American Journal of Psychiatry, 164*(12), 1832–41.

Sockalingam, S. & Abbey, S. E. (2009). Managing depression during hepatitis C treatment *Canadian Journal of Psychiatry*, *54*(9), 614–25.

Steele, K. (2002). *The day the voices stopped: A schizophrenic's journey.* New York, NY: Basic Books.

Stein, D. J., & Rauch, S. L. (2008). Neuropsychiatric aspects of anxiety disorders. In S. C. Yudofsky and R. E. Hales (Eds.), *American psychiatric publishing textbook of neuropsychiatry and behavioral neurosciences* (5th ed., pp. 1025–44). Arlington, VA: American Psychiatry Publishing.

Velligan, D. I., Weiden, P. J., Sajatovic, M., Scott, J., Carpenter, D., Ross, R., & Docherty, J. P. (2009). The expert consensus guideline series: Adherence problems in patients with serious and persistent mental illness. Journal of Clinical Psychiatry, 70(Suppl. 4), 1–46.

WEBSITES

http://www.annafoundation.org

http://www.healingselfinjury.org/

http://www.mentalhealth.samhsa.gov/cmhs/womenandtrauma/wcdvs.asp

http://www.sidran.org

Index